Country Breads
of the World

Linda Collister
& Anthony Blake

Country Breads of the World

To John Thorne

Published in the US in 2000 by The Lyons Press
First published in 2000 by Conran Octopus Ltd

Text copyright © 2000 Linda Collister
Photography copyright © 2000 Anthony Blake
Design and layout copyright © 2000 Conran Octopus Ltd

Commissioning Editor Stuart Cooper
Project Editor Norma MacMillan
Art Editor Paul Welti
Production Controller Suzanne Sharpless

ISBN 1 58574 112 4
Library of Congress Cataloging-in-Publication data is available
upon request

Colour origination by Sang Choy International, Singapore
Printed in China

*Page 1: Rare and unusual dough-rising baskets from all over
the world collected by Maurice Bichard (see page 63), who is
a leading member of the Basketmakers Association.*

*Page 2: At the old mill in Blatten, Switzerland (see page
42), freshly baked rye loaves are cooled on a rack suspended
from the ceiling, to thwart mice.*

Right: Wheat ready to harvest.

In the recipes, measurements for ingredients are given in
standard U.S. cups and spoons as well as in metric
weights and volume measures. Use either all metric
or all standard U.S., as the two are not interchange-
able. Flour is measured spooned into cups.

Contents

2 Leavening the dough 46

3 Working and shaping the dough 82

4 Baking bread 112

5 Celebration breads 144

For me, as for many others, the food writer John Thorne is an inspiration and a catalyst. In his newsletter, "Simple Cooking," and books (see bibliography, page 172), he modestly, learnedly, and thoughtfully describes his experiences preparing food and eating it. His apparently casual meditations could be described as the yeast with which the rest of us make bread. One remark of his resonates throughout this book: how, he asks, can making a loaf of bread be "at once an ordinary and an extraordinary event?"

Introduction

When I met John Thorne, in a coffee shop near his home in New England, I asked what fascinated him about bread – and of course he explained what fascinates me as well: "Bread is important and nurturing in a way that other foods are not. The baked dough ultimately nourishes the body, but the dough itself has to be fed by the baker, and the process of making and then baking is intellectual and psychological nourishment."

He no longer makes bread, just pizza dough and sourdough English muffins. "When I had a wood-fired bread oven, I was thrilled to be making bread as good as any that I had ever eaten. But I found, after I lost access to the oven, that I was now all the happier to support local artisanal bread bakers, knowing the difficulties they face. Craft-bakers often encounter resistance because their bread costs twice that of supermarket loaves ('after all, it's only bread', I heard someone mutter, faced with a $3.50 loaf that in substance and flavor could have wiped the floor with any $2 supermarket loaf, especially the pseudo-artisanal breads many such hypermarkets are churning out). Most people prefer a loaf with real flavor – the flavor of bread."

Opposite the coffee shop was an organic market, so we talked about flour as well. What interested John most is the effect made by different flours. "If you are making wine, you need the right grapes to start, however skilled the winemaker." And we brooded together on the significance of the rest of the process: making the dough, kneading, and baking.

By the time we finished our second cup of coffee, the plan for this book was clear in my mind. It would try to answer John's question: what makes breadmaking at once ordinary and extraordinary? It would try to describe the combination of physical and psychological nourishment that breadmaking provides. It would explore the different stages of breadmaking – milling flour, making dough, kneading, and baking – to reveal what each contributed to the perfect loaf.

Good bread demands good flour, thorough kneading, and congenial conditions for rising.
For baking, enthusiasts like Paul Merry (see page 120) prefer a wood-fired oven.

As John Thorne says: "Making your own bread teaches many things, and one of them is to treasure it and those who make it above almost all other things."

Anthony and I decided to start with the main ingredient, flour. We've met many incredibly gifted, skilled, and enthusiastic breadmakers, amateurs as well as professionals, and the one belief they shared was that you could not make good bread without excellent flour. Mills vary in their operations and their products, and we have been inspired by the wide range of flours now available. The many craft-bakers we spoke to said that they are no longer limited in the style of breads they can bake.

Making good bread begins with the dough. Once you have learned to use fresh or dried baker's yeast, got the feel of the dough, understood why it behaves as it does, you will have a good loaf. The next challenge is to try naturally leavened, or sourdough, bread. Sourdough is unpredictable; each loaf takes a leap of faith. But by learning and modifying ancient methods, by slightly changing the proportions of traditional ingredients, by tinkering with fermentation and baking times and temperatures, breadmakers can produce loaves that reflect their own tastes and skills as well as centuries of tradition.

The bread you bake today is a slice of history; it is also a piece of your own personality. There is no one recipe: each baker has his or her own ideas, and we have plenty of different ones for you to try. Find which of them works for you – not everyone enjoys sourdoughs, or yeasted breads, or whole-wheats, or ryes. But it is fun to experiment, and the basic ingredients are not expensive.

The way the risen dough is cooked also determines the result. It is usually baked in a conventional oven, but we wanted to look at the alternatives. John Thorne and many other bakers find the oven is central to the perfect loaf, so we have included environment-friendly wood-fired brick ovens, stovetop griddles, and a few more unusual ovens.

We were struck by the link between bread and spirituality, the fact that bakers in many countries felt that what they were making was more than mere food. We visited places where bread is not taken for granted – but well-made bread is. In a remote village in Sardinia, we discovered women bakers continuing an ancient craft. In America, we witnessed the legacy of the Shakers. We learned about the festive traditions of Scandinavia; the return of the slowly-made, hand-crafted loaves to France; the country breads of Luxembourg and Germany; some ancient and modern loaves from Russia and Japan. We have been blessed with a wealth of recipes, and blessed too with the discovery that for many bakers, as for us, making bread brings peace and replenishment.

Of all the basic cooking processes, the baking of bread is the most obviously transcendent. In no other does the raw material so little resemble the finished product. You begin with an unappetizing, indigestible lump of dough. Magically, miraculously, you finish with beautiful, nutritious, delicious food.

1 Milling the grain

ALL BAKERS, whether professional or amateur, agree on one thing: you cannot make good bread without good flour. The same simple truth is heard in every kitchen and bakery: "I couldn't make this quality of bread without the best flour" … "If I make the best, my customers will gladly pay for it" … "You can really taste the wheat in this bread" … "When my sourdough breads wouldn't rise properly, I realized it had to do with the flour" … "I work hand-in-glove with the miller, and respect him like a father."

For craft-bakers, the choice of flours is both dazzling and inspiring; specialty mills now use a huge range of grains and produce flours with different textures. Wheat may be the most common grain used, but there are many varieties to choose from – spelt, kamut, and durum are similar, but each has its own taste. Rye flour has a deep, strong, earthy flavor, and very different properties; it can be used alone or can be added to a dough to boost the taste. So can barley and oats.

The wooden bag chute at the Augsberger mill in Switzerland (see page 36) is both elegant and functional.

Wheat flours vary in protein content as well as flavor. The protein content determines whether there will be enough gluten when the flour is mixed with water to allow it to be transformed into bread. The more protein, the stronger the flour, and the stronger the gluten that can be developed during kneading.

Flours vary from mill to mill, so the same recipe made with different flours can produce bread that varies in taste, size, and texture. As a result of this variation in flours, recipes usually give an approximate quantity of flour (or liquid), and an indication of the consistency of the final dough.

Look for organic and specialist flours and grains in larger supermarkets, and whole- food and specialist stores. You can also buy direct from mills – see the Directory on page 172 for details. Store flour in a cool, dry cupboard and take note of the "use-by" date. To avoid flour going stale or encouraging bugs, buy little and often.

I HAVE NEVER MET more enthusiastic bread lovers than John Lister and Clive Mellum, one the idealistic miller and the other the perfect baker. John has been milling grain, most of it locally grown and organic, at Shipton Mill in Gloucestershire, England, since 1981. Grain has always been milled here – a watermill on the site was recorded in the Domesday Book – and when John discovered a derelict mill building, down the end of a narrow winding lane by a tributary of the River Avon, he set about restoring the machinery. Today the river no longer provides enough water to power the mill, so the three sets of stones run on electricity.

Good flour, good bread

Above: Hidden in a valley, down a winding country lane, Shipton Mill is not easy to find.
Opposite: Millers for the Prince of Wales – the organic flour is used to make Duchy shortbread – Shipton Mill is proud to display the crest and royal warrant over the door.

My first question to John was what made the perfect loaf of bread. "Time," was his characteristically modest answer. Without mentioning flour, he was off: "Time is the key to good bread, not time as in preparation, working in the kitchen or bakery, but the timespan of the loaf from making the dough to taking it out of the oven. A good baker allows the dough to develop at its own optimum pace. It takes less working time to make a good loaf than it does to make one of those so-called fast breads." John believes that breadmaking has come full circle. "As the old craftsman-bakers retire, and there are fewer young bakers prepared to start work at three in the morning – it's a tough, isolating way of life – so more and more people who want to eat good bread rather than an industrialized product make it themselves."

But flour is important, too. Nearly every baker we spoke to said that you can't make really good bread from ordinary flour. And nearly every baker we met in the U.K. has some Shipton Mill flour in the kitchen. John is generally revered: "He's the key to the renaissance of the craft-baker in England"; "He's done a Richard Branson – taken on the big boys of the flour world and beaten them at their own game"; "He's done the food world a great service"; and "John's helped make quality organic flour a mainstream ingredient."

The other half of Shipton's team is Clive Mellum. Following his grandfather, father, and uncle, he started work at age 11, tying fagots of wood for the bread oven (and looking after the pigs) at a bakery in Blindley Heath, Sussex, England. This was followed by a four-year apprenticeship. But unlike previous generations, he was able to combine the theory and science of bakery learned in college with the practical knowledge from a traditional handcraft bakery. At 21, he opened his own bakery. After 20 years running it, he and his wife bought a bed-and-breakfast, and he went into the flour business.

Now, 35 years after he began, his love of breadmaking is still as fresh as one of his new-baked loaves. The day we met, he had been up at 3a.m., helping a distant bakery with a sourdough problem; 12 hours later he was still happy to teach us, still eager for us to see and try another exceptionally good loaf. His knowledge of flours and breadmaking is encyclopedic. When I have a problem with a recipe, a call to Clive provides an immediate solution.

*Grains of wheat drop down onto
the stone for milling.*

*John Lister prefers Maris Widgeon
wheat for its good, deep flavor.*

Clive is patriotic about his bread: "Everybody has been influenced by the trendy European breads, which have a lot more flavor than our everyday breads have had. As expectations change, the craft-baker is coming back. In my grandfather's day, English bread was based on a sponge dough skilfully made with proper flour, which gave bread with a good brittle, crunchy crust and proper taste [see his favorite recipe on page 16]." Thanks in no small part to Clive and John, this is now becoming true once more.

Shipton Mill's quality control is meticulous. All the whole-wheat flour is stone-ground, whereas the white flour is milled on standard rollers, but carefully regulated for low extraction (that is, the least possible proportion of the grain removed) and high protein content. The white flour has a protein content of 12.1%, the 100% whole-wheat 11.6%. The unique flavor of both the whole-wheat and white flours comes from the use of the wheat variety, Maris Widgeon, using a blend of Canadian and local wheats. John explained that he chooses large, round, glossy wheat berries for their good flour to bran ratio and their deep flavor. Smaller, darker, cheaper berries yield a dark, slightly bitter flour higher in bran, which is difficult to bake with.

The untreated white bread flour is very creamy in color, as it has not been as heavily crushed and heated as most commercial brands. Many of these other flours work best with speedy dough processes, but Shipton's is ideally suited to a long fermentation, and comes into its own with sourdough starters and slow rises.

In addition to their organic white and 100% whole-wheat flour, Shipton Mill produces a large range of other flours and cereals that are mostly unknown to the home baker, only being available by mail order from the mill. A white flour, produced only from French wheat, is suitable for baguettes; it is exported to many French *boulangeries*. The Italian ciabatta flour, made from a blend of Canadian and other hard-wheat varieties, is a rough and granular flour that produces a lively dough capable of retaining the large air bubbles that develop during fermentation. There's also an extra-coarse whole-wheat flour that can be mixed with others to add flavor and texture, and an organic Irish soda coarse brown bread flour, which is neither whole-wheat nor white but halfway between. Its attractive flecked appearance comes from large flakes of bran and pieces of rolled wheat berries. It can be used, of course, for soda bread, but can also be mixed with white flour to make farmhouse-style yeasted loaves with a nutty flavor.

I was most interested in the range of rye flours, as it is very difficult to make German-style loaves at home without authentic ingredients. The organic light rye is pale, with just some of the bran, and is used by German bakers to make the traditional, and still popular, light rye breads. The organic dark rye is the equivalent of a brown flour, and makes a coarser, livelier dough. This is perfect for darker loaves, ones made with a rye "sponge," and sourdoughs. A very dark, coarse rye, the equivalent of whole-wheat flour, is also available – John says this is not for the faint-hearted, as it is quite tricky to work and needs a sourdough starter for the best results (see Bakhaus Loaf, page 69). For pumpernickel, as well as for adding texture to other breads (see Vanskapsbrød, page 160), there is cracked rye – whole rye berries cut into two or three pieces – and also cracked wheat berries, plus malted wheat flakes, cracked malted rye berries, and Shipton's five-cereals blend (a mix of malted wheat flakes, barley flakes, sunflower seeds, hulled millet, and oats).

Clive had a useful tip for me. He said it's virtually impossible to overknead any dough by hand – your arms give up before the dough does. But if you knead a dough by machine, with a dough hook, he suggests using a low speed and the minimum time. And ignore the myth that if you knead stoneground whole-wheat flour, the pieces of bran would shred the strands of gluten you are trying to develop.

THIS *is just brilliant bread, according to John Lister of Shipton Mill. The dough, made with a very small proportion of yeast to flour, is left to ferment for 16 hours, then shaped and left to rise for another hour or so before baking. The result is a really well-flavored loaf, with a crisp crust and nice chewy crumb. The malt helps to feed the yeast and keep it going during the prolonged fermentation, rather than adding flavor to the dough.*

Clive Mellum always uses fresh yeast — he is not happy with the idea of using dry yeast.

Sixteen-hour bread

MAKES 2 MEDIUM LOAVES

$^1/_2$ 0.6-oz cake fresh yeast (8g)

$2^1/_4$ cups (560ml) water (see recipe)

$^1/_4$ teaspoon malt extract syrup

2 teaspoons (10g) lard or other hard white fat

$8^1/_4$ cups (1kg) organic unbleached white bread flour

1 tablespoon fine sea salt

2 baking sheets, dusted with flour

Crumble the yeast into a mixing bowl (Clive uses a plastic one that comes with a lid). Measure the water. Clive wants the finished dough to be about 82°F, so calculates the water temperature as 164°F minus the temperature of the flour. If the flour is at room temperature (around 68°F), then the water should be 98°F, just a little less than luke-warm; in very hot weather it may be necessary to use chilled water. Pour the water into the bowl and mix with the yeast to make a lump-free liquid. Work in the malt extract and the lard, then add the flour and salt, and work all the ingredients until they just come together.

Turn out onto a work surface and knead very thoroughly for 10 minutes, until the dough is very pliable, silky, and smooth. Return to the bowl and cover with a lid or plastic wrap. Leave to rise slowly for 12 hours at room temperature. At this point, punch down the dough to deflate it, then cover again and leave for up to 4 hours, as Clive does, or up to 8 hours at a cool temperature.

Punch down the risen dough to remove the large bubbles of air, then divide into two equal pieces. Knead each piece for 2 minutes — the dough should "squeak" as you work it. Cover with a sheet of plastic wrap and leave to relax for 15 minutes.

Quickly shape each piece of dough into a round, ball-shaped loaf and place on the prepared baking sheets. Put the sheets into large plastic bags, slightly inflate the bags, then tuck the ends under to close tightly. Leave to rise in these mini greenhouses for $1^1/_2$–3 hours, depending on room temperature, until the dough has almost doubled in size.

Toward the end of the rising time, preheat the oven to 425°F.

Uncover the loaves, quickly slash the tops with a small, sharp knife (Clive uses a serrated baker's knife), and put into the oven. Create a little steam by throwing about $^1/_4$ cup of water onto the floor of the oven (or pouring it into a heated roasting pan sitting on the bottom of the oven); the steam helps to give a thin, crisp, and glossy crust. Bake for 35–40 minutes until the loaves sound hollow when tapped underneath. Cool on a wire rack.

The bread is best eaten within 5 days. Once thoroughly cooled, it can be frozen for up to a month.

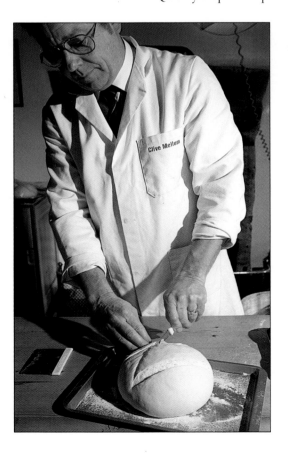

Clive slashes a diamond shape in the top of the risen loaf before baking it.

T HIS *is the London bloomer recipe Clive Mellum of Shipton Mill feels so strongly about: "It is bread as my grandfather made. It should be on the supermarket shelves with a big Union flag on it. It has the best flavor, texture, and crust of any bread. We should be proud to have this as our national loaf." The French-style sponge starter gives a deep flavor, and a crumb and crisp crust similar to a Vienna loaf. Little work is involved — the sponge can be mixed, then left overnight, and the dough quickly finished the next day.*

Clive Mellum's favorite loaf

MAKES 3 MEDIUM LOAVES, OR
12 LARGE ROLLS

SPONGE:

¹/₂ 0.6-oz cake fresh yeast (8g)

2¹/₄ cups (560ml) lukewarm water

8¹/₄ cups (1kg) organic unbleached white
    bread flour

1 tablespoon fine sea salt

TO FINISH:

4 cups (500g) organic unbleached white bread
    flour

¹/₂ tablespoon fine sea salt

2 0.6-oz cakes fresh yeast (30g)

1¹/₄ cups (290ml) lukewarm water

several baking sheets, well floured

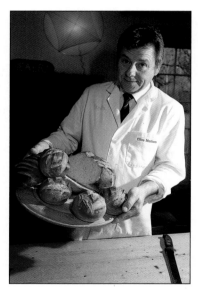

The dough for Clive's Favorite Loaf can be shaped into a round ball-shaped loaf, a bloomer, or rolls.

Make the sponge: Crumble the yeast into a large mixing bowl and mix to a smooth liquid with the water (see Sixteen-Hour Bread, page 15, for information on water temperature). Work in the flour and salt. Turn out onto a work surface and knead thoroughly for 10 minutes. Return the dough to the bowl, cover tightly with the lid or with plastic wrap, and leave to ferment at room temperature for 12 hours.

The next day, turn the dough out of the bowl and set aside. Mix the second quantity of flour and salt in the bowl, then make a well in the center. Crumble the yeast into the well, then mix with the water to make a smooth liquid. Work in the flour from the sides of the bowl, followed by the sponge, to make a smooth but not sticky dough. Turn out onto a work surface and knead thoroughly for 10 minutes. Cover the dough with a sheet of plastic wrap, or the upturned bowl, and leave to rest for 15 minutes.

Cut the dough into three equal pieces and shape each into a round, ball-shaped loaf. Put onto the prepared baking sheets.

Alternatively, to form long bloomer loaves, pat out each piece of dough into a rectangle, fold in the short ends, and then roll up the dough from one long side. Place seam-side down on the prepared baking sheets.

Knead the dough thoroughly for 10 minutes to give a good texture to the bread.

Clive makes the traditional 13 slashes in the risen bloomer before baking.

To make bread rolls, cut each piece of dough into four, and shape into neat balls. Place on the prepared baking sheets spaced well apart, then lightly dust the tops of the rolls with flour.

Put the baking sheets into large plastic bags, slightly inflate them, and close tightly. Leave to rise for 35 minutes to 1 hour or until slightly less than doubled in size. Clive says that slight under-rising is more beneficial, as it gives a better oven-spring than slight over-rising.

Toward the end of the rising time, preheat the oven to 425°F.

Uncover the loaves and quickly slash with a small, sharp, serrated knife — a London bloomer traditionally has 13 diagonal slashes. Put into the oven and throw a splash of water onto the floor of the oven (see Sixteen-Hour Bread, page 15). Bake for 35–40 minutes for loaves, 20–25 minutes for rolls, until a good golden brown and they sound hollow when tapped underneath. Cool on wire racks.

The bread is best eaten within 5 days of baking. Once thoroughly cooled, the loaves can be frozen for up to a month.

*T*HIS *loaf, made from a thick-batter sourdough starter, has the flavor of a San Francisco sourdough bread. Clive Mellum has been keeping his starter going for 10 years — he gives away as much as he uses. He suggests using tap water that has been filtered and boiled to remove the chlorine. (See pages 48–49 for more information on starters.)*

Clive's sourdough loaf

MAKES 1 LARGE OR 2 SMALL LOAVES

SOURDOUGH STARTER:

³/₄ cup (200ml) lukewarm water

1³/₄ cups (200g) organic unbleached white
    bread flour

additional white or rye flour for feeding

TO FINISH:

1 cup (250ml) lukewarm water

4 cups (500g) organic unbleached white bread
    flour

¹/₂ tablespoon fine sea salt

a baking sheet, well floured

Make the starter: Mix the water with the flour to make a thick batter. Cover the bowl with a wet dish towel and leave at room temperature until fine bubbles are clearly visible on the surface — usually 4–5 days, but up to 7 days in cool weather. The batter can then be fed: Measure it, and add an equal quantity of lukewarm water as well as 1¹/₂ teaspoons (10g) of flour for every 2 teaspoons of water. If the batter does not seem very bubbly and lively, replace a little of the white flour with rye flour. Feed in this way every day for 3 days. The starter is now ready to be used.

Once you have established a good lively starter it can be kept, covered with plastic wrap, at room temperature. Feed it at least once every 5 days, even if you are not using it. If you feed and water your starter on a daily basis, the yeast level will be higher and the acidity lower than if you feed it less often, so you can regulate your starter by varying the feeding timetable — if you like a well-risen loaf with a mild flavor, feed the starter every day; for a stronger flavor, feed less often and allow longer for the dough to rise.

When you want to bake, give the sourdough starter two feeds, about 12 hours apart, so it is vigorous.

Combine ¹/₂ cup (125ml) of the starter with the second quantities of water and flour and the salt in a large bowl. Mix to make a smooth but not sticky dough. Turn out onto a work surface and knead thoroughly for 10 minutes. Return to the bowl and cover with a lid or plastic wrap. Leave to rise at room temperature until the dough is doubled in size — the time depends on the vigor of your starter as well as the room temperature; allow 2–8 hours.

Turn the dough out onto a work surface. Punch down the dough to remove the large air bubbles and knead for a minute. If making two loaves, cut the dough in half. Cover with a sheet of plastic wrap and leave to rest for 15 minutes.

Shape the dough into one or two round loaves and put onto the prepared baking sheet. Slide the sheet into a large plastic bag, slightly inflate, and close the end. Leave to rise at room temperature until the loaf is almost doubled in size — about 2 hours or up to 6 hours.

Toward the end of the rising time, preheat the oven to 425°F.

Uncover the loaf and quickly slash the top with a small, sharp knife, then put into the heated oven. Throw a little water onto the floor of the oven, or pour water into a hot roasting pan to create steam. Bake until the bread is golden brown and sounds hollow when tapped underneath — 35–40 minutes for a large loaf or 25–30 minutes for two smaller loaves. Cool on a wire rack.

The bread is best eaten within 6 days. Once thoroughly cooled, it can be frozen for up to a month.

BEAUTIFULLY *silky, aromatic sunflower flour is a mixture of roasted, finely ground sunflower seeds and white bread flour. Very popular in Austria, it makes a remarkable and highly nutritious loaf – light yet satisfyingly chewy, with a rich, unique flavor and seductive aroma. It slices well, makes excellent sandwiches and toast, and can be used with sweet or savory toppings. Use sunflower flour quickly after purchase – due to the high oil content of sunflower seeds, the flour will go rancid if kept for long.*

Sunflower-flour loaf

MAKES 1 LARGE LOAF

6¹/₃ cups (700g) sunflower flour

2 teaspoons fine sea salt

1 0.6-oz cake fresh yeast (15g)*

1³/₄ cups (400ml) lukewarm water

a loaf pan, about 10 x 5 x 3 inches, greased

Mix the flour and salt in a large mixing bowl and make a well in the center. Crumble the yeast into a measuring cup, add the lukewarm water, and stir until all the lumps of yeast have disappeared. Pour into the well in the flour, then gradually work the flour into the liquid to make a smooth dough that is slightly soft but not sticky. If the dough sticks to your fingers or the bowl, work in extra flour a tablespoon at a time; if there are dry crumbs in the bowl, or the dough seems dry and hard, work in extra water a tablespoon at a time.

Turn out the dough onto a lightly floured work surface and knead thoroughly for 10 minutes. The dough will feel very silky – it is a real pleasure to knead, and will leave your hands feeling soft.

Return the dough to the bowl, then cover with a damp dish towel or put the bowl into a large plastic bag. Leave to rise at room temperature until the dough is doubled in size – 1¹/₂–2 hours.

Punch down the dough to remove the large pockets of air, then turn out onto the work surface. Knead for a minute. Pat the dough out to a rectangle the length of your pan, then roll up tightly like a jelly roll. Put the dough into the pan, seam-side down and folding the ends under the roll to make a neat, rectangular shape. Cover as before and leave the dough to rise until almost doubled in size – about 1 hour.

Toward the end of the rising time, preheat the oven to 425°F.

Uncover the loaf and bake for 30–35 minutes until it turns golden brown and sounds hollow when turned out of the pan and tapped underneath. Unmold and cool on a wire rack.

The bread is best eaten within 5 days, or toasted. Once thoroughly cooled, it can be frozen for up to a month.

Gradually work the flour into the yeast liquid.

The dough will be slightly soft in texture.

After thorough kneading it will be firmer.

* You can use 1 envelope (2¹/₂ teaspoons) rapid-rise active dry yeast instead of the fresh yeast. Mix the dry yeast with the flour and salt, then add the water and continue with the recipe.

Sunflower-Flour Loaf (left) and Mixed-Grain Sunflower Loaf are both made from aromatic and nutritious sunflower flour.

I REALLY *like this combination of ingredients. It produces a loaf packed with nutrients, yet it is not dense and heavy to chew; the bread is full of flavor and light enough to make moist, satisfying sandwiches. For a good breakfast-time bread, you could add a tablespoon of honey with the yeast liquid. I use Shipton Mill's five-cereals blend with sunflower flour, but you could substitute the King Arthur Flour 10-grain cereal baking blend.*

Mixed-grain sunflower loaf

MAKES 1 LARGE LOAF

5³/₄ cups (600g) sunflower flour

³/₄ cup five-cereals blend

2 teaspoons fine sea salt

1 0.6-oz cake fresh yeast (15g)* (see opposite)

1³/₄ cups (400ml) lukewarm water

extra five-cereals blend for rolling

a loaf pan, about 10 x 5 x 3 inches, well greased

Make the dough as given for Sunflower-Flour Loaf, opposite, mixing the five-cereals blend into the flour with the salt. If the dough sticks to your fingers or the bowl, work in a little more flour. On the other hand, if the dough seems stiff and won't come together, add a little more water.

Rise and shape the dough as for the Sunflower-Flour Loaf, then roll the loaf in a little extra five-cereals blend to coat lightly. Put the loaf in the pan and sprinkle with any five-cereals mix that has fallen off, to give an even topping. Leave to rise and then bake as given.

This makes very good toast.

Juicy black olives and marjoram flavor this delicious bread.

MADE *in a roasting or baking pan, this upside-down loaf comes out about 2 inches deep, with a moist, rich topping of black olives — Kalamata for choice — marjoram and olive oil. The bread is flavored with more marjoram and is richly aromatic and light. This simple-to-make bread is designed for entertaining. Serve it warm with salami, Serrano ham, roasted sweet peppers, and salads, or use for bruschetta.*

Sunflower and olive bread

MAKES 1 LARGE LOAF

1 cup (150g) black olives, pitted

$^1/_3$ cup (150ml) virgin olive oil

a strip of fresh lemon peel

2 tablespoons chopped fresh marjoram

6$^1/_3$ cups (700g) sunflower flour

2 teaspoons fine sea salt

1 0.6-oz cake fresh yeast (15g)*

1$^3/_4$ cups (400ml) lukewarm water

a roasting pan, about 9 x 12 inches, oiled with
    olive oil

a baking sheet

Put the olives in a jar with the olive oil, lemon peel, and half of the marjoram. Close tightly, then shake well. Leave to marinate for 3–4 hours, or overnight if possible.

To make the bread, put the flour, salt, and remaining marjoram into a mixing bowl and thoroughly combine. Make and rise the dough as given for Sunflower-Flour Loaf on page 18.

Discard the lemon peel, then pour the olives and the flavored oil into the bottom of the prepared roasting pan. Distribute evenly.

Punch down the risen dough and turn out onto a lightly floured work surface. Pat or roll out the dough to a rectangle to fit your pan. Carefully place the dough on top of the olives — they will move about however hard you try not to disturb them, but don't worry. Pat the dough down so it fits the pan neatly and evenly. Cover as before and leave to rise at room temperature while heating the oven to 425°F.

Uncover the loaf and bake for 20 minutes until firm and golden. Carefully invert the loaf onto the baking sheet, then return to the oven to bake for a further 5–10 minutes so the olive-topped crust becomes golden and slightly crunchy. Cool on a wire rack or serve straight from the oven.

The bread is best eaten within 48 hours, and is not suitable for freezing.

* You can use 1 envelope (2$^1/_2$ teaspoons) rapid-rise active dry yeast instead of the fresh yeast. Mix the dry yeast into the flour with the salt and marjoram, then continue with the recipe.

I F *you normally make bread with whole-wheat flour, try using spelt flour. I think you will become hooked on its rich, slighty nutty taste. Spelt grain has been discovered on several pre-historic sites — it was cultivated long before wheat, and was popular with the Romans, who prized good bread. It is highly nutritious, and although it does contain gluten, some people with wheat allergies find they are able to use it in baking (check with your doctor if this is of interest to you). Here I've mixed it with white flour and a five-cereals blend of malted wheat flakes, barley flakes, sunflower seeds, hulled millet, and oats.*

Spelt and multi-cereal loaf

MAKES 1 LARGE LOAF

2 cups (250g) unbleached white bread flour

2^1/$_2$ cups (250g) spelt flour, preferably stoneground

scant 2 cups (250g) five-cereals blend

2 teaspoons fine sea salt

1 0.6-oz cake fresh yeast (15g)*

1^3/$_4$ cups (400ml) lukewarm water

2 teaspoons olive oil

a loaf pan, about 10 x 5 x 3 inches, greased

Mix the white and spelt flours with the cereals mixture and the salt in a large mixing bowl. Make a well in the center. Crumble the yeast into a small bowl and mix to a smooth liquid with a little of the water. Pour into the well in the center of the flour. Add the oil and the remaining water, then gradually work the flours into the liquid to make a soft, slightly sticky dough — it should not stick to the bowl or your fingers, so add a little more flour if necessary. If the dough is dry and stiff to work, add a little more water.

Turn out onto a floured work surface and knead thoroughly for 10 minutes. Return the dough to the bowl and cover with a damp dish towel, or put the bowl into a large plastic bag and close tightly. Leave to rise at room temperature until the dough has doubled in size — about 2 hours.

Punch down the risen dough with your knuckles to deflate it, then turn out onto a work surface. Pat out to a rectangle the length of your pan. Roll up tightly like a jelly roll, then put into the prepared pan, seam-side down, tucking the ends under to make a neat shape. Cover and leave to rise until almost doubled in size — 1–1^1/$_2$ hours.

Toward the end of the rising time, preheat the oven to 425°F.

Uncover the loaf and bake in the heated oven for about 35 minutes until it turns golden brown and sounds hollow when turned out of the pan and tapped underneath. Cool unmolded on a wire rack.

The bread is best eaten within 3 days, or is excellent toasted. Once thoroughly cooled, it can be frozen for up to a month.

* You can use 1 envelope (2^1/$_2$ teaspoons) rapid-rise active dry yeast instead of the fresh yeast. Mix the dry yeast with the flours, salt, and cereal mix.

A mixture of flours, cereals, and seeds makes this loaf special.

Westmill's in Bishop's Stortford, Hertfordshire, England, is home to Allinson flour, currently the UK's favorite bread flour, outselling its nearest competitor by five bags to one. The Allinson name goes back to 1895, when Dr. Thomas Allinson opened his first flour mill in Castleford. White flour was then the norm, and bran was generally considered harmful, so bread made with 100% whole-wheat flour was thought to be just for cranks or those on special diets.

Giants of milling

Wheat grains go through four different roller mills to grind them finer and finer before sieving and bolting.

Thomas Allinson, an early health crusader, was determined to educate people about bread and flour, asserting that the white flour produced from the new roller mills was not as nutritious as flour made from the whole grain. So dedicated was he that he even bought flour mills to produce the stoneground whole-wheat flour he believed to be so vital to good health. He wrote: "Whole-wheat bread is a necessity for all classes of the community. The rich should eat it, so that it may carry off some of their superfluous food and drinks; and the poor must eat it, then they will not need to buy so much flesh foods and other expensive articles of diet. If a law could be passed forbidding the separation of the bran from the fine flour, it would add very greatly to the health and wealth of our nation, and lessen the receipts of the publican, tobacconist, chemist, dentist, doctor, and undertaker."

My mother, now well over 80, recalls that her parents were convinced by Thomas Allinson's radical views and decided, for reasons of flavor as well as health, that they would only eat bread made with Allinson flour. The family was considered, to put it kindly, unusual.

Today the range of Allinson's flour includes: the best-selling white bread flour; the second most popular, softgrain white bread flour (with added rye and wheatgrains to give a lightly textured white loaf); stoneground organic 100% whole-wheat; harvester strong brown bread flour (with the addition of malted wheat flakes); plus four types of Tiger chapatti flour – high extraction white, medium, brown, and 100% whole-wheat (all fortified with vitamins). Allinson also markets a rapid-rise dry yeast – a fine powder in preweighed envelopes that is mixed directly with flour (rather than needing to be dissolved in warm water first), which makes life simpler for the home baker.

Marketing manager Gulam Uddin told us it was easy to see that breadmaking was on the increase: "While flour sales overall are falling by 11% in volume, bread flour sales are actually up 14% year on year. Our research tells us breadmaking is seen as a family activity. It is very popular with children, and we offer quality unadulterated flour to health-conscious bakers." A full organic range will be available soon. To increase customer loyalty and to bring families in to breadmaking, Allinson have launched a Baking Club, to answer queries, solve problems, and provide recipes.

The mill buys the best locally grown wheat – mainly Rialto, Mercia, and Herewood varieties – with 12% protein. Before a load of wheat is accepted, it is minutely checked for pesticide residues, and protein and moisture content, inspected for damage, and then graded. "We need a consistently high, quality product – you can't make decent bread with poor flour." Mill technician Caroline Brown also told me that from each batch of flour milled, a loaf of bread is made by hand at the mill test kitchen to provide a practical quality control.

This is milling on a vast scale: each hour seven tons of wheat are cleaned, ground and then sieved using computerized rollers, sifters, and bolters to produce 6,500 bags of flour. The flours are readily available in supermarkets and healthfood stores in Britain.

THIS *is a very simple bread, based on the Italian* pugliese, *with a good open texture and plenty of flavor. I get the best results when I use Allinson's softgrain flour — unbleached white bread flour mixed with rye and wheat berries — and a well-flavored, not too acidic, olive oil.*

Italian ring loaf

MAKES 1 LARGE LOAF

8^1/$_3$ cups (1kg) unbleached white bread flour
    with rye and wheat berries

2 teaspoons fine sea salt

1^1/$_2$ 0.6-oz cakes fresh yeast (20g)*

about 2^1/$_2$ cups (600ml) lukewarm water

^{1}/$_2$ cup (100ml) extra virgin olive oil

a large baking sheet, floured

Draw the flour into the liquid, adding the olive oil as you mix.

Gently join the ends of the dough sausage together to make a ring.

Mix the flour and salt in a large mixing bowl and make a well in the center. Crumble the yeast into a small bowl and mix with about 4 tablespoons of the water into a smooth liquid. Pour into the well in the flour, then add nearly all the remaining water. Quickly draw the flour into the yeast liquid, then pour in the oil and continue mixing until the dough comes together. Gradually add the rest of the water if necessary (it is hard to predict exactly how much water you will need, as flours vary so much) — the dough should be fairly soft, but should hold its shape and not stick to your fingers or the bowl.

Turn out onto a lightly floured work surface and knead thoroughly for 10 minutes. The dough should be very elastic and silky in texture. Return the dough to the oiled bowl and cover with a damp dish towel, or put the bowl into a large plastic bag and close securely. Leave to rise at cool to normal room temperature, rather than in a warm kitchen, until doubled in size — 2–3 hours.

Tip out the risen dough onto a floured work surface. Do not punch down or knead the dough. Handling it as gently as possible, carefully shape into a sausage about 22inches long. Join the ends together to make a ring — don't worry if it is not terribly neat. Transfer to the prepared baking sheet and cover as before with a damp dish towel or large plastic bag. Leave to rise until almost doubled in size — about 1 hour.

Towards the end of the rising time, preheat the oven to 450°F.

Uncover the bread and lightly dust with flour. Bake for 10 minutes, then reduce the oven temperature to 375°F and bake for a further 20 minutes or until the bread sounds hollow when tapped underneath. Cool on a wire rack.

The bread is best eaten within 2 days. Once thoroughly cooled, it can be frozen for up to a month.

*You can use 4 teaspoons rapid-rise active dry yeast instead of the fresh yeast. Add the dry yeast to the flour with the salt, then continue with the recipe.

A MAJOR PART OF THE DIET of early Americans were jonnycakes made from cornmeal. Jonnycakes, also called journey cakes as they were easy to pack for a trip, may no longer be the daily bread for Americans, but it is heartening to discover that traditionally milled native organic corn is now prized by the best bakers in New England.

Best in Boston: part one

Gray's Grist Mill

A weather-beaten gray-shingled building, Gray's Grist Mill is right on the border of Westport, Massachusetts, and Adamsville, Rhode Island. A mill has operated continuously here since 1675, making it the oldest in the U.S.A. The current miller is Tim McTague.

Tim started working at the mill 17 years ago, when he was 23. After much perseverance he persuaded the semi-retired mill owner, John Hart, to teach him the craft. He says it only took about three months of daily appearances before Hart, a true Yankee, finally started talking to him, and Tim gradually set about learning the ropes, or rather the stones. Tim was captivated by the old relic of a mill and, as the last link in the mill's 300-year history, invested his heart and soul into milling. He has a band of devoted customers, including Jeff Paige (see page 129) and Rene Becker (below).

Tim stone-grinds organic corn, wheat, and rye. In particular, he makes cornmeal from crib-dried Rhode Island White Cap Flint corn, which is descended from corn grown by the Narragansett Indians. The mill houses two sets of stones, one for animal feed, the other – 200 years old – for bread flour. The mill pond no longer powers the stones, and Tim has set up a vintage tractor engine to do the job.

Rene Becker

Rene Becker is a pedigree baker: "My grandmother on my mother's side was Polish, and a baker in Detroit, and although she had sold up by the time I was born, there was always a lot of good bread in our house." Rene put himself through the last couple of years in college with freelance baking. "I really wanted to be a journalist, but bread is such a fascinating puzzle – there are really only four ingredients, but the result varies so much. So, when the time came that I knew people would pay for a hand-crafted loaf, I quit writing and got a loan." He took a year off to work on the recipes, and almost four years ago opened the Hi-Rise Bakery in Cambridge, Massachusetts.

His bread has been named "Best in Boston" and has a national reputation: Julia Child is a regular, and Carol Field pops in when she's in town. "I have to credit Julia to a certain extent," Rene told me. "I learned how to make baguettes using her recipe in *Mastering the Art of French Cooking.*" Rene has fulfilled his goal to make simple things, do them very well, and make them distinctive – his doughs are fermented slowly, and the breads really taste of the grains used. "All my organic whole-wheat berries, rye, and corn come from Linley Mills in North Carolina, and are ground for me at Gray's Grist Mill, so they have real flavor and texture."

The bakery is a working theater: customers can watch and smell the progress of the bread as it is made. Sacks of Italian flour are stacked by the entrance. The dough is mixed in small batches and risen in baskets on a table behind the coffeepots. At the moment of baking, the loaves are unmolded, slashed, and loaded into the oven on a rollered canvas stretcher in seconds. Later, the baker empties the oven as rapidly, shovelling the unbearably hot, crackling loaves into large woven-wood baskets, ready to fill the shelves. But there's nothing romantic about it – it's hard work. "I make a point of hiring people who know nothing about baking, but just have a passion for bread."

Rene Becker (below) says: "I feel breads are like my children, they are so distinctive." At the Hi-Rise Bakery, the breads are baked in a massive oven. In the shop (bottom) you can enjoy the delicious breads, rolls, and buns all day.

The Hi-Rise Bakery's home made soup with rolls is a popular lunch for locals. To make cornbread rolls (the round ones in the basket), cut the cornbread dough into golfball-size pieces, shape into neat balls, and leave to rise. Then glaze and bake for 15–20 minutes.

Rene becker's *is the best cornbread we have ever eaten, a yeasted bread made with newly milled cornmeal — never more than 2 weeks old — and fresh sweetcorn kernels for a real burst of flavor. As always, the quality of the ingredients makes all the difference: the corn oil is organic cold-pressed and the corn fresh from the cob in late August or September. This bread is best made in an electric mixer, although it can also be made by hand. You might need a little more or a little less flour, depending on its strength.*

Cornbread

MAKES 3 MEDIUM LOAVES

2 0.6-oz cakes fresh yeast (30g)*

$^3/_4$ cup (200ml) warm water (104°F)

$^3/_4$ cup (200ml) cool water (61°F)

2 extra large eggs, lightly beaten

$^1/_4$ cup (80g) clear honey

2 tablespoons corn oil

about 7 cups (850g) unbleached white bread flour

1$^1/_2$ cups (175g) fine cornmeal

1 cup (150g) fresh corn kernels off the cob

4 teaspoons fine sea salt

1 egg white, lightly beaten with 2 teaspoons water, for glazing

3 loaf pans, about 8$^1/_2$ x 4$^1/_2$ x 2$^1/_2$ inches, well buttered

Crumble the yeast into the mixer bowl. Add the warm water and stir until thoroughly dispersed, then leave to stand for a minute. Add the cool water, the eggs, honey, and oil, and stir well. Add the flour, cornmeal, and corn kernels, and mix on low speed for 4 minutes (or mix by hand for 5 minutes). Leave the dough to rest, uncovered, for 10 minutes.

Add the salt. Mix on low speed for 4 minutes (5 minutes by hand), then 1 minute on medium speed (2 minutes by hand). The dough should be firm but still a little tacky because of the corn; it should not be wet. Cover with the lid of the bowl or plastic wrap and leave to rise in a warm, draft-free place until doubled in size – about 1$^1/_2$ hours.

Punch down the risen dough and turn out onto a lightly floured work surface. Divide into three equal portions. Pat each portion into a rectangle, then roll it into the shape of a log just big enough to fit your prepared pans. Put into the pans, place in a large plastic bag, and inflate slightly. Close tightly, then leave to rise as before until almost tripled in size – about 1$^1/_2$ hours.

Toward the end of the rising time, preheat the oven to 375°F.

Uncover the loaves and lightly brush with the egg-white wash, then bake for about 40 minutes or until golden and the unmolded loaves sound hollow when tapped underneath. Leave to cool on a wire rack.

The bread is best eaten within 4 days. Once thoroughly cooled, it can be frozen for up to a month.

*You can use 2 envelopes (5 teaspoons) rapid-rise active dry yeast instead of the fresh yeast. Mix the dry yeast with the dry ingredients in a mixing bowl, then work in the wet ingredients and continue with the recipe.

"THE *key to this loaf is good grain and unsulfured molasses," is Rene Becker's advice. This local loaf, which gets its shape from the coffee can in which it is traditionally steamed, was always eaten with baked beans and frankfurters on a Friday night. Rene's recipe has converted me — this is delicious. Rather than the usual raisins, he uses tart dried blueberrries:"I discovered they were the first export from Plymouth. The Native Americans used to dry them by the ton. Molasses and rye flour add to the distinctive flavor and to the bread's authenticity, as these are what the first Bostonians would have had available."*

If you can find the large cans used for coffee, or catering-size cans, these are ideal. I found that loose-based deep cake pans, about 4¹/₂ inches in diameter, also work fine if extended in height by 4 inches with a collar of buttered heavy-dutyaluminum foil secured with a paper clip.

Boston brown bread

MAKES 2 MEDIUM LOAVES

1¹/₂ cups (180g) unbleached white bread flour

2¹/₄ cups (225g) rye flour

1¹/₃ cups (160g) whole-wheat flour

scant 1 cup (110g) cornmeal

¹/₃ cup (50g) oat flour (or rolled oats finely ground in a food processor)

1¹/₂ teaspoons baking powder

1 tablespoon baking soda

1 teaspoon fine sea salt

²/₃ cup (220g) molasses

3²/₃ cups (900ml) milk, gently warmed

³/₄ cup (110g) dried blueberries (or raisins or dried cranberries)

2 clean coffee cans, about 4¹/₂ inches across and 6 inches tall, well buttered

Preheat the oven to 300°F.

Combine all the dry ingredients in a large bowl and mix well. Make a well in the center. Mix the molasses with the milk until thoroughly blended. Using a wooden spoon, gradually work enough of the milk mixture into the dry ingredients to make a thick paste, beating well. Then beat in the rest of the milk to make a very thick batter. Finally, fold in the blueberries using a large metal spoon until evenly distributed.

Spoon the batter into the buttered cans, which should be three-quarters full. Bake for about 1¹/₂ hours until a skewer inserted into the center comes out clean. Leave to cool for about 5 minutes, then gently remove the bread from the cans while still warm. Leave to cool on a wire rack.

The bread is best eaten within 3 days. Once thoroughly cooled, it can be frozen for up to a month.

WHOLE-WHEAT *berries are soaked until they almost sprout, then combined with coarse whole-wheat flour plus a sourdough starter, to give a loaf with real texture and a deep flavor. "We use a very powerful starter, which has the consistency of a porridge or very thick soup," Rene Becker told me. "Knowing when your starter is at the peak of its power is the key to making any sourdough-style bread. If you don't have a starter that you use regularly, or refresh regularly, you can substitute* $^1/_3$ *0.6-oz cake fresh yeast (5g) dispersed in* $^1/_2$ *cup water at 104°F."*

Huron loaf

MAKES 2 LARGE OR 3 MEDIUM LOAVES

$^2/_3$ cup (130g) whole-wheat berries

SPONGE:

1$^1/_2$ cups (320ml) cool water, preferably spring water (61°F)

2 tablespoons (30g) thick-batter sourdough starter (see page 49)

2 cups (230g) organic unbleached white bread flour

DOUGH:

1$^1/_4$ cups (300ml) cool water, preferably spring water (61°F)

3$^1/_2$ cups (400g) organic whole-wheat bread flour

about 4 cups (450g) organic unbleached white-bread flour

4 teaspoons fine sea salt

2 baking sheets, or 2 loaf pans, about 10 x 5 x 3 inches, well greased

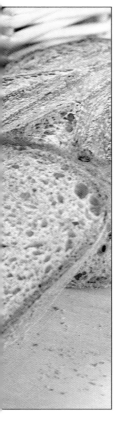

Soak the whole-wheat berries in cold water for 24 hours, then drain and place them in a large jar. Cover the top of the jar with cheesecloth or muslin and set aside at room temperature. Leave them for at least a day. They will have more flavor when slightly sprouted, which will take 2–3 days. Grind the berries in a food processor, as coarse or fine as you like.

Make the sponge 13 hours before you intend to mix the dough: Combine the water, sourdough starter (or yeast mixture), and flour in a medium bowl and mix well together. Cover with plastic wrap and let sit at room temperature.

To make the dough, put the bubbly sponge in the bowl of an electric mixer, or into a larger mixing bowl. Pour the water into the bowl used for the sponge and swirl around to dissolve as much of the sponge left on the sides as possible, then add to the large bowl. Add the flours and processed whole-wheat berries, and mix on low speed for 4 minutes (or work by hand for 5 minutes) to make a firm but not stiff dough. Leave to rest for 15 minutes.

Add the salt, and mix for 4 minutes on low speed (or 5 minutes by hand), then for 1 minute on medium speed (3 minutes by hand). If necessary, turn out the dough into a large bowl. Cover with plastic wrap, or put into a plastic bag. Leave to rise at warm room temperature until doubled in size – 3–4 hours, depending on the vigor of your starter and the room temperature.

Turn out the dough onto a work surface and divide into two or three equal pieces. Shape each into a round or oblong loaf and place in floured cloth-lined baskets or pleated floured cloths. Or, shape and put into the prepared loaf pans. Cover with a dry cloth or plastic wrap and leave to rise as before until the loaves have slightly more than doubled in size – 2–3 hours.

Toward the end of the rising time, preheat the oven to 450°F. If baking the loaves on baking sheets, put the sheets into the oven to heat.

If the loaves have been risen in floured cloths, turn them onto the hot baking sheets. Use a razor blade to score the top of each loaf in a simple pattern. Bake for 35–40 minutes for small loaves, 40–50 minutes for larger ones, spraying the loaves with water every 5 minutes for the first 15 minutes of baking. The bread is done when the crust is hard and the loaves sound hollow when tapped underneath. Cool on a wire rack.

The bread is best left for at least 12 hours before eating and can be kept for up to 5 days. Once thoroughly cooled, it can be frozen for up to a month.

Boston Brown Bread (on the left), the classic accompaniment for baked beans, is traditionally steamed or baked in a large coffee can. Huron Loaf (on the right) gets its wonderful flavor and texture from a sourdough starter and sprouted whole-wheat berries.

The nutty texture of Oat Bread (on the rack) makes it a perfect partner for soup. Oat and Sour Cherry Loaf (on the board) is delicious with cheese or cold cuts.

I'M *a fan of the catalog from King Arthur Flour (see Directory, page 172), which contains many gems for the home baker. As well as hard-to-find ingredients, some esoteric items of equipment, and things you have never heard of, there is an excellent range of basics such as good-quality Irish oatmeal and steel-cut oats.*

I use organic oats and organic white bread flour for this simple recipe made with fresh yeast. Eat with soup, or with butter and honey.

Oat bread

MAKES 1 MEDIUM LOAF

²/₃ 0.6-oz cake fresh yeast (10g)

1³/₄ cups (400ml) lukewarm water

1¹/₂ cups (250g) steel-cut oats, coarsely ground in a food processor

about 2 cups (250g) unbleached white bread flour

¹/₂ tablespoon fine sea salt

extra coarse oat meal for sprinkling

a baking sheet, floured

Crumble the yeast into a large mixing bowl. Add the water and mix with your hand to make a smooth liquid. Pour in the oat meal and quickly mix to make a thin, gritty, lump-free batter. Cover the bowl with plastic wrap and leave at warm room temperature for about 4 hours — the mixture should become thick and spongy.

Work in the white flour and salt to make a soft, very slightly sticky dough — it will feel rather more gluey than a white flour dough. If the dough sticks to your hands or the bowl, add a little more flour. If there are dry crumbs in the bowl or the dough feels stiff and dry, add a little more water.

Turn the dough out onto a work surface and knead thoroughly for 10 minutes. Cover the dough with a damp dish towel, an upturned bowl, or a sheet of plastic wrap and leave for 15 minutes.

Crumble the fresh yeast into a
mixing bowl, then add the water.

Shape the dough into an oval loaf about 9 inches long and put onto the prepared baking sheet. Put the sheet into a large plastic bag or cover lightly with a damp dish towel. Leave to rise until almost doubled in size – 1–2 hours.

Toward the end of the rising time, preheat the oven to 425°F.

Sprinkle the top of the loaf with a little oat meal. Then, using kitchen scissors, snip the top in a zig-zag pattern. Bake for about 35 minutes until the loaf turns a light golden brown and sounds hollow when tapped underneath. Cool on a wire rack.

The bread is best eaten within 3 days, or toasted. Once thoroughly cooled, it can be frozen for up to a month.

VARIATION: *Oat and sour cherry loaf*
This is excellent with cheese or cold ham. Make the dough as for Oat Bread, adding $^1/_2$ cup (75g) dried sour cherries with the salt. Knead and rest the dough, then shape into a neat round loaf and leave to rise. Sprinkle with a little oat meal and slash the top of the loaf with a sharp knife. Bake as given, allowing 30–35 minutes.

Quickly stir the oat meal into the
yeast mixture. Leave until spongy.

Work in the flour and salt. The
dough will be soft and a bit sticky.

Snip the top of the loaf in a
zig-zag pattern, then bake.

Turn the dough out onto a work
surface and knead thoroughly.

After shaping and rising, sprinkle
the loaf lightly with oat meal.

ALTHOUGH THE ROMANS brought the watermill with them to Britain, the first English record of a windmill was in 1191. By the late Middle Ages, there were over 10,000 windmills in England.

Best in Boston: part two

The Maud Foster windmill was built in 1819. It stands right by the Drain, close to the center of Boston in Lincolnshire. The mill was named after a large landowner in the area in the mid-sixteenth century, a woman of some local importance. At the time she owned the land the Drain ran through, and it continued to be called the Maud Foster Drain until this century.

If you have the energy, you can climb all the seven floors of the mill to see the action. It grinds five tons of local organic wheat each week, and the flours produced are sold in the mill shop and used to make the breads and cakes enjoyed in its wonderful, surprisingly quiet tearoom. The flours are also shipped to small bakeries, restaurants, and specialist stores around Britain.

The Maud Foster windmill in Boston, Lincolnshire, stands by the Drain, the canal that provides a drainage system for the local flood plains.

M Y *favorite flour from the Maud Foster windmill is the stoneground organic four-grain. It is a coarse, slightly gritty blend of wheat and rye flours with malted wheat barley and oat flakes, and makes a truly delicious, well-textured loaf. Here I have mixed the simple flour, salt, and yeast dough with soured milk to enhance the taste and the performance of the rye — it rises better in an acidic mixture. Soured milk used to be part and parcel of daily baking. Today, with rocket-science dairy technology and rapid deliveries, it takes ages for milk to sour naturally, so to speed things up, add a teaspoon of lemon juice or white wine vinegar to warm milk and leave to stand for an hour or so. Wheaten or scofa flour, or a coarse stoneground whole-wheat flour, can also be used in this recipe.*

Windmill loaf

MAKES 1 MEDIUM LOAF

4 cups (500g) stoneground organic four-grain
    flour

$^1/_2$ tablespoon fine sea salt

$^2/_3$ 0.6-oz cake fresh yeast (10g)*

about 1$^1/_4$ cups (300ml) soured milk,
    lukewarm

a baking sheet, floured

Combine the flour and salt in a large mixing bowl and make a well in the center. Crumble the yeast into a small bowl and stir to a smooth liquid with half of the milk. Pour into the well in the flour, then add the remaining milk. Work the flour into the liquid to make a soft and very slightly sticky dough — it is important that the dough is not stiff, dry, or solid at this stage, so add more milk as necessary. The dough will firm up considerably as you knead it, so don't worry if it feels wetter than a usual dough.

Turn the dough out onto a work surface and knead thoroughly for 10 minutes — it should feel firm and pliable and no longer sticky and wet. If you have added too much liquid, and the dough is sticky at this stage, work in a little extra flour. Return the dough to the bowl, cover with a damp dish towel, and leave to rise at normal to warm kitchen temperature until doubled in size — 1$^1/_2$–2 hours.

Punch down the risen dough to deflate it, then turn out onto the work surface. Shape into a round loaf. Set on the prepared baking sheet and cover loosely with a damp dish towel, or place the sheet inside a large plastic bag. Leave to rise as before until doubled in size — 1–1$^1/_2$ hours.

Toward the end of the rising time, preheat the oven to 425°F.

Uncover the loaf and cut a cross on the surface. Bake for about 30 minutes until the loaf is golden brown and sounds hollow when tapped underneath. Cool it on a wire rack.

The bread is best eaten within 4 days, or toasted. Once thoroughly cooled, it can be frozen for up to a month.

* You can use 2 teaspoons rapid-rise active dry yeast instead of the fresh yeast. Combine the dry yeast with the flour and salt, then work in the milk and continue with the recipe.

Desna Greenhow mills only one kind of flour at her lovingly restored watermill — organic stoneground whole-wheat — and she does it all herself.

DESNA GREENHOW is rightly proud of her mill at Otterton, near Budleigh Salterton in East Devon, England "It's one of the 500 or so cornmills mentioned in the Domesday survey compiled soon after the Norman Conquest. Its machinery has been turned by the Otter river ever since, except for the 20 years it lay derelict in the Fifties and Sixties."

The mill has a fascinating history. Desna, a historian, has traced its 1000 years. "Otterton and its lands were granted by William I to the abbots of St. Michel in Normandy [France] – we have details of how the priory was run. The monks were bound to provide 16 shillings' worth of bread each week for the poor who came and asked for it. The bread would have been made from flour ground at the manor mill and baked in the priory ovens." In 1260, Prior Geoffrey Legat wrote that the prior had the right to every porpoise caught on the Otter estuary in exchange for 12 pence, and had to give a loaf of white bread to every sailor and two to the master of the fishing boat that caught it. At the Dissolution in 1539, Henry VIII gave Otterton to one of his clerks, Richard Duke. Although the fishing declined, the mill flourished.

A thousand-year-old watermill

Next to the mill is the Barn Bakery, where Lydia Greenaway (above) and Brenda Davis bake about 100 loaves of bread a day. Their award-winning cakes can be enjoyed in the tea shop.

It appears again on record at the sale of the manor to the Rolle family in 1785, and by the middle of the last century the miller, John Uglow, was a man of some local importance. His flour was delivered by coasting vessels as far away as Plymouth. But roller mills were soon to undermine the livelihoods of small millers, and in the late 1950s, Otterton was declared uneconomic and left to rot in peace.

Desna and George Polson, a judge, rescued the mill in 1977, and set about careful restoration with the help of a trained millwright. The two water wheels, over three yards across, were made in Exeter 150 years ago. The oldest parts of the machinery are 200 years old, and the stones are the ones used when the mill closed in 1959.

So now the mill is anything but peaceful. It is a noisy, creaking, restless place, full of the rushing of water, the slapping of the wooden buckets of the water wheel, the rhythm of the cast-iron machinery, and the churning of the great pair of quartz burr stones. "It has been fascinating doing something with a natural power source. Water-powered milling is an enthralling occupation," said Desna. The fineness of the flour is regulated in two ways: by raising and lowering the top millstone to alter the gap between the stones, and by using sluices to control the speed of the water – the greater the force of water, the faster the stones turn and the finer the flour produced. The speed of production is controlled by the rate the grain is fed down onto the stones.

Desna only mills organic wheat grown in England's West Country, and she only makes whole-wheat flour. She buys for quality rather than wheat variety, looking for a 12% protein level and the low moisture content that prevents clogging between the stones. "There are no manuals about this kind of milling. I had help from two millers who had worked here in the past, the rest was trial and terror."

Alongside the mill is a bakery, open and baking seven days a week. The loaves and cakes are sold in the mill shop and restaurant and also in wholefood stores in Exeter. Home bakers travel from all over the county to stock up with Desna's flour – I now use her flour for my whole-wheat breads, as it has an exceptionally deep but not bitter flavor and a light sandy texture that is easy to work with. She has strong views on how to treat whole-wheat flour: "It should be freshly ground, like pepper or coffee, so buy as you need it; stale whole-wheat flour tastes rancid and bitter. Handle the dough very gently, not as much or as vigorously as you would do normal doughs. Mix just until the dough leaves the sides of the bowl, then knead as little as possible."

*Organic stoneground whole-wheat flour from
Otterton Mill gives this whole-wheat cob a
superb and nutty flavor.*

WHEN *Women's Institute baker Rosemary Rowson (see also page 84) makes a traditional
Devon whole-wheat loaf, she uses stoneground organic flour from Otterton Mill and fresh
yeast, because "you can taste the difference with good ingredients." Her family likes the nutty flavor
of a 100% whole-wheat loaf, but for a lighter result she suggests using half whole-wheat flour
and half unbleached white bread flour. Rosemary is a fine teacher and this is the ideal recipe to
start you breadmaking — it is straightforward and fool-proof, and you are bound to enjoy the
results. This loaf has a superb flavor; it's moist and doesn't fall apart when you try to cut it.*

*Rosemary has a good tip for using whole-wheat flour: she makes sure the flour is thoroughly
warm before starting, by leaving the measured flour in a large mixing bowl near her range for a
couple of hours. This gives a lighter, less dense loaf.*

Rosemary Rowson's whole-wheat cob

MAKES 2 MEDIUM LOAVES

6 cups (750g) whole-wheat flour, preferably
   stoneground
2 teaspoons fine sea salt
2 tablespoons (30g) butter, diced
2 teaspoons clear honey or sugar
1¹/₂ 0.6-oz cakes fresh yeast (25g)*
1³/₄ cups (450ml) lukewarm water

1 or 2 baking sheets, greased

Warm the flour (this can also be done by putting it in a heatproof bowl in a very low
oven, or in the microwave on high for 15 seconds). Mix in the salt, then rub in the
butter using the tips of your fingers until the mixture looks like coarse crumbs with
no big lumps. If using honey, make a well in the center of the flour mixture and add
the honey. If using sugar, stir it into the flour mixture, then make a well in the center.

Crumble the yeast into a cup or bowl, add a little of the measured water, and stir
until thoroughly dispersed. Pour into the well. Using a wooden spoon or your hand,
gradually mix in the flour and the remaining water to make a soft but not sticky dough
– the dough will feel very different from one made with white flour. If the dough feels
stiff or dry and is hard to work, add a little more warm water — it is better to have a
whole-wheat dough that is slightly soft rather than slightly dry; the latter would result

Rosemary prefers to use a wooden spoon to mix the dough.

Before putting the loaf to rise, she cuts a deep cross in the top.

in a baked loaf that is crumbly and dry. Rosemary says: "If it is nice and soft, even slightly sticky, then you will get a good rise."

Turn out onto a floured work surface. Don't worry if the dough looks a mess at this stage. Pick up the dough from underneath and swish it around to make a soft ball of dough. Then knead thoroughly for 5 minutes, stretching the dough really well. The dough will feel firmer and be very smooth and pliable. Return the dough to the bowl and cover with plastic wrap – Rosemary feels this is better than a damp dish towel for keeping the dough moist. Leave to rise in a warm but not hot spot until doubled in size – about 1 hour in a warm farmhouse kitchen.

Remove the dough from the bowl and knead gently on a lightly floured work surface for half a minute to expel all the large bubbles of air and return the dough to its original size. Cut into two equal pieces and shape each into a ball about 6 inches across, tucking the outer edges under the loaf to make a neat cushion. Put onto the prepared baking sheet or sheets with the gathers underneath. Cut a deep cross into the top of each loaf. Put the sheet into a large plastic bag and leave to rise as before until doubled in size – about 45 minutes in a warm kitchen. Do not let the loaves become more than double or they will collapse in the oven.

Toward the end of the rising time, preheat the oven to 450°F.

Uncover the loaves and bake for 15–20 minutes until they turn a healthy brown and sound hollow when tapped underneath. Cool on a wire rack.

The bread is best eaten within 4 days, or toasted. Once thoroughly cooled, it can be frozen for up to a month.

* You can use 4 teaspoons rapid-rise dry yeast instead of the fresh yeast. Mix the dry yeast into the warm flour with the salt, then continue with the recipe.

VARIATION: *Hazelnut cob*
To make the ideal bread to eat with cheese, follow the recipe for Whole-Wheat Cob, but omit the butter and add $1/4$ cup hazelnut oil to the warm water. While the dough is rising for the first time, toast $1^1/4$ cups (150g) hazelnuts in the oven preheated to 350°F until golden brown; cool, then rub off the skins in a dish towel and coarsely chop the nuts in a food processor or by hand. Before shaping the loaves, knead the nuts into the dough until evenly distributed. Bake as given.

In Hazelnut Cob, chopped toasted hazelnuts and hazelnut oil add wonderful richness and crunch.

THE SIMPLON PASS CONNECTS BRIG AND GANDO in the southern Swiss Alps. Since the Middle Ages it has been a busy trading and communications route between northern Europe and Italy, so Brig has always been open to travelers. But the first real tourists arrived at the end of the nineteenth century when an Englishman opened a hotel on the mountain top (the locals had to carry the guests up several hundred feet from the road). Now the population of 900 swells by 10,000 at the height of the season, and skiers in winter, walkers and hikers in summer, are the main source of income. They all eat bread – French baguettes, Italian loaves with durum semolina, light whole-wheat, 100% rye sourdoughs – and the local millers and bakers like to keep everyone happy and well fed.

Hearty grains from the Swiss Alps

At Bernhard Augsberger's mill, in the southern Alps, wood is used for the structure and some of the milling machinery. The result is both elegant and functional.

Bernhard Augsberger

Although the Augsberger flour mill sits on the bank of the Rhône in Naters-Brig, it never used water power. "We have always used electric roller mills. Many people knock roller mills, but with the right raw materials and care, you can produce superb flour. For instance, we set the rollers slightly farther apart and use lower pressure than normal; this reduces the heat and you get a better result. The way we use the rollers produces large flattened flakes of wheat or rye, which gives a speckled, textured flour. You can't get the same result with a stone mill – you get an even-textured sandy flour."

The mill produces 50 different flours. "We have 15 base flours; the rest are mixtures, different combinations, different textures. Ten years ago we could only sell 100% whole-wheat rye flour and farmer's flour [a blend of 20% rye and 80% wheat], but when I came into the business I realized that the special flour market was important. The specialist craft-baker will take the rest of the truck [of basics] if he can buy the unusual or special flours he needs. Now our best seller is half-white flour."

The specialty of the Valais canton is a sturdy wholegrain rye loaf. Rye is not particularly Swiss, but a third of all the Swiss rye is grown in this valley, with its acidic soil, well over three thousand feet above sea level. "We have the largest choice of rye flours in Switzerland; in this canton rye is five times more important than in the rest of the country. All our rye is locally grown, but only a quarter of the wheat we need. We buy the entire crop grown by the most important organic farmer. Some of our organic farmers cultivate tiny, handkerchief plots the size of your back yard. They are so important to us."

Because Switzerland is not part of the E.U., the agricultural system is tightly controlled. Bernhard has to buy 85% of his grain from Swiss farmers and is only allowed to import 15% from French and Canadian growers.

Right: Bags of Augsberger flour are stacked next to the spiral chute. The mill produces 50 different flours, each with its own color-coded lettering on the bag.

Below: Fine wholegrain rye flour is used to make Walliser Roggenbrot, *a bread special to this Swiss canton.*

Tʜɪs *round wholegrain rye loaf with a thick, crazy-cracked, floury crust is the special bread of the canton — Wallis (in German) or Valais (in French). Until relatively recently, it was difficult to grow wheat in this area, and imported wheat flour was expensive, so sourdough rye became the everyday bread. The more compact the loaf, the longer it kept.*

Bernhard Augsberger says the dough needs plenty of humidity while rising, and a vigorous sourdough starter. If the shaped dough does not crack sufficiently, it usually means the sourdough was not lively enough.

Walliser roggenbrot

MAKES 2 MEDIUM LOAVES

INITIAL DOUGH:

1 cup (250ml) lukewarm water

4oz (125g) soft-dough sourdough starter
   (see page 49)

3 cups (325g) fine wholegrain rye flour

TO MAKE THE BREAD:

2 cups (500ml) lukewarm water

2 teaspoons fine sea salt

about 6 cups (650g) fine wholegrain rye flour

2 baking sheets

For the initial dough, put the water, sourdough starter, and flour into a large bowl, and mix with your hand until thoroughly combined and you have a slightly soft dough. Cover the bowl with a damp dish towel and leave in a warm place for about 1 hour.

To make the bread, combine the initial dough with the water, then work in the salt and enough flour to make a slightly soft dough. It will feel sticky because it is made only from rye flour, but it should not be so soft that it doesn't hold its shape, or so firm that it is hard to work — you may have to work in extra flour or water accordingly.

Turn the dough out onto a lightly floured work surface and knead thoroughly until pliable — about 5 minutes. Shape the dough into two neat balls. Put each ball of dough into a bowl, cover, and leave as before for about 1 hour.

Turn out the balls of dough onto a floured work surface. Dust them heavily with flour, then gently flatten to make two round loaves, each about 7 inches across. Place on the baking sheets, then set inside plastic bags. Leave to rise in a warm place until well cracked on top and almost doubled in size — 4–8 hours, depending on the vigor of your starter and the temperature.

Toward the end of the rising time, preheat the oven to 400°F. Put a baking dish with hot water on the oven floor, to create a steamy atmosphere.

Uncover the loaves and bake in the heated oven for 50–60 minutes until they sound hollow when tapped underneath. Cool on a wire rack.

The bread is best eaten within a week. Once thoroughly cooled, it can be frozen for up to a month.

Urs Arnold-Theiler bakes different loaves for Swiss and Italian customers.

He gets all his flour from Bernhard Augsberger's mill, and uses the Augsberger bags for delivering the baked loaves.

The Arnold-Arnold Bakery

Over six thousand feet up, along the Simplon Pass from Brig in Switzerland toward the Italian border, is the small, isolated village of Simplon-Dorf. It was a surprise to find a good-sized traditional family bakery and tearoom here, in a village of just 300 people. The baker, Urs Arnold-Theiler, and his wife Mathilda sell 80% of their breads and pastries to hikers, skiers, and passers-by. Local villagers, hotels, and restaurants buy the rest. Here, as in Brig, tourism is vital.

Old-fashioned rye loaves are the most popular in the village. "In the old days each family was able to use the village oven for two days three times a year," Urs told me. "The loaves were marked with the family stamp to differentiate them. We still make rye bread in the same way: 100% wholegrain rye flour, a saved-dough starter or 'chef' [150g per kilo of flour], and a 20-hour rise. All the other bakeries in the area were after our secret because our bread was so popular. Eventually I gave my recipe to a friend in Zermatt. But he could never get the same result, because the water, conditions, and flour there were all different from ours."

Almost 70% of Urs's customers are Italian, and they prefer his whole-wheat, graham flour, and half-white flour loaves and rolls. All the flour comes from Bernhard Augsberger's mill (see page 36).

T HE *village symbol in Simplon-Dorf — a horn — is the inspiration for these good-flavored bread rolls. Urs uses a half-white flour from Augsberger's mill. You can achieve a similar result by mixing unbleached white bread flour and a fairly fine whole-wheat flour.*

Little horns

MAKES 10 ROLLS

7 cups (800g) half-white flour,(or 6$^{1}/_{2}$ cups (760g) white bread flour and $^{1}/_{2}$ cup (40g) whole-wheat flour

1 tablespoon fine sea salt

$^{2}/_{3}$ 0.6-oz cake fresh yeast (10g)*

1oz (25g) soft-dough sourdough starter (see page 49)

about 2 cups (500ml) lukewarm water

several baking sheets

Combine the flour and salt in a large mixing bowl. Crumble the yeast into another bowl, add the starter and three-fourths of the water, and stir until thoroughly combined. Add to the flour mixture and work together, adding enough of the remaining water to make a fairly firm dough.

Turn out onto a lightly floured work surface and knead thoroughly for 10 minutes until the dough is very elastic. Return the dough to the bowl, cover with a sheet of plastic wrap, and leave to rise in a warm place until doubled in size — about 1 hour.

Punch down the risen dough and turn out onto a lightly floured work surface. Divide the dough into 20 equal pieces. Roll each piece with your hands to make a neat sausage shape about 6$^{1}/_{2}$ inches long. Form x-shaped rolls on the baking sheets, using two sausages for each. Cover and leave to rise as before until the rolls are doubled in size — about 15 minutes.

Meanwhile, preheat the oven to 425°F.

Uncover the little horns and bake for about 20 minutes until a good golden brown. Cool on wire racks.

The rolls are best eaten within 24 hours. Once thoroughly cooled, they can be frozen for up to a month.

* You can use 2 teaspoons rapid-rise active dry yeast instead of the fresh yeast. Combine the dry yeast with the flour and salt, then work in the water, and continue with the recipe.

Little Horns, shaped to resemble the symbol of Simplon-Dorf, have a good flavor and texture.

Fields of organic spelt and wheat grow side by side in the hills above Brig in Switzerland.

A T T H E *Arnold-Arnold Bakery, Urs Arnold-Theiler makes these rolls using a rough whole-wheat flour, called graham flour, which he buys from Bernhard Augsberger's mill. An Irish wheaten flour or coarse brown Irish-style flour will also do very well. A combination of fresh yeast and sourdough starter gives the rolls a light, crumbly texture and plenty of flavor. They are excellent for breakfast or with cheese and pâtés.*

Graham rolls

MAKES 12 ROLLS

4 cups (500g) graham flour

1/2 tablespoon fine sea salt

1 tablespoon (15g) butter, diced

1 0.6-oz cake fresh yeast (15g)*

1/2 cup (50g) soft-batter sourdough starter
   (see page 49)

about 1 1/3 cups (330ml) lukewarm water

several baking sheets

Combine the flour and salt in a large mixing bowl. Add the butter and rub in with your fingertips until the mixture looks like coarse crumbs. Crumble the yeast into another bowl, add the sourdough starter and three-fourths of the water, and stir until you have a smooth liquid. Add to the flour mixture. Gradually work the flour into the yeast liquid, adding enough of the remaining water to make a soft but not sticky dough — the amount of water you need will depend on the type of flour and the consistency of the sourdough.

Turn out onto a lightly floured work surface and knead thoroughly for 5 minutes, until the dough is pliable and elastic. Return the dough to the bowl, cover with a sheet of plastic wrap, and leave in a warm place until doubled in size — about 1 hour.

Punch down the dough to deflate, then turn out onto a lightly floured work surface. Divide into 12 equal pieces. Shape each piece into an oval about 4 x 2 1/2 inches. Set well apart on the baking sheets. Dust with a little extra flour, then cover and leave to rise as before until the rolls have doubled in size — about 30 minutes.

Toward the end of the rising time, preheat the oven to 425°F.

Uncover the rolls. Using a sharp knife, make a shallow slit down the length of each one. Bake the rolls for about 20 minutes until a good golden brown. Cool on a wire rack.

The rolls are best eaten within 24 hours. Once thoroughly cooled, they can be frozen for up to a month.

* You can use 1 envelope (2 1/2 teaspoons) rapid-rise dry yeast instead of the fresh yeast. Mix the dry yeast with the flour and the salt, then rub in the butter and work in the water and the sourdough.

U RS ARNOLD-THEILER *makes this surprising rye loaf, called* bio roggenbrot, *using a coarse organic rye flour that has tiny flakes of bran mixed with a rough wheat flour rather like the one used in Irish soda bread. It is important to warm all the ingredients, and to knead the dough for the full 10 minutes. The loaf only has one rising, for 30 minutes in a warm place, and should not be left much longer than that or it will crack.*

Organic rye bread

MAKES 1 LOAF

3¹/₂ cups (400g) organic very coarse
   whole-grain rye flour

scant 1 cup (100g) organic coarse whole-wheat
   flour

¹/₂ tablespoon fine sea salt

2oz (50g) soft-dough sourdough starter (see
   page 49)

1¹/₂ 0.6-oz cakes fresh yeast (25g)*

about 1¹/₃ cups (330ml) lukewarm water

a baking sheet

Combine the flours and salt in a large mixing bowl. Add the sourdough starter, and the yeast dispersed in three-fourths of the water. Mix together, working in as much extra water as you need to make a slightly soft and sticky dough.

Turn out onto a lightly floured work surface and knead thoroughly for 10 minutes. Shape into a flat, round loaf about 7 inches across. Place on a floured baking sheet, then put the sheet into a large plastic bag and close the ends. Leave in a really warm place for 30 minutes.

Meanwhile, preheat the oven to 400°F. Put a baking dish of hot water in the oven to create steam.

Uncover the bread, and score it or stamp a pattern in the center. Put it in the oven and spray or sprinkle with water. Bake for 1 hour until the loaf sounds hollow when tapped underneath. Leave to cool on a wire rack.

The bread is best eaten within a week. Once thoroughly cooled, it can be frozen for up to a month.

* You can use 4 teaspoons rapid-rise active dry yeast instead of the fresh yeast. Combine the dry yeast with the flours and salt, then continue with the recipe.

Breads from the Arnold-Arnold Bakery include Little Horns (left), Graham Rolls (front), and Organic Rye Bread (back right), here marked in traditional fashion with Urs Arnold-Theiler's family stamp.

THE SMALL VILLAGE OF BLATTEN, high in the mountains above Brig in Switzerland, was devastated by avalanches early in 1999. On a hot summer's day, six months later, we had to make several detours to avoid the massive blocks of compacted snow that still filled the roads. The parking lot at the base of the ski lift was completely filled with tree trunks piled six high, the mountain side was scarred and bare. Luckily there were no casualties, but over 30 houses and old wooden chalets disappeared. One of the oldest and smallest buildings, a mill and bakery built 300 years ago, survived.

Manna from the mountaintop

The original stone mill at Blatten in Switzerland was built 300 years ago. The mill wheel is powered by water diverted from a mountain stream.

The stone mill, powered by water diverted from a mountain stream down onto the mill wheel, was installed in the mid-nineteenth century, and the bakehouse a few years later. Villagers brought their own rye to the mill, then one family at a time would use the bakehouse to make enough bread to last them for six months. By 1960, most families were able to travel down the mountain and buy bread from a bakery, so the mill closed.

The disused buildings and equipment were rescued in 1991 by a group of dedicated local bread enthusiasts, who set about restoring everything to full working order. For the last seven years they have spent a day here each weekend in summer and each month in winter. They mill the rye they grow themselves on a nearby handkerchief plot, firing the oven (no shortage of suitable wood), and then mixing the resulting flour into bread dough in 90-pound batches, using the massive kneading trough. While the dough rises, they light the barbecue and open a few of the bottles of wine that were cooled in the stream. Then their wives arrive – to do the cleaning up.

Making and shaping the dough into 60-odd loaves is team work, and very hot – the bakehouse felt like a sauna at 93°F, with windows and door tightly closed. Loading the oven with the risen loaves is a three-man job – one holds the light, another the peel, the third fills the oven. Then it's time to eat and open a few more bottles. The baked loaves are stacked on the work bench that doubles as a lid to the kneading trough, and on a vertical wooden cooling rack suspended from the ceiling to thwart mice. Wrapped in paper bags, the loaves are eagerly bought by the local hotels and ski chalets.

The chief miller and baker is Rolf Eggel, whose day job is with the area teachers' union. We heard that he also made the best soup in the village. He started making bread when he discovered he was diabetic, and had to take care what he ate. Rolf had a number of tips to offer us: use a lot of fine-cut wood for a fast fire; warmth is vital to rye bread, so keep the room hot; and warm the flour, water, and saved "chef" (the saved-dough sourdough starter). In common with many of the other bakers we talked to, he said that sourdoughs work best with organic ingredients and spring water rather than chemically treated water.

R OLF EGGEL *and his friends mix the dough in 90-pound batches, so this is a scaled-down recipe. Each time they save a portion of the dough (before the fruits are incorporated) as the "chef" to raise the following week's batch. (See also page 48.) They use a mixture of ready-to-eat dried fruits — prunes, apricots, nectarines, apples, and pears — or, sometimes, a mixture of toasted nuts instead of (or with) the fruit.*

This bread has an excellent flavor and texture, and a very thick crust. It's good on its own or with a rich, creamy cheese.

Rye bread with dried fruit

MAKES 3 SMALL LOAVES

2oz (50g) saved-dough starter (see recipe introduction)

8¹/₂ cups (1kg) wholegrain rye flour

scant 1 cup (125g) cracked rye

1 cup (125g) unbleached white bread flour

4 teaspoons fine sea salt

3¹/₂ cups (850ml) lukewarm water, preferably still spring water

about 1 cup (100g) dried fruits or toasted nuts, or a combination, roughly chopped and tossed with flour to coat

several baking sheets

If necessary, bring the saved-dough starter, or "chef," back to warm room temperature – it should feel soft, slightly sticky, and warm. Combine the dry ingredients in a large bowl, and warm gently in a low oven or microwave.

Put the chef into the center of the flour mixture, then pour the water over and "get stuck in," as Rolf puts it. Mix all the ingredients to make a soft, sticky dough, then work the dough for about 10 minutes until it feels slightly stiffer and more supple. Cover with a damp dish towel and leave in a warm place (Rolf recommends a stifling 86°F) for 1 hour, longer in a cooler place.

Turn out the dough onto a floured work surface, and divide it into three equal pieces. Flour your hands, then form the dough into neat balls. Make three deep cuts in each dough ball and push the fruit or nuts into the slits. Remold the dough into balls with your hands. Put the loaves on a sheet or board dusted with flour and leave, uncovered, to rise. Rolf sets the loaves above a giant *pot-au-feu*, which provides a steamy atmosphere to help the yeasts to thrive. In a hot room (around 95°F) it will take about an hour to almost double in size, but allow up to 4 hours in a warm kitchen. The dough will crack on the surface.

Toward the end of the rising time, preheat the oven to 400°F. Put the baking sheets in to heat.

Transfer the loaves to the hot sheets and bake for 1 hour or until the loaves sound hollow when tapped underneath. Cool on a wire rack.

The loaves are best cooled and then wrapped to be cut the next day, and will last up to a week. They can be frozen for up to a month.

Top left: The oven takes about 5 hours firing to reach the initial 450°F.
Top center: Mixing the dough in the kneading trough is 30 minutes of hot, sweaty team work. Top right: 65 loaves are shaped from each batch of dough.
Left: Rolf proudly presents the freshly baked rye loaves.

*This easy-to-make Wheat-Free Loaf
is tasty and has a good texture.*

THERE *are a number of wheatless flour mixes on sale in wholefood and specialist food stores. Most are multi-purpose, and can be used for muffins, cookies, pastry, and cakes. A few can also make really tasty bread with a good texture. The flour I like best is a combination of barley, rye, oats, rice, and corn flours; another excellent one is organic and the same mix without the rye. As each wheat-free flour has its own characteristics and flavor, use this recipe as the basis for your own experiments. The water is slightly warmer than I normally use — it helps to gelatinize the starches in the flour. It should not be more than "hand hot" or it will kill the yeast, but if it is cool or lukewarm, the baked loaf will be too heavy.*

We and — more importantly — our friends who react badly to wheat flour were thrilled with the flavor and texture of this loaf.

Wheat-free loaf

MAKES 1 MEDIUM LOAF

about 5 cups (550g) wheat-free flour (a mix
    of barley, oats, rice, and corn, with or
    without rye)
$^1/_2$ tablespoon fine sea salt
1 0.6-oz cake fresh yeast (10g)*
about 2 cups (530ml) hand-hot water
1 teaspoon clear honey

a loaf pan, about $8^1/_2$ x $4^1/_2$ x $2^1/_2$ inches, well
    greased

Combine the flour and salt in a large mixing bowl and make a well in the center. Crumble the yeast into a small bowl. Mix in $^1/_2$ cup of the water and the honey to make a smooth liquid. Pour into the well in the flour and mix in enough flour to make a sticky paste. Gradually pour in the remaining water in a slow trickle as you mix in the flour with your other hand — you should end up with a heavy, sticky, slightly gritty batter, quite unlike a normal bread dough. If it seems stiff and doesn't flow, add a little more water. (If the baked loaf has a split along one side, rather than the top, it is an indication that the batter was too stiff, so add a little more water the next time you make this bread.) The batter-dough does not need to be kneaded or worked any further.

Pour the batter into the prepared pan and cover with a damp dish towel or put the pan into a large plastic bag. Leave at warm room temperature for 20 minutes.

Meanwhile, preheat the oven to 425°F.

Uncover the loaf — it will have risen slightly — and bake for 30 minutes until golden brown and firm. Turn the loaf out of the pan and put it back into the oven, straight onto the shelf. Bake for a further 10 minutes. Cool on a wire rack.

Pour the yeast, honey, and water mixture into the well in the flour.

Trickle in the remaining water, mixing with your hand as you go.

The mixture will be more like a heavy batter than a bread dough.

Pour the batter-dough into the pan and smooth the surface to level it.

The bread is best eaten within 4 days. Once thoroughly cooled, it can be frozen for up to a month.

* You can use 1 envelope (2^1/$_2$ teaspoons) rapid-rise active dry yeast instead of the fresh yeast. Mix the dry yeast with the flour and salt. Dissolve the honey in the water and then continue with the recipe.

VARIATIONS: Once you have made the loaf to your satisfaction, you can add seeds, nuts, herbs, olives, sun-dried tomatoes – whatever you fancy for a change.

Some specialist millers produce an all-purpose gluten-free flour milled from a blend of rice, potato, buckwheat, and corn. Available from healthfood stores, it can be used for cakes, pastry, and muffins, as well as this bread, which is suitable for people allergic to wheat, gluten, soy, dairy, and yeast.

Gluten-free, yeast-free loaf

MAKES 1 MEDIUM LOAF

about 4 cups (400g) gluten-free flour

1 tablespoon baking powder

^{1}/$_2$ teaspoon fine sea salt

1 teaspoon clear honey

1^1/$_2$ teaspoons sunflower oil

1^1/$_2$ cups (350ml) water

a loaf pan, about 8^1/$_2$ x 4^1/$_2$ x 2^1/$_2$ inches, well greased

Preheat the oven to 400°F.

Sift the flour, baking powder, and salt into a mixing bowl. Make a well in the center. Mix the honey and oil into the water, then pour into the well. Using a wooden spoon, mix the flour into the liquid to make a smooth, thick, soft batter. It should be more like a soft cake batter rather than a biscuit or soda bread dough.

Pour the batter into the prepared pan. Bake for about 30 minutes until a light golden brown; a skewer inserted in the center should come out clean. Unmold and leave to cool on a wire rack.

The bread is best eaten within 2 days, or lightly toasted. Once thoroughly cooled, it can be frozen for up to a month.

2 Leavening the dough

ANUMBER OF METHODS are used to leaven bread doughs. The most ancient is fermentation by wild yeasts, in a sourdough starter. For the yeasts naturally present in the atmosphere, a moist, warm mixture of flour and water is the perfect environment for reproduction. As they multiply, the yeasts produce carbon dioxide and alcohol, which change the texture and the flavor of the dough. The starter is alive – it must be "fed" to keep it effective and vigorous – and it is unpredictable: rising times depend on its vigor, and the flavor of your bread can vary wildly from mild and tangy to almost inedibly acidic. But this near-magical complexity is what attracts and entrances many bakers.

Other bakers prefer the tractability of commercial baker's yeast that comes as a moist gray-brown cake or fine dry granules. This works in much the same way as wild yeast, but it is much easier to predict the rising times and the final result. Because the fermentation is quicker, the bread has slightly less flavor than a sourdough. Some

Home bread maker Maurice Bichard (see page 62) uses a thick-batter sourdough starter made from high-protein Canadian wheat flour to leaven his loaves.

bakers prefer this, while others use a combination of sourdough and fresh yeast to get the best of both worlds, a light-textured loaf with plenty of flavor.

Yeasts thrive at around 79°F. At cooler temperatures, they slow down and then become dormant; at higher temperatures, and if mixed with water that is too hot, they may die. Bakers use temperature to slow or hasten the fermentation of the dough. Recipes sometimes give an indication of the best conditions for fermentation: cool room temperature (about 60°F), normal (about 68°F), and warm (about 86°F).

The simplest and quickest way to leaven a bread dough is to add chemical leavening agents – baking powder, baking soda, and cream of tartar. When in contact with a suitable liquid (the baking soda needs something acidic, the cream of tartar something alkaline) and warmth, they produce gases. The dough does not have to be kneaded, but it must be baked quickly before the chemical reaction is complete. The bread will stale more quickly than yeasted bread.

SOURDOUGH STARTERS – also called "chefs," "mothers," *levains*, or *bigas* – come in a number of forms. Although all starters do the same thing – raise and flavor bread dough – bakers tend to prefer one starter to another, having spent years finding the one that works best for them, and each baker is quite specific about the kind to use. However, for most home bread makers it is a case of trial and error, experimenting and enjoying the variety of sourdough starters.

Taming wild yeasts

The best way to store a saved-dough starter is in an airtight container in the fridge.

The main types of sourdough starters are:

• naturally fermented (i.e. without commercial baker's yeast): a soft dough or a thick, runny batter made from white, whole-wheat, or rye flour and water. A white sourdough starter is multi-purpose and can be used in any mixture; a light rye is useful for flavoring doughs other than rye (see Maurice Chaplais's breads, page 94).

• *biga*: a saltless soft-dough starter that includes a small quantity of baker's yeast (typically 5g yeast to 2 cups (250g) flour and ½ cup (100ml) water) to encourage the fermentation. The mixture is left for 12 hours to mature – it must rise by two or three times its volume and then collapse. *Bigas* are used by Italian bakers to flavor their doughs.

• saved-dough: literally that – after a dough has been risen and punched down, a piece is cut off and stored in a plastic box or sealed glass jar in the fridge (it will keep for up to a week). It is then worked into the next batch of dough, to raise and flavor it. The saved-dough starter can be naturally fermented or yeasted, or a combination, and it can be made from white flour or a mixture. It should not contain eggs or dairy products, which could cause it to go moldy.

If using a recipe that calls for a saved-dough starter, make up a batch of yeasted dough. Cut off a piece, about 8 ounces (250g), and store overnight in the fridge to "mature." Use the rest of the batch of dough to make a smaller loaf or rolls.

Sourdough starters give rich, deep flavor to the breads they leaven.

THE *aim is to capture the yeasts naturally present in the air and the wheat, and encourage them to grow and produce bubbles of gas. This fermentation is a natural process, with carbon dioxide and lactic acid as by-products. The gas raises the dough, the lactic acid adds the flavor.*

For the best chance of success, use organic flour (never bleached) and spring (not chlorinated) water. If you do use tap water, filter, boil to remove the chlorine, and cool to room temperature. The kitchen work surface works best for my starters — the room is usually quite warm (around 77°F) and, because of all the fruit and vegetables there as well as all the cooking, the air seems to be full of yeasts.

Naturally fermented sourdough starter

scant 1 cup (100g) organic unbleached white bread flour

¹/₂ cup (115ml) water (see recipe introduction)

EACH REFRESHMENT:

scant 1 cup (100g) organic unbleached white bread flour

After 24 hours.

After 48 hours.

After 72 hours.

Ready to use or store.

Combine the flour and water in a small bowl to make a sticky paste.

Cover with a damp dish towel or piece of cheesecloth, not plastic wrap. Leave on the kitchen work surface, away from drafts, for 3 or 4 days until the mixture looks bubbly. Dampen the dish towel as necessary, to keep it moist.

After this time, your starter should have a milky smell and look bubbly. If it smells bad, rather than just slightly sour, or has patches of mold, or doesn't look at all active, then throw it away and start again. (This applies to all starters, not just new ones.) As Patrick LePort (page 103) says, a good starter should smell milky, not make your eyes water.

Once your starter looks bubbly, you can start to refresh or "feed" it. Add another scant 1 cup (100g) organic bread flour and enough water to make a thick, sticky paste. Work the dough with your hand or a wooden spoon to get plenty of air into the mixture. Cover again with a damp dish towel and leave for 24 hours.

The starter should look very active and bubbly now. Remove and discard half of it. Add another cup (100g) organic bread flour and enough water to make the paste as before. Cover and leave for 12 hours.

If the starter looks very bubbly and active at this point, it is ready to use. If it still seems to need a boost, halve the mixture once again and feed as before. It should then be ready to use in 6 hours.

Feed your sourdough starter regularly, even if you are not using it, and store in the fridge in a plastic container or glass jar. Bring back to room temperature before a final refreshment and using it for baking — most recipes recommend feeding the starter 6–8 hours before using. Unless you make a lot of bread, you may find you give away — or throw away — as much as you use. Here are a few more tips:

• The wetter and warmer the mixture, the more rapid the fermentation. Some bakers like a wet, batter-like sourdough starter because it works faster (and is easier to incorporate into flour to make a dough). Others prefer a starter in the form of a ball of soft dough, so that fermentation will be slower. This recipe makes a thick-batter starter. For a soft-dough starter, at the final refreshment before storage, add enough flour to make a very soft, slightly sticky dough.

• To make a vigorous but fairly mild-tasting sourdough, halve and feed your starter every 6 hours until it is very frothy. (If your starter has become rather stale, slow working, and very acid, you can get it back to health quite easily this way — too much acidity diminishes the power of the natural yeasts.)

• If you prefer a stronger-flavored but slightly slower-working starter, feed less often, every 3 or 4 days, until you get the balance you like.

• Never use milk, yogurt, or salt in a sourdough starter.

• Some bakers recommend adding a pinch or two of rye flour or a little beer to encourage a tired starter to become more active.

THE *great thing about this recipe is that it can be adapted to make any kind of bread. You can use white bread flour (organic for choice), stoneground whole-wheat bread flour, spelt flour, kamut, or a combination. My favorite combinations are: equal quantities of white and whole-wheat; 50% white and 25% each whole-wheat and rye; 50% whole-wheat, 30% white, and 10% each rye and coarse whole-wheat. Once you are used to the recipe, you can add up to 15% of grains such as cracked wheat or rye, or a cereal mix. Seeds such as sesame, pumpkin, sunflower, flax, and millet can be added or used as a topping. The dough can be shaped into a round or oval loaf and baked on a baking sheet, as here, in a 10 x 5 x 3 inch loaf pan.*

Simple yeasted bread

MAKES 1 LARGE LOAF

6 cups (700g) bread flour (see recipe introduction)

$^1/_2$ tablespoon fine sea salt

1 0.6-oz cake fresh yeast (15g)*

about 1$^3/_4$ cups (430ml) lukewarm water

a large baking sheet, floured

Mix the chosen flour(s) and salt in a large mixing bowl. In cold weather, it is a good idea to warm the flour by putting the bowl into a low oven (300°F) for a few minutes, or into the microwave on high (100%) for 15 seconds. The warmth encourages the yeast to work – cold flour will retard its growth. Make a well in the center of the flour.

Break up the fresh yeast by crumbling it into a small bowl or jug. Add about 4 tablespoons of the water. (The water should feel just warm and comfortable to touch: if it is cool, it will slow the growth of the yeast – which is sometimes desirable if you want a very slow rise – but if it feels slightly hot, then you risk killing the yeast altogether.) Stir until thoroughly dispersed. Pour the yeast liquid and the rest of the water into the well in the flour.

Using your hand, gradually draw the flour into the liquid in the well and mix until the dough comes together into a ball. The dough should leave the sides of the bowl clean and be firm. Because each type of flour is different, it is impossible to give an exact quantity of water (or flour). If the dough seems sticky or wet and won't hold its shape, work in extra flour a tablespoon at a time; if the dough feels stiff, dry, and hard to work, or there are dry crumbs at the bottom of the bowl, work in extra water a tablespoon at a time.

Turn the dough onto a work surface – only sprinkle with a little flour if the dough feels too soft. Knead the dough for 10 minutes, using as little flour as possible. Shape

If using fresh yeast: squeeze and crumble it between your fingers into a small bowl.

Add a little of the measured lukewarm water (or other liquid) and stir to mix with the yeast.

When the yeast is completely dispersed, pour the liquid into the well in the flour mixture.

If using rapid-rise dry yeast: sprinkle the granules directly onto the flour mixture.

Mix until the yeast granules are thoroughly blended with the other dry ingredients.

Make a well in the center and pour in all of the lukewarm water (or other liquid).

the dough into a ball and return to the cleaned mixing bowl. Cover the bowl with a damp but not wet dish towel or cover with its lid. Or set the bowl inside a very large plastic bag that has been greased inside. The idea is to keep the dough in the warm and humid conditions that yeast likes best. Leave the dough to rise in a draft-free spot until doubled in size. The time this takes depends on the temperature of the dough and of the room – allow 2 hours at 60°F, 1 1/2 hours at 68°F, about 1 hour at 77°F. The dough can also be left to rise overnight in the fridge.

When the dough has properly risen, it won't spring back after you stick in your finger. If not left to rise for long enough, the loaf will be heavy. Over-rising, however, is a bigger problem – if a dough is seriously distended by being left too long, it tends to collapse in the oven. If the dough is only slightly over-risen, you can usually save it by kneading again for a couple of minutes before shaping and rising again.

Deflate the risen dough by punching it down. Turn the dough out onto a work surface, only flouring the surface if the dough feels soft or sticky. Shape the dough into a round or oval loaf. Put the shaped loaf onto the baking sheet. Cover as before and leave to rise until almost doubled in size – 1–1 1/2 hours at 68°F.

Toward the end of the rising time, preheat the oven to 425°F.

Uncover the loaf. With a very sharp knife or razor blade, slash the top three times without dragging the blade. Bake the loaf for 15 minutes or until golden, then lower the oven temperature to 375°F, and bake for a further 20–25 minutes or until it sounds hollow when tapped underneath. If the loaf sounds dense rather than hollow, return it to the oven directly onto the shelf, bake for 5 minutes, and then test again. Don't undercook. Transfer to a wire rack to cool.

* You can use 1 envelope (2 1/2 teaspoons) rapid-rise active dry yeast instead of the fresh yeast. Stir the dry yeast into the flour and salt mixture until thoroughly blended. Make a well in the center, then pour in all the water and continue with the recipe.

V ERY FEW BAKERIES make bread as good as homemade. Too often if the crust is good, the crumb lacks flavor or substance. Luxembourg is blessed with two of the best commercial bakers we've encountered. The bakers, good friends, produce their bread in very different conditions with very different, but equally satisfying, results.

Artisans and technicians

Opposite: In their restaurant shop on the outskirts of Luxembourg, Jeff Oberweis (on the left) and his father Pit sell ten different breads as well as exquisite pastries and cakes. Above: One of the four Oberweis shops is in the Grand Rue.

Jeff and Pit Oberweis

When Pit Oberweis set up his bakery in 1963, he wanted to be the best in the Grand Duchy. His son Jeff spent five years in Paris, with a stint at Fauchon, honing the skills needed to create a prize-winning business. Now, with four shops and a glamorous restaurant at the bakery in the midst of a high-tech industrial estate, Jeff says they have no intentions of getting any bigger. "It's a family business – both my parents, my brother, and our wives all work here. On Saturday, when most of the pâtissiers and bakers are off, my father runs the ovens, lifting the loaves and pastries in and out. It is very hard work for an older man." Jeff devises all the recipes, and supervises the baking. He and his father still like to meet and greet the customers, chat about their purchases, discuss the order for a wedding cake, make sure everyone is satisfied.

The bakery is very new, gleaming and quiet, with no discernible scents of cooking and baking. Yet there is little in the way of machinery – some mixers, whisks, and rollers, but no large vats or industrial robotics. There are rows of stainless steel and granite tables, gas burners for warming and melting, racks of cake and tart pans, stacks of yard-square baking sheets. This is a bakery where everything is worked by hand – artisanal but on a large and efficient scale. "Our customers want thick, crusty bread that looks hand-done. Each loaf looks a bit different, but we have had to be realistic. With all the food and hygiene regulations you can't work in the old way. You have to have the

The old town of Luxembourg.

cleanest, smartest bakery, yet produce goods that taste like those the best old craftsmen made. So we use local Luxembourg flour, which has its own properties and characteristics, fresh eggs, and the best-quality butter."

Jeff leaves nothing to chance. Although the pastry ovens are electric, the bread ovens are gas-fired. And all the breads, with one exception, are baked straight on the floor of the oven for the best crust. Oberweis makes ten different breads, many with *levain blanc* – a portion of dough saved from the previous day's batch. The *baguette au levain* is made with coarse rye, white flour, and *levain blanc*; the *pain au levain* is made with white flour, wheatgerm, and bran mixed with *levain blanc*. But the best known loaf is the *pain complet*, a deeply flavored, well-textured loaf that manages not to sink to the bottom of your stomach.

Pain complet is real Luxembourg bread – good on its own, but even better with *charcuterie*. It is made with a white soft wheat flour (which has more flavor than the harder wheat flour), rye flour, cracked wheat, cracked rye, and barley flour, plus flax seed, sesame seeds, and millet. *Levain blanc* is added for flavor and fresh yeast for a lighter texture. Because the dough is quite soft – the wheat flour is fairly low in gluten – it is shaped and put straight on baking sheets ready for the oven.

Good bread is central to meals in Luxembourg, and every bread shop offers a wide selection.

Baker Patrick Gross removes a batch of pain complet *from the oven at the Oberweis bakery. This deeply flavored bread is made from a mixture of grains and flours.*

J EFF O BERWEIS *gave me guidelines for making this bread, but the exact proportions of the flours and seeds remained a mystery. After watching Patrick Gross, the baker, prepare a couple of batches, and then tasting the results, I had a better idea. I arrived at this recipe by testing again and again, slightly altering the proportions of the ingredients, until I was happy. Of course, each batch will taste a little different because of the unpredictability of the starter, in this case* levain blanc *— a piece of dough saved from a previous batch of white bread dough.*

Jeff says the best dough temperature for developing taste is 64°F, and he achieves this by varying the temperature of the water he uses: in hot weather, cold or iced water; in warm weather, room-temperature water; in cold weather, lukewarm water.

Oberweis pain complet

MAKES 1 MEDIUM LOAF

7oz (200g) saved-dough starter (see recipe introduction), at room temperature

1 cup (220ml) water (see recipe introduction)

²/₃ 0.6-oz cake fresh yeast (10g)*

1 teaspoon fine sea salt

¹/₂ cup (50g) stoneground whole-wheat flour

¹/₄ cup (25g) unbleached all-purpose flour

1¹/₄ cups (150g) stoneground unbleached white bread flour

¹/₂ cup (50g) rye flour

¹/₂ cup (50g) hulled barley flour

¹/₄ cup (50g) hulled millet seeds

2¹/₂ tablespoons (25g) flax seed

2¹/₂ tablespoons (25g) sesame seeds

3¹/₂ tablespoons (25g) cracked wheat

2¹/₂ tablespoons (25g) cracked rye

¹/₂ cup (25g) rolled oats

a baking sheet, greased

Put the starter dough, water, and crumbled yeast into a large mixing bowl, and beat with your hand to make a thick batter. Beat in the salt, then gradually work in the rest of the ingredients to make a soft but not sticky dough.

Turn out onto a lightly floured work surface and knead for 5 minutes. Cover with the upturned bowl or a damp dish towel, and leave for 45 minutes at room temperature. (In warm weather, use a cool spot so the dough doesn't rise too quickly.)

Knead the dough again for a minute, then shape into a neat round loaf. Place on the baking sheet. Score the top with a sharp knife, cover lightly with a damp dish towel, and leave to rise until doubled in size — 1¹/₂–2 hours at room temperature. The bread will taste better if it rises slowly.

Toward the end of the rising time, preheat the oven to its hottest setting.

Uncover the loaf and put it into the oven. Reduce the oven temperature to 425°F and bake for about 35 minutes until the loaf is a good golden brown and sounds hollow when tapped underneath. Cool on a wire rack.

The bread is best eaten within 4 days, or toasted. Once thoroughly cooled, it can be frozen for up to a month.

*You can use 2 teaspoons rapid-rise active dry yeast instead of the fresh yeast. Mix the dry yeast with the whole-wheat flour before adding to the starter and water batter.

Fernand Bock is well known in Luxembourg for his trademark bread, pain de Ruecht, *made from a mixture of white and rye flour.*

Fernand Bock

Several hundred feet closer to the city, in the rue de Gasperich, is the small, smart *boulangerie* of Fernand Bock. The bakery itself is tiny – a wall of ovens, a dough-rising chamber, two tables, and a mixing machine. Monsieur Bock has two younger bakers to help him produce 500 loaves a day during the week, and almost 1000 for the weekend. Not all the bread is sold through the *boulangerie* by Madame Nicole Bock; Fernand Bock also supplies several distinguished and Michelin-starred restaurants, including that of Lea Linster. Monsieur Bock comes from a family of bakers – his father started this bakery in 1936, and he took over in 1963. The bread he makes comes from two lifetimes of experience.

All the bread produced at the bakery is made by hand, and Bock has strong views: "After mixing and kneading, handle the dough as little as possible. The dough should be soft, almost sticky. Leave it to rest almost half an hour, then shape it roughly, touching it as little as possible and using plenty of flour on your hands and table. Then give it a good long, cool rising. This gives the best texture and flavor. And, of course, it gives the loaf a good crust. A good crust is nicer to eat, but also helps the loaf keep longer, and it develops more flavor. If you overhandle, overknead, or over-shape the dough, it becomes too hot and this makes for a tough loaf."

Fernand Bock is known everywhere in the region for his special bread, *pain de Ruecht*. Like all the bread he makes, it is designed to accompany well-flavored food, especially *charcuterie*. It is a large cushion-shaped loaf, baked to a very, very dark brown, to produce a crisp rather than chewy crust and a tender, fairly light, and open crumb. It is made by combining the local white wheat flour with rye flour, leavened with a very little fresh yeast plus a portion of dough saved from the previous day's batch. Bock says the addition of the fresh yeast makes a tender, light loaf with a good flavor – using just a saved-dough starter, would yield a dense and compact bread. The flavor of his bread comes from the quality and blend of the flours, the proportion of the starter, and a very long rising time – usually 15 hours. The shaped dough is left on well-floured roller-sheets in the dough-rising chamber for about 12 hours at 35°F. Then the temperature slowly rises to 45°F. After a couple of hours it climbs slowly to 90°F, so the dough is at warm room temperature when it goes into the oven.

Bock also produces a wonderful *pain ancien*, again with a good crisp crust and a high crust to crumb ratio, but the texture is more open than *pain de Ruecht*. It is made with all white flour and a saved-dough starter plus a very little fresh yeast. The dough is even more sticky than that for the *Ruecht*, and, once cut, is dropped with floured hands onto the roller rising tables to give a free-form loaf or roll.

THIS *is my scaled-down version of Fernand Bock's delicious loaf. Use the best flours you can find, stoneground and organic if possible, and allow for a long rising time at a cool temperature.*

Pain de Ruecht

MAKES 1 LARGE LOAF

8oz (250g) saved-dough starter (see recipe),
    at room temperature
4 cups (990ml) lukewarm water
$^2/_3$ 0.6-oz cake fresh yeast (10g)*
about 10 cups (1.2kg) stoneground
    unbleached white bread flour
$2^3/_4$ cups (300g) stoneground rye flour
$1^1/_2$ tablespoons fine sea salt
extra flour for dusting

a large baking sheet, floured

Put the starter dough, water, and crumbled yeast into a large mixing bowl. Beat with your hand to make a stringy, liquid batter. Gradually work in the flours and salt to make a soft dough — it should be firm enough to hold its shape and not stick to the sides of the bowl, so add a little more flour if necessary.

Turn out onto a floured work surface and knead thoroughly for 10 minutes. The dough should feel a lot firmer, and keep its shape. Cover with the upturned bowl or a damp dish towel and leave to rise for 30 minutes.

Cut off a piece of dough the size of your original starter — about 8 ounces (250g) — and save for the next batch. With well-floured hands, lift the rest of the dough onto the prepared baking sheet and gently pull out the sides of the dough; then push them underneath to make a neat cushion-like round loaf. Do this several times, but avoid the temptation to knead the dough, punch it down with your knuckles, or turn it over. If the dough has spread or quickly loses its shape, then work in extra flour as necessary. (The dough can also be left to rise in a large basket lined with a floured cloth, and then turned onto the baking sheet for baking.) Cover with a damp dish towel or place the baking sheet in a very large plastic bag, oiled inside. Leave to rise in a cool place until doubled in size — overnight or up to 12 hours. The time will depend on the weather, room temperature, and the vigor of your saved-dough starter (see Note).

Preheat the oven to its hottest setting. For an extra crisp crust, put a roasting pan half-filled with hot water on the floor of the oven.

Uncover the loaf and lightly dust with flour, then quickly slash the top with a razor blade or sharp knife. Bake for 15 minutes, then reduce the oven temperature to 375°F and bake for a futher 35 minutes until the loaf sounds hollow when tapped underneath and is a good dark brown. Cool on a wire rack.

The bread is best eaten within 5 days, or toasted. Once thoroughly cooled, it can be frozen for up to a month.

*You can use 2 teaspoons rapid-rise active dry yeast instead of the fresh yeast. Mix the dry yeast with the flour before adding to the starter batter.

Note: When I first tried the recipe I found the dough had spread out alarmingly after the overnight rise, but I had already heated the oven and was ready to bake. So I just re-tucked in the sides of the dough to make a plump cushion shape, then quickly slashed the top and put it into the oven. The bread was not perfect, but not a total disaster either. If you are worried about gauging the consistency of this dough, then consider rising it in a cloth-lined basket, at least for the first attempt. As always when I have a technical problem, I spoke to baker Clive Mellum at Shipton Mill (see page 13). He told me that my saved-dough starter was not vigorous enough. If you suspect this to be the case, either add more starter or more fresh yeast.

Above: After kneading, the dough should be very soft, elastic, and pliable.
Right: A well-baked pain de Ruecht *has a dark brown crust.*

I N *the Deep South, biscuits are traditionally served as the simple yet perfect partner to a juicy stew or meat with plenty of thickened gravy. The flavor in biscuits usually comes from the buttermilk or sour cream used to bind the dough, the lightness from the leavening agent normally used — baking soda. But biscuits are usually boring, only an acceptable accompaniment, not something to eat on their own.*

A sourdough starter usually grows at such a rate that there is enough for something other than a loaf of bread every day. Used to make biscuits, the starter gives a puffy texture and a deep, rich flavor. The biscuits can be baked right away, but for the best flavor, make them and then wait a couple of hours before baking.

Sourdough biscuits

MAKES 9 BISCUITS

3 cups (450g) unbleached all-purpose flour, preferably stoneground

1 teaspoon fine sea salt

$^{1}/_{2}$ teaspoon baking soda

$^{2}/_{3}$ cup (150ml) thick-batter sourdough starter (Clive Mellum's, page 17, Maurice Bichard's page 64, or mine, page 49), at room temperature

1 extra large egg, beaten

about 1 cup (250ml) light cream or half-and-half

a 3$^{1}/_{2}$-inch round biscuit or cookie cutter, floured

a baking sheet, lightly greased

Sift the flour, salt, and baking soda into a large mixing bowl. Mix the starter with the egg, then add to the bowl. Using a large, round-bladed knife or your hand, gradually bring the ingredients together, adding as much of the cream or half-and-half as necessary to make a very soft but not sticky dough.

Turn the dough onto a lightly floured work surface and gently knead just for a couple of minutes until the dough looks fairly smooth. With floured hands, pat out the dough 1 inch thick, then cut out rounds with the cutter. Gather up the trimmings, knead lightly, and pat out, then cut more rounds until all the dough is used up. Arrange the rounds on the prepared baking sheet, spacing them well apart if you like crusty biscuits or almost touching, for ones with softer sides. Cover with a dry, clean cloth and leave to rise in a warm kitchen for a couple of hours (or overnight in the fridge, closely covered with plastic wrap) until slightly puffy. The biscuits can also be left to rest just for the time it takes to heat your oven.

When ready to bake, preheat the oven to 450°F. Uncover the biscuits and bake for 12–15 minutes until well risen, light, and a good golden brown. Eat warm as soon as possible.

Once thoroughly cooled, the biscuits can be frozen for up to a month.

VARIATION: To make sweet biscuits or scones, to eat with butter and jam, add a tablespoon of clear honey with the cream or half-and-half.

Eat Sourdough Biscuits warm from the oven, with a juicy stew or casserole.

Work the ingredients into a very soft but not sticky dough.

Measure the sourdough starter, then mix in the beaten egg.

Gradually pour in the cream, mixing with a metal spatula.

On a floured surface, press out the dough to 1-inch thickness.

Cut out rounds with a floured 3½-inch-diameter biscuit cutter.

L IGHT rye and dark rye flours mixed with cut rye grains and a small portion of white flour make this an interesting, moist, and substantial loaf. The batter-like sourdough starter helps to develop and deepen the flavors of the rye flours. You can use the starter on page 49, Clive Mellum's on page 17, or Maurice Bichard's on page 64.

Mixed rye sourdough

MAKES 1 LARGE LOAF

1/2 cup (125ml) thick-batter sourdough starter
(see recipe introduction), at room
temperature

1 cup (250ml) lukewarm water

scant 1 cup (100g) unbleached white bread
flour

2 cups (200g) light rye flour

1 1/3 cups (200g) dark wholegrain rye flour,
preferably stoneground

5 tablespoons (50g) chopped rye berries

1/2 tablespoon fine sea salt

a baking sheet, floured

Mix the starter and the water to make a smooth liquid. Combine the three flours, chopped rye berries, and salt in a large mixing bowl and make a well in the center. Pour in the starter mixture and gradually work in the dry ingredients to make a slightly sticky dough. It is important that the dough is not stiff, dry, or hard, so add more lukewarm water as necessary.

Turn out onto a lightly floured work surface and knead thoroughly for 10 minutes – this is quite hard work, as the dough will not be as pliable as one made with all wheat flour. Return the dough to the bowl and cover with plastic wrap, or put the bowl into a large plastic bag and close tightly. Leave to rise overnight, or up to 12 hours, at cool to normal room temperature – the dough should double in size.

Next day, punch down the dough with your knuckles to deflate it, then turn out onto a work surface. Shape into a round loaf and put onto the prepared baking sheet, or place the loaf in a cloth-lined and well-floured dough-rising basket. Put the sheet or basket into a large plastic bag and close tightly. Leave at normal kitchen temperature to rise until almost doubled in size – 3–5 hours, depending on the room temperature and the vigor of the dough.

Toward the end of the rising time, preheat the oven to 425°F. If you have used a basket for rising the dough, put an unfloured baking sheet or baking stone into the oven when you switch it on.

Heat a little water until boiling. Uncover the risen dough. If a basket was used for rising, swiftly turn the loaf onto the hot baking sheet or stone. Brush the loaf with the boiling water, then quickly slash with a sharp knife or blade. Bake for about 35 minutes until the loaf sounds hollow when tapped underneath. Cool on a wire rack.

This loaf tastes best if wrapped and left for a day before slicing, and is best eaten within a week – the flavor deepens as the bread ages. Once thoroughly cooled, the loaf can be frozen for up to a month.

Turn the loaf out of the dough-rising basket onto a heated baking sheet.

If the cloth-lined dough-rising basket has been well floured, it should lift off easily.

Score the top of the loaf with a razor-sharp knife to avoid dragging the crust.

*I*F *you don't like sourdoughs, or you don't have a sourdough starter, the same combination of flours in the recipe opposite can be used to make a yeasted loaf that has plenty of flavor.*

Yeasted mixed rye bread

MAKES 1 LARGE LOAF

1 0.6-oz cake fresh yeast (15g)*

1¹/₃ cups (330ml) lukewarm water

scant 1 cup (100g) unbleached white bread
    flour

2 cups (200g) light rye flour

1¹/₃ cups (200g) dark wholegrain rye flour,
    preferably stoneground

5 tablespoons (50g) chopped rye berries

¹/₂ tablespoon fine sea salt

a baking sheet, floured

Crumble the yeast into a medium-sized bowl. Mix in the water, then stir in the white flour and half the light rye flour to make a smooth batter. Cover the bowl with a damp dish towel or plastic wrap and leave to "sponge" for 20–30 minutes — until the batter looks thick and foamy.

Mix together the rest of the light rye flour, the dark rye flour, chopped rye berries, and salt in a large mixing bowl. Make a well in the center. Pour in the sponge liquid, then work in the dry ingredients to make a slightly sticky dough. If the dough is hard to bring together or work, and feels dry and stiff, work in a little more lukewarm water. If the dough is very wet and sticky, work in a little more white flour.

Turn out onto a lightly floured work surface and knead thoroughly for 10 minutes until the dough feels more pliable and elastic. Return the dough to the bowl and cover with a damp dish towel or plastic wrap. Leave to rise at normal kitchen temperature until doubled in size — 2–3 hours.

Punch down the dough, then shape into a round loaf. Put onto the floured baking sheet, or into a basket lined with a well-floured cloth. Put the sheet or basket into a large plastic bag and close tightly. Leave to rise until almost doubled in size — about 2 hours.

Toward the end of the rising time, preheat the oven to 425°F. If you have used a basket for rising the bread, put an unfloured baking sheet or stone into the oven to heat up.

Heat a little water until boiling. Quickly uncover the loaf. If a basket was used for rising, turn out the loaf onto the hot sheet or stone. Brush the loaf with the water and slash the top with a blade or sharp knife. Bake for about 35 minutes until the loaf sounds hollow when tapped underneath. Cool on a wire rack.

The bread is best eaten within 5 days. Once cooled, it can be frozen for up to a month.

* You can use 1 envelope (2¹/₂ teaspoons) rapid-rise active dry yeast instead of the fresh yeast. Mix the dry yeast with the white bread flour and half the light rye flour, then stir in the water. Leave to sponge for about 30 minutes, then continue with the recipe.

Since his retirement, livestock geneticist Dr. Maurice Bichard has put his formidable scientific training to good use. Although he has always eaten good bread, and learned to make a decent loaf at his mother's knee, his interest in home baking became really serious only a few years ago.

The scientific baker

Maurice Bichard (pictured in his converted barn in Oxfordshire, England) believes that the yeasts in sourdough starters derive from the flour itself, and are not airborne. He keeps his sourdough cultures in glass jars (above) and in plastic containers, often letting them lie dormant — without "feeding" — for months

As a scientist, Maurice holds very different views from other bakers I have met. He maintains that most bakers' lore has little scientific value, and he enjoys a lively discussion with so-called "purist" bakers. For example, although he has bought several different sourdough starter cultures from around the world (through Sourdoughs International; see Directory, page 172), Maurice believes whatever culture you use your bread will become characteristic of you, your flour, water, and conditions. He has kept liquid starter cultures in his cellar for much longer than recommended – some have lain for a couple of years without fresh flour and water to "feed" them. In fact, he doesn't hold with the idea that a sourdough starter is made by allowing the flour and water batter to absorb natural yeasts from the air and surroundings – he believes they develop from yeasts in the flour itself.

He has also experimented with a range of flours with differing gluten (protein) content, from medium to very high, to find out whether the unvarying advice to knead thoroughly for 10 minutes is valid. He discovered no discernible difference between doughs kneaded thoroughly for 3 or 7 or 10 minutes, whatever the strength of the protein over 10% – they all rose the same, and the baked loaves had similar textures.

For his bread, he likes to use a mixture of Doves Farm white bread flour and an extra-strong Canadian-wheat bread flour. The Canadian bread flour is also his choice for his sourdough starters.

Maurice brushes his rye loaves with egg yolk before baking, to give a good glazed finish to the crust.

Tapping loaves on the base is a traditional way to test if they are done — they should sound hollow.

The scientist also checks using a meat thermometer to read the internal temperature of the loaf.

For Maurice Bichard, "variety is one of the delights of bread," and he makes white, rye, whole-wheat and granary loaves in many different shapes and sizes.

Aᴼᴛᴇʀ *a series of experiments to find the perfect loaf, Maurice Bichard happened upon an early Bon Viveur recipe from London's* Daily Telegraph *newspaper. It gave instructions for making a "sponge" as the first step in breadmaking — mixing the yeast with the water and enough of the flour to make a thick batter, then leaving this mixture until it becomes thick and foamy, or sponge-like, as the yeast grows and produces bubbles of gas. The rest of the flour is then worked into the sponge, and the dough kneaded, risen, shaped, risen again, and finally baked as usual.*

The discovery of longer fermentation was the key for Maurice. After a couple of courses with Paul Merry and Andrew Whitley at The Village Bakery (see page 114), his bread began to change and evolve, becoming more and more sour in taste. With his retirement came the chance to buy a mid-Victorian farmhouse, with a barn containing a brick oven that predates the house by a century. Maurice cleared out the oven and slowly, by trial and error, learned how to work it. In the process, he perfected his loaf, with its good thick crust and the scent of wood ash.

Maurice Bichard's sourdough white bread

First make the starter. Mix the flour and water in a bowl, cover lightly with a wet dish towel, and leave for 4–6 days at room temperature, stirring gently once a day and dampening the towel as necessary, until the batter has small bubbles and has become slightly gray with a whiff of sourness.

Add the flour and water for the first refreshment and mix to make a smooth, thick batter. Cover and leave as before for 12 hours — the batter should look quite foamy.

MAKES 2 LARGE LOAVES

STARTER:

1 cup (110g) unbleached white bread flour

³/₄ cup (175ml) water, at room temperature

FIRST REFRESHMENT:

1¹/₂ cups (185g) unbleached white bread flour

1 cup (225ml) water, at room temperature

SECOND REFRESHMENT:

4 cups (500g) unbleached white bread flour

2¹/₂ cups (600ml) water, at room temperature

FIRST PROOF:

7¹/₂ cups (900g) unbleached white bread flour

4¹/₂ cups (1.1 liters) water, at room
    temperature

TO MAKE THE BREAD:

6–7 cups (750–800g) unbleached white bread
    flour

2 teaspoons fine sea salt

1 cup (250ml) water, at room temperature

2 tablespoons olive oil

2 baking sheets

Mix in the flour and water for the second refreshment until smooth and thick again. Leave, lightly covered as before, for 12 hours until foamy.

Measure 4¹/₂ cups (1.1 liters) of the starter batter and discard the rest (or use it for biscuits, page 58). Add the flour and water for the first proof and mix to make a smooth, very thick batter. Leave as before for 12 hours until very foamy.

Measure 4 cups (1 liter) starter batter from the first proof (see Note), and mix with the flour, salt, water, and olive oil. The dough should not be dry and tough, but not soft and sticky either, so add more water or flour as necessary. Knead the dough thoroughly until smooth, glossy, and very elastic. Cut in half and shape into two round loaves. Put into baskets lined with a well-floured cloth and leave to rise until doubled in size – 4–8 hours depending on the vigor of your starter and the temperature.

Toward the end of the rising time, preheat the oven to 450°F. Put the baking sheets in the oven to heat.

Turn the loaves onto the hot baking sheets and quickly slash across the top of each. Put into the oven and reduce the temperature to 425°F. Bake for about 35 minutes until the bread is deep brown and well-risen and sounds hollow when tapped underneath. Maurice says you can also test if the bread is cooked by checking the internal temperature: it should be 194–203°F in the center of the loaf. You can use an instant-read thermometer to test. Cool on a wire rack.

VARIATIONS: *Rye bread*

Mix 4 cups (1 liter) of the starter from the first proof with 3¹/₂ cups (360g) rye flour, about 2 cups (240g) unbleached white bread flour, 2 teaspoons fine sea salt, 1 cup (250ml) water at room temperature, and caraway seeds to taste. Make the dough, knead, shape, and rise as given, brushing with egg yolk to glaze before baking.

Whole-wheat bread

Mix 4 cups (1 liter) of the starter from the first proof with 4 cups (480g) whole-wheat flour, about 2 cups (240g) white bread flour, 2 teaspoons fine sea salt, 1 cup (250ml) water, and 2 tablespoons walnut oil. Make the dough, knead, shape, rise, and bake as for sourdough white bread, above.

Note: Leftover starter batter from the first proof can be kept in a covered jar in the fridge until needed. When ready to use, measure it and add an equal quantity of water, then work in enough flour to make a batter of a similar consistency – the ratio is usually 11 parts original starter batter, 11 parts water, and 9 parts flour. Leave at room temperature until very thick and frothy before using to make a loaf of bread.

For baking in his wood-fired oven, Maurice turns the risen loaf out onto a wooden peel.

The basket used for rising has given this loaf an attractive pattern on its surface.

A quick cross cut in the top of the loaf, and it is ready to be slid onto the oven floor.

A SWEET *rye bread, this is light in color, flavor, and texture. It makes excellent breakfast toast as well as sandwiches. Use your favorite rye flour or experiment with stoneground, a very light rye, or the heavier dark wholegrain type.*

Honey rye bread

MAKES 1 MEDIUM LOAF

2 tablespoons clear honey

$^2/_3$ cup (140ml) hot water

$^2/_3$ cup (140ml) lukewarm water

1 0.6-oz cake fresh yeast (15g)*

3 cups (350g) unbleached white bread flour

$1^1/_2$ cups (150g) rye flour

$^1/_2$ tablespoon fine sea salt

extra rye flour for dusting

a loaf pan, about $8^1/_2$ x $4^1/_2$ x $2^1/_2$ inches, greased

Dissolve the honey in the hot water, stirring well. Leave to cool until lukewarm, then add the measured lukewarm water. Crumble in the fresh yeast and stir until you have a smooth liquid.

Put the flours and salt in a large mixing bowl and mix thoroughly, then make a well in the center. Pour in the yeast liquid and gradually mix in the flour to make a soft but not sticky dough. If the dough sticks to your fingers or the bowl, add a little more white flour; add a little more water if the dough is stiff and dry or there are dry crumbs in the bottom of the bowl.

Turn out onto a lightly floured work surface and knead thoroughly for 10 minutes. Return the dough to the bowl and cover with a damp dish towel or put the bowl into a large plastic bag and close tightly. Leave to rise at room temperature until doubled in size – about 2 hours.

Punch down the dough to deflate it, then turn out onto a lightly floured work surface. Pat out to a rectangle the length of your pan. Roll up tightly like a jelly roll and dust with a little rye flour. Put into the prepared pan, seam-side down, tucking the ends under to make a neat loaf shape. Cover as before and leave to rise until almost doubled in size – about $1^1/_2$ hours.

Toward the end of the rising time, preheat the oven to 425°F.

Uncover the risen loaf and bake for about 35 minutes until it is brown and sounds hollow when turned out of the pan and tapped underneath. Cool on a wire rack.

The bread is best eaten within 6 days, or toasted. Once thoroughly cooled, it can be frozen for up to a month.

* You can use 1 envelope ($2^1/_2$ teaspoons) rapid-rise active dry yeast instead of the fresh yeast. Add the dry yeast to the flours with the salt and mix well, then add the honey and water mixture and continue with the recipe.

Honey gives this rye bread a delicate sweetness.

F OUND *all across France, this honey-rich spice bread dates from medieval times, when it was a costly celebration treat. The use of baking powder is obviously a modern adaptation. Recipes vary from region to region — this one comes from Dijon and uses rye flour. In recent years, the reputation of* pain d'épices *has suffered badly from the cheap industrial products found in supermarkets. The best ones are still made by artisans using a high proportion of honey and chopped nuts or candied peel.*

Pain d'épices is flavored with quatre épices, *a ready-made mixture of spices found in French food stores. If you can't get it, make up your own blend and store it in a screwtop jar. Jane Grigson suggested using seven parts ground black pepper to one part each ground cloves, ground ginger, and grated nutmeg.*

Pain d'épices

MAKES 1 MEDIUM LOAF

1²/₃ cups (200g) unbleached all-purpose flour

1 cup (100g) rye flour

¹/₄ teaspoon fine sea salt

¹/₂ teaspoon ground cinnamon

¹/₂ teaspoon ground cloves

¹/₂ teaspoon *quatre épices*

2 teaspoons baking powder

²/₃ cup (100g) blanched almonds, toasted and
    roughly chopped

1 cup (300g) well-flavored clear honey, gently
    warmed

2 extra large egg yolks

5 tablespoons milk

GLAZE:

2 tablespoons sugar

3 tablespoons milk

a loaf pan, about 8¹/₂ x 4¹/₂ x 2¹/₂ inches,
    greased and bottom-lined

Preheat the oven to 350°F.

Sift the flours, salt, spices, and baking powder into a mixing bowl. Stir in the almonds. Pour in the liquid honey, egg yolks, and milk, and mix everything together to make a heavy, sticky cake batter.

Spoon into the prepared pan and bake immediately for about 45 minutes until the loaf turns golden brown and a skewer inserted in the center comes out clean. Unmold onto a wire rack.

Heat the sugar in the milk until dissolved, then simmer for 1–2 minutes to make a sticky glaze. Brush the hot loaf with the hot glaze and leave to cool.

Wrap the loaf and keep for a day before cutting. It is best eaten within 8 days. The unglazed loaf can be frozen for up to a month.

Sweet and spicy Pain d'Épices is a traditional French treat.

"GERMANS ARE CONSERVATIVE about food," Gert Kusche told me. "They are keen on quality and tradition. At Bakoven, we make proper German bread with proper materials." At this bakery near the German school in Surrey, England, the rye flours, liquid sourdough starter, even the oven and bakers come from Germany. Most of their bread is bought by expatriates. Bakoven also supplies the German and Austrian embassies in London, selling bread from a strategically parked van.

Proper German bread

At Bakoven, Gert Kusche (top right) bakes good heavy rye bread for his fellow expatriates, putting the loaves in traditional bread-rising baskets from Germany (above).

Two craft-bakers are behind Bakoven. Gert Kusche comes from Kassel in Germany, "where the heavy rye bread comes from." His 40 years in baking began with four years training, then a lengthy spell at Unilever in the research and development bakery. This led to consultancy baking in Africa, India, and the Gulf countries. When the Berlin wall came down, Gert opened his own craft bakery in Leipzig. It was popular and expanded rapidly, but became bigger than Gert wanted. So he took up an invitation from Lufthansa's catering arm to open a bakery in London. This didn't work out as he had planned, but he met Marcus Hampton, an American who had gained a reputation in London making hand-shaped sprouted wheat and whole-wheat breads. They decided to join forces.

At Bakoven, the breads are made in small batches on a 16-hour production cycle, with every stage and procedure carefully controlled and monitored. "We are producing five or six thousand loaves a night, using a live liquid rye sourdough starter," Gert said, "so we need to be accurate about its strength and the quantity, as well as the temperature and conditions."

Gert gave me a brief but invaluable lesson in the chemistry of sourdough starters: "Rye flour, unlike wheat flour, has very little gluten, and is mostly starch, so it needs to be treated differently. Adding a sourdough starter is very important in avoiding a dense, tight loaf. The starter gives flavor and creates a more open texture. The starches in the rye flour are cracked by the lactic acids in the starter, and this allows water to be absorbed and retained, otherwise the dough becomes heavy and sticky. Yogurt and buttermilk do a similar job. The amount of starter you need depends on its acidity and also on the weather."

Gert explained that a sourdough starter contains more than 100 different microorganisms, a combination of acidifiers (bacteria), and budding fungi (otherwise known as yeasts), with different functions. The acidifiers produce lactic acid and acetic acid; the yeasts produce alcohol and carbon dioxide. Keeping a balance requires experience – the sourdough needs enough acetic acid to break down the rye flour, but not so much as to inhibit the yeasts from growing and producing the carbon dioxide needed to aerate the loaf. Lactic acid, which adds flavor, forms in soft dough at around 95–104°F, while acetic acid forms in firm dough at around 68°F. The yeasts grow best in soft dough, well kneaded to incorporate oxygen, at around 75–78°F.

"Sourdough bread doughs should be made on the soft side, but not too soft or the bread will be flat. On the other hand, if the dough is too firm, the baked loaf will be tight and tough. The bread initially needs a steamy atmosphere in the oven to give the crust flexibility, so it doesn't crack. The bread finishes cooking in its own humidity."

THIS is Gert Kusche's favorite loaf, made with three parts rye flour (organic wholegrain, but very finely ground) to one part organic white bread flour. Gert uses a pungent rye sourdough starter, which gives the loaf a great depth of flavor. The acid bacteria also help to break down the starches in the rye flour to enable the water to be thoroughly absorbed and the loaf to rise well. Fresh yeast provides additional rising power, so the bread is relatively light despite the rye content. I recommend making the loaf using a blend of light and dark rye flours plus white flour, to get a result very similar to Gert's. To give the loaf its characteristic, undefinable taste, Gert also adds a touch of "bread" spice, a combination of ground caraway, coriander, and anise or fennel seeds, which is widely available in Germany.

Bakhaus loaf

MAKES 2 LARGE LOAVES

5¹/₂ cups (600g) organic rye flour

1³/₄ cups (200g) organic unbleached white
    bread flour

1 tablespoon fine sea salt

¹/₄ teaspoon ground bread spice, or a few
    pinches each of ground caraway, coriander,
    and fennel seed

1¹/₃ cups (320ml) thick-batter sourdough
    starter (see page 49)

1 0.6-oz cake fresh yeast (10g)*

1³/₄ cups (400ml) lukewarm water

2 very heavy baking sheets or 2 loaf pans,
    about 10 x 5 x 3 inches, greased

Combine the flours, salt, and spice in a large mixing bowl and make a well in the center. Pour in the sourdough starter. Crumble the yeast into the water and stir until smooth, then pour into the mixing bowl. Work the ingredients together to make a very soft and quite sticky dough.

Turn onto a work surface and knead very thoroughly for 8–10 minutes – the dough will change in consistency as you work it, and should become firmer and more pliable. Return the dough to the bowl, cover with a dish towel or heavy cloth, and leave to rise for 1 hour at normal to warm kitchen temperature. The dough will become even firmer as it's left to rest.

Without kneading or punching down the dough, divide it into two equal pieces and quickly form each into a rough, round loaf – do not mold or shape them. Put into floured dough-rising baskets or baskets lined with a well-floured cloth, or into the greased loaf pans, if using. Cover as before and leave to rise for 20–30 minutes until almost doubled in size.

Toward the end of the rising time, preheat the oven to its hottest setting. If you are using dough-rising baskets, put the ungreased baking sheets into the oven to heat up.

Turn out the dough onto the hot sheets and quickly score the top of each loaf with a blade or sharp knife, then put into the oven; uncover the loaves in pans and put straight into the oven. An initial burst of steam is important when baking rye bread – it stops the crust from forming too quickly and inhibiting the oven-spring – so mist the loaves with water or sprinkle the floor of the oven with a little water. Bake for 5 minutes, then reduce the oven temperature to 400°F and bake for a further 35 minutes until the loaves sound hollow when tapped underneath. Cool (unmolded) on a wire rack.

The bread is best eaten within 6 days, or toasted. Once thoroughly cooled, it can be frozen for up to a month.

* You can use 1 envelope (2¹/₂ teaspoons) rapid-rise active dry yeast instead of the fresh yeast. Mix the dry yeast with the dry ingredients, then continue with the recipe.

A NTHONY BLAKE *says this is one of his favorite loaves. "I particularly like bread with grains and crunchy pieces. If you don't have all the different grains, then increase the ones you do have to make up the same overall weight. I get all my flours, grains, and seeds from Shipton Mill, though health food stores usually have most of them. I like to experiment with various combinations – that's the fun of breadmaking."*

Anthony's grain bread

MAKES 3 MEDIUM LOAVES

TO START:

1 cup (100g) malted wheat flakes

5 tablespoons (50g) chopped rye berries

$^1/_2$ cup (50g) cracked wheat

$^1/_4$ cup (50g) steel-cut oats, roughly chopped

$^1/_4$ cup (40g) rye berries

1 tablespoon (10g) pearl barley

2 tablespoons molasses

2 cups (500ml) boiling water

TO FINISH:

2 cups (200g) dark rye flour

1$^3/_4$ (200g) coarse whole-wheat flour,
   preferably stoneground

4 cups (500g) unbleached white bread flour

2 teaspoons fine sea salt

3 0.6-oz cakes fresh yeast (50g)*

$^2/_3$ cup (150ml) lukewarm water

$^2/_3$ cup (150ml) stout, at room temperature

1 tablespoon sunflower or light olive oil

3 loaf pans, about 8$^1/_2$ x 4$^1/_2$ x 2$^1/_2$ inches,
   well greased

Start by combining the first six ingredients in a large bowl. Add the molasses to the measured boiling water and stir until dispersed, then add to the dry ingredients and mix well. Cover with plastic wrap and leave for 24 hours.

The next day, the soaked mixture should resemble coarse, sloppy porridge. Add the rye, whole-wheat, and white flours and the salt. Crumble the yeast into the lukewarm water and stir until dispersed, then add the stout. Pour the liquid into the grain and flour mixture, and mix thoroughly to make a firm but not stiff dough. Add a little more water if necessary, or, if the dough feels very sticky, work in a little extra white flour.

Turn the dough out onto a work surface and knead thoroughly for 10 minutes (dust your hands and the work surface with flour only if the dough is sticky). Shape the dough into a ball. Put the oil into a clean, large bowl, add the ball of dough, and flip it over so it is coated in oil. Cover with plastic wrap and leave at room temperature until doubled in size – about 2 hours, but allow more time in cold weather, less in hot.

Punch down the risen dough and divide it into three equal portions. Shape each into an oblong to fit the pans, then put the dough neatly into the pans. Cover and leave as before until doubled in size – allow 1$^1/_2$ hours.

Toward the end of the rising time, preheat the oven to 425°F.

Uncover the loaves and dust with a little rye or whole-wheat flour. Bake for 30–35 minutes until the loaves sound hollow when unmolded and tapped underneath. Turn out and cool on a wire rack.

The bread is best if left for a day before slicing, and will keep for 5 days, or can be toasted. Once thoroughly cooled, it can be frozen for up to a month.

*You can use 3 envelopes (7$^1/_2$ teaspoons) rapid-rise active dry yeast instead of the fresh yeast. Combine the dry yeast with the flours and add to the soaked grain mixture, then add the water and stout.

After soaking for 24 hours the grain mixture feels like a coarse porridge.

If the dough is too sticky, dust with a little flour to help you knead.

Allow at least 2 hours of rising for the dough to double in size.

A NTHONY'S *large garden provides him with abundant fruit and vegetables year round. In a good year, mine provides 20 plums, about 4 pounds of Gardener's Delight tomatoes, and enough lovage to feed a regiment. I grow lovage because it is one of the few herbs that will thrive for me, and because it goes so well with potatoes — I love potatoes. This bread, leavened with baking powder, is very simply made using freshly cooked or leftover floury mashed potato plus fried bacon and the herbs. It has an excellent flavor and a good light texture — eat it with soups or with ham and eggs for brunch.*

Lovage potato bread

MAKES 6 TRIANGLES

scant 1 cup (125g) unbleached all-purpose flour

2 teaspoons baking powder

$^1/_4$ teaspoon each salt and ground pepper, or
    to taste

$^1/_2$ cup (125g) mashed potato

2 tablespoons (25g) unsalted butter, chilled
    and diced

4oz (125g) sliced bacon, fried until crisp and
    crumbled

1 heaped tablespoon chopped fresh lovage

1 extra large egg, beaten

a little extra beaten egg or milk for glazing

a large baking sheet, lightly greased

Preheat the oven to 425°F.

In a large bowl, thoroughly mix the flour, baking powder, seasoning, and potatoes. Add the butter and rub in using the tips of your fingers until it looks like coarse crumbs. Stir in the bacon and lovage, then add enough beaten egg to make a soft but not sticky dough.

Turn out onto a floured work surface and pat out to a circle about 8 inches across and $^3/_4$ inch thick. Cut into six triangular wedges with a sharp knife. Arrange, spaced slightly apart, on the prepared baking sheet.

Lightly brush with beaten egg or milk to glaze, then bake for about 15 minutes until firm and golden. Eat hot, straight from the oven, or warm on the day of baking. Do not freeze.

VARIATIONS: The lovage can be replaced by chopped parsley or chives, and the bacon with diced ham or cooked mushrooms.

With your fingertips, rub the butter into the flour and mashed potato mixture.

Mix in enough beaten egg to make a soft but not sticky dough.

Cut the circle of dough into six equal wedges using a sharp knife.

Brush the wedges with egg or milk so the crust bakes to a shiny, golden brown.

Until recently, for most families in rural Ireland, travel meant infrequent trips to the nearest livestock market. So yeast was hard to obtain and bought bread was a rarity. The traditional bread of Ireland was made at home, baked in a heavy iron pot set over a peat fire, with hot peats covering the lid. These breads are quickly made, with no lengthy kneading or rising required. They are given a light texture and a wonderful taste by a combination of acidic buttermilk or soured milk and the alkaline baking soda. Self-rising flour is a simple alternative and avoids the nasty tang of excess chemicals that results when you get the proportions wrong. Soda breads are made to be eaten soon after baking.

Irish soda breads

Top: A lake in Connemara.
Above: Anthony Kaye dresses one of the millstones at Isinglass mill in Wexford.
Right: This white soda loaf is speckled with lumps of rich dark chocolate.

THE *coarse brown wheaten flour that is traditionally used for this appealing loaf is neither whole-wheat nor white — it's a combination. The flecked, speckly look and wonderful nutty flavor come from large flakes of bran and rolled wheat berries added to the flour. This medium-strength gluten flour, readily available in Ireland, can be difficult to come across elsewhere, though King Arthur Flour makes an excellent Irish–style flour (see Directory, page 172). An acceptable alternative is to mix 2 1/2 cups (300g) coarse stoneground whole-wheat flour with scant 1 cup (35g) bran and 2 1/2 tablespoons (15g) wheatgerm. The bread is wonderful with soups and good cheeses.*

Irish wheaten bread

MAKES 1 MEDIUM LOAF

3 cups (350g) coarse wheaten flour (see recipe introduction)

2/3 cup (100g) unbleached all-purpose flour

1 teaspoon fine sea salt

1 teaspoon baking soda

2 1/2 tablespoons (35g) butter, diced

1 1/4–1 3/4 cups (300–400ml) buttermilk or soured milk

a baking sheet, greased

Preheat the oven to 425°F.

Mix the flours, salt, and the well-crushed baking soda in a mixing bowl. Add the diced butter and rub into the flour using the tips of your fingers, lifting your hands high over the bowl so plenty of air gets into the mixture. When the mixture looks like bread crumbs, gradually stir in the buttermilk or soured milk using a large, round-bladed knife, adding enough to make a soft, slightly sticky dough.

Turn out onto a work surface well floured with wheaten flour and, with floured hands, gently knead a couple of times. Shape into a neat round loaf about 8 inches diameter and 1 inch thick. Put onto the prepared baking sheet and sprinkle with more flour, then cut a deep cross to mark the loaf into four "farls."

Bake immediately for 35–45 minutes until well browned and the loaf sounds hollow when tapped underneath. Cool on a wire rack, and eat while still warm, the same day, or toasted.

This loaf can be frozen, but may be rather dry and crumbly when thawed.

PLAIN *white soda bread gets a Sunday-best glamor when you knead in chunks of good-quality chocolate. Eat warm for breakfast with butter and a big pot of coffee.*

Speckled white soda loaf

MAKES 1 MEDIUM LOAF

3 cups (450g) self-rising white flour

1 teaspoon fine sea salt

2 teaspoons sugar

3 tablespoons (40g) butter, diced

4 squares (100g) semisweet chocolate coarsely chopped

about 1 1/4 cups (300ml) buttermilk to mix

a baking sheet, greased

Preheat the oven to 425°F.

Sift the flour, salt, and sugar into a mixing bowl. Add the diced butter and rub in using the tips of your fingers, lifting your fingers well above the bowl to get plenty of air into the mixture. When the mixture looks like bread crumbs, stir in the chocolate, then mix to a soft dough with the buttermilk.

Turn out the dough onto a floured work surface and knead for a few seconds. Shape into a round loaf about 1 1/4 inches thick. Put onto the prepared baking sheet and score into 8 triangles.

Bake immediately for 30–35 minutes until the loaf turns a good golden brown and sounds hollow when tapped underneath. Eat warm, straight from the oven.

Once thoroughly cooled, the loaf can be frozen for up to a month. Thaw completely, then warm through before eating.

Malted Raisin Loaf (on the left) and Dried Fruit Cider Bread are
both good sliced, buttered, and eaten with cheese or preserves.

THIS *fruited loaf leavened with baking soda comes from Rosemary Rowson (see page 84).*
Not as rich or sweet as the Dried Fruit Cider Bread opposite, it is good sliced, buttered, and
eaten with ham or cheese, or with preserves for breakfast.

Malted raisin loaf

MAKES 1 MEDIUM LOAF

3 tablespoons malt extract

1$^1/_2$ tablespoons light corn syrup

$^2/_3$ cup (150ml) whole milk

2 cups (225g) whole-wheat flour,
    preferably stoneground

1 teaspoon baking soda

$^1/_8$ teaspoon fine sea salt

$^1/_3$ cup (50g) golden raisins

1 extra large egg, beaten

a loaf pan, about 8$^1/_2$ x 4$^1/_2$ x 2$^1/_2$ inches,
    well greased

Preheat the oven to 350°F.

Put the malt extract and corn syrup into a saucepan with the milk and heat gently until melted. Leave to cool until lukewarm. Mix the flour with the baking soda, salt, and raisins. Add the milk mixture and the egg, and mix thoroughly with a wooden spoon to make a slack dough.

Pour or spoon into the prepared pan. Bake for about 35 minutes until a skewer inserted into the center comes out clean. Keep an eye on this loaf when making it for the first time, or if you are unsure of your oven's heat — it quickly dries out if left to bake too long.

Loosen the loaf with a round-bladed knife, then unmold onto a wire rack and leave to cool.

The loaf improves in flavor if wrapped and kept for a day before slicing, and is best eaten within 5 days. Once thoroughly cooled, it can be frozen for up to a month.

I HAVE *adapted this simple recipe for a well-flavored loaf leavened with baking powder from Rosemary Rowson. She uses the stoneground organic whole-wheat flour from Otterton Mill (see page 33) and the local medium-dry hard cider. The taste of the cider survives the cooking process, and provides a delicious contrast with the sweetness of the dried fruit. Try the loaf thickly sliced with a piece of sharp, slightly moist cheese.*

Dried fruit cider bread

MAKES 1 MEDIUM LOAF

1 cup (150g) mixed dried fruit

²/₃ cup (150ml) medium-dry hard cider

1¹/₄ cups (150g) whole-wheat flour, preferably stoneground

³/₄ teaspoon baking powder

¹/₈ teaspoon fine sea salt

¹/₃ cup (70g) firmly packed light brown sugar

¹/₄ cup (25g) walnut pieces

1 extra large egg, beaten

a loaf pan, about 8¹/₂ x 4¹/₂ x 2¹/₂ inches, well greased

Put the fruit and cider into a non-aluminum pan and slowly bring to a boil. Simmer for 2 minutes, then remove from the heat and leave for 2–4 hours until cold and the fruit has become swollen.

Preheat the oven to 350°F.

Mix the flour, baking powder, salt, sugar, and walnuts in a mixing bowl. Using a wooden spoon, stir in the fruit and cider mixture and the egg. When thoroughly combined to a stiffish dough, spoon into the prepared pan and smooth the surface.

Bake for about 45 minutes until a skewer inserted into the center comes out clean. If the top is browning too quickly, cover with a piece of wax paper. Leave to cool in the pan for a couple of minutes, then loosen the loaf with a round-bladed knife and gently unmold onto a wire rack. Leave to cool completely.

The bread is best eaten within a week. Once thoroughly cooled, it can be frozen for up to a month.

Work in the cider-soaked fruit and the beaten egg.

Combine the dry ingredients with your hand.

When everything is thoroughly blended, spoon into the loaf pan.

Check the loaf is cooked by inserting a skewer into the center.

THIS BREAD COMES FROM Ya-yoi Tsuchitani, a Japanese-American who lives in New York. "Green tea breads are derived from a sweet confection found on Iwaishima island in the Inland Sea. Three hundred and fifty or four hundred years ago, an ancestor of my father's was given the island, then called Izo, by a grateful Shogun. Many years ago I visited the island during the Izo festival – a traditional feast held twice a year. The highlight of the festivities is the presentation of the Izo confections.

Japanese green tea bread

"On the island, people for many, many generations have lived to well over a hundred. It's generally thought that this was because green tea, red beans, and chestnuts were eaten every day. Now we know that these have great antioxidant properties. My mother and her friends in the States were anxious to share the health benefits of green tea, and through trial and error transformed this traditional delicacy for Occidental taste. The benefits are spiritual as well as physical – this bread represents both ying and yang, or the feminine and masculine we all need to function as humans. The green tea is the yang, the chestnut the ying."

Ya-yoi explained that the sweet yeasted bread, made from two doughs rolled together, is served very thickly sliced at teatime, on its own or with a ginger preserve.

The *cha maccha*, or powdered green tea, must be of excellent quality, one prepared for the traditional Japanese tea ceremony. Its consistency is similar to cake flour.

The recipe for this unusually flavored bread is fairly complicated, so be sure to read through before starting.

Top: A temple outside Tokyo. Left: For Green Tea and Chestnut Bread, two doughs are made, one flavored with the powdered green tea used for the traditional tea ceremony in Japan and the other with sweetened chestnut purée.

THIS *bread, called* kahlo, *uses Japanese green tea, which is a fine, bright green powder. Ya-yoi adds sour cream to the dough to balance the bitter flavor the tea imparts. She recommends using French sweetened chestnut purée, available in cans, and peeled and cooked chestnuts, also in cans. When you prepare this bread, start the green tea dough while the chestnut dough is having its first rise, as the tea dough needs only one rise.*

Green tea and chestnut bread

MAKES 2 MEDIUM LOAVES

CHESTNUT DOUGH:

1½ 0.6-oz cakes fresh yeast (25g)*

4 tablespoons lukewarm water

3 tablespoons sugar

¾ cup (175ml) milk, scalded and cooled

1 teaspoon fine sea salt

about 3½ cups (400g) unbleached white bread flour

4 tablespoons (60g) unsalted butter, melted

1 cup (225ml) sweetened chestnut purée

1 425g-can (285g) cooked whole chestnuts, drained

GREEN TEA DOUGH:

1½ 0.6-oz cakes fresh yeast (25g)*

4 tablespoons lukewarm water

3 tablespoons sugar

¾ cup (175ml) sour cream, at room temperature

4 tablespoons (50g) unsalted butter, melted

1 teaspoon fine sea salt

¼ teaspoon baking soda

about 2½ cups (300g) unbleached white breadflour

3 tablespoons Japanese green tea

GLAZE:

1 egg yolk

1 tablespoon mirin (Japanese cooking wine) or a light white wine

1 tablespoon soy sauce

1 tablespoon water

2 loaf pans, about 8½ x 4½ x 2½ inches, well greased

To make the chestnut dough, crumble the yeast into the water in a large bowl and stir until dispersed. Add the sugar, milk, and salt. Add half the flour and mix well, then work in the melted butter, chestnut purée, and the rest of the flour to make a soft but not sticky dough. Work in extra flour if necessary. Leave to rest for 5 minutes.

Turn out onto a floured work surface and knead thoroughly for 10 minutes. Return the dough to the cleaned and lightly buttered bowl, then turn the dough so it is coated with a thin layer of butter. Cover with plastic wrap and leave the dough to rise until doubled in size — about 45 minutes in a warm kitchen.

Meanwhile, make the tea dough. Crumble the yeast into a cup, add the water and sugar, and stir until dispersed. Combine the sour cream, melted butter, salt, and baking soda in a large bowl. Stir in the yeast mixture. Sift the flour and powdered tea into the yeast mixture and mix thoroughly to make an even-colored, soft but not sticky dough. If the dough feels very sticky, work in extra flour; if there are dry crumbs in the bottom of the bowl or the dough feels dry, work in extra water. Knead and leave to rise as given for the chestnut dough — allow 1 hour.

Punch down the risen chestnut dough to deflate, then knead gently five or six times in the bowl. Leave the dough to rise again, just as before, until doubled in size.

Punch down the chestnut dough and turn out onto a lightly floured work surface. Knead lightly two or three times, then work in the chestnuts one at a time — they will start to crumble and the dough will become almost like plastic, but just keep adding and folding. Leave to relax for 5 minutes.

Punch down the risen tea dough, turn out onto a work surface, and knead for 1 minute. Cut the dough in half, and reserve one half for the second loaf. Roll out the piece of tea dough to a rectangle 8 x 12 inches, and wedge shaped — about ½ inch thick at one end tapering to ¼ inch at the other. Repeat with half of the chestnut dough.

Stack the chestnut dough on top of the tea dough, with the thin end of one dough on top of the thick end of the other — let the thicker end of the chestnut dough extend slightly over the green tea dough. Roll up the rectangle from a short side to make a neat cylinder rather like a jelly roll. Put into a prepared pan with the seam underneath, tucking the ends under. This forms a swirl or a wave (in Japanese, a *tsunami*) when the bread is sliced. Repeat with the second halves of the tea dough and the chestnut dough. Cover the loaves and leave to rise as before until doubled in size — allow 45 minutes in a warm kitchen.

Toward the end of the rising time, preheat the oven to 375°F. Mix together the ingredients for the glaze.

Uncover the loaves and brush with the glaze (you can use a simple egg yolk and water glaze, if you prefer). Bake for 30–35 minutes until golden and the loaves sound hollow when unmolded and tapped underneath. Turn out and leave to cool on a wire rack. The bread is best eaten within 3 days. It does not freeze very well.

* Rapid-rise active dry yeast is not recommended.

T IS IMPOSSIBLE to walk along Charlotte Street in London without noticing the Rasa Samudra restaurant. However, the shocking pink exterior is just a foretaste of what is inside. To the owner Das Sreedharan, colors and aromas are an important part of South Indian culture. Each dining area has its own vibrant decor and atmosphere, and you can pick a table according to your mood. But the food is far from fanciful – my husband, who was brought up in the Subcontinent, couldn't remember when he had eaten a better fish curry.

Flatbreads from South India

Rasa Samudra serves authentic seafood and vegetarian dishes from Kerala, South India, where Das was born. "It is a wonderful place for food – there are spice plantations in the highlands, and most spices are indigenous to Kerala. In the lowlands there are paddy fields, and, of course, Kerala is the coconut capital of India. We have over 200 different kinds of bananas. In South India, fish-eating is a way of life – fishing is almost a religion, as the fish are regarded as a gift, a blessing." Das learned early how good food should be: "My mother was known in Kerala for her imaginative, fresh, colorful pickles and chutneys. She was always coming up with lighter, brighter combinations."

The highlight of my lunch with Das was the dazzling array of fresh pickles and poppadums served while we read the menu. When I told Das, he laughed, because his mother trained all his chefs before they came to London. Despite his love and interest in good food, it was considered unusual for boys to go into the kitchen, so he took an honors degree in accountancy at Kerala University. Working in front of house at a five-

star hotel in New Delhi, then in restaurant management, he realized the importance of service and hospitality. "It's not enough just to have the best food, you must become good friends with your customers."

After serious research into Keralan cooking with the help of his mother, Das opened his first London vegetarian restaurant in 1994 (he now also has one in Dering Street, London W1). (See Directory and bibliography, page 172, for details of Rasa Samudra and of Das's book, *Fresh Flavors of India*.)

Das is proud of his flatbreads, which are cooked on heavy metal griddles or on traditional bowl-shaped shallow pans. For Das, as a life-long vegetarian, these breads are a staple of his diet, as they are for millions of other Indians.

Das Sreedharan (opposite) is a welcoming host
in his colorful restaurant Rasa Samudra.

"THIS is a favorite breakfast bread in South India, where the light, spongy texture comes from 'toddy' or coconut liquor," Das Sreedharan told me. "Here we use yeast to ferment the batter. The appam is traditionally cooked in a quad or kadai, a cast-iron bowl or wok-shaped metal pan set over the heat, though you could use a large non-stick frying pan or a wok.

"Appam is usually eaten with an egg cooked in the center, or can accompany a stew — an Easter specialty with the Christian community is chicken stew with appam. We make at least 50 a day and often give it away to our customers. I'm so proud of this bread, I just want everyone who comes in to taste it."

Das has a great tip for cooking with a quad or kadai: use a halved onion dipped in oil to grease the pan between breads, to prevent them from sticking.

Appam

MAKES ABOUT 14 BREADS

1¹/₃ cups (250g) basmati rice

2³/₄ cups (650ml) cold water

1 cup (125g) packed freshly grated coconut, or
    1¹/₃ cups dried shredded coconut

¹/₃ 0.6-oz cake fresh yeast (10g)*

2 tablespoons lukewarm water

1 teaspoon sugar

1 cup (75g) semolina flour

1 teaspoon fine sea salt

oil for greasing

a quad, kadai, non-stick frying pan, or wok

Rinse the rice thoroughly, then put it into a bowl with 2 cups (500ml) of the cold water and leave to soak for 1 hour.

Drain the rice, reserving the water. Put the rice, coconut, and 1 cup (230ml) of the reserved rice-soaking water into a powerful grinder, blender, or food processor and work to a fine consistency.

Crumble the yeast into a small bowl, add the lukewarm water, and the sugar, and stir until dispersed.

Put the semolina flour and remaining cold water into a pan and cook over medium heat, stirring, until the mixture is thick — about 5 minutes. Remove from the heat and leave to cool slightly.

Add the yeast and semolina mixtures to the rice mixture in the food processor and work to make a smooth, thick, and creamy batter, adding a little more of the reserved rice-soaking water as necessary. Transfer to a large bowl. Cover with a damp dish towel and leave to ferment until the mixture has doubled in volume and is slightly bubbly — about 4 hours, or longer in cold weather.

Incorporate the salt thoroughly but gently, to avoid knocking the air out of the mixture. The batter should be the consistency of heavy cream, so add a little more water if necessary.

Heat the quad or other pan and grease lightly. Add a ladle of the batter, and tip and swirl the pan — as if making crêpes — so that the batter covers the bottom in a thin layer. Cover the pan with a lid and cook for 2–3 minutes. The bread will have a crisp, golden base and a soft, spongy white top. Remove from the pan with a small spatula, and make more breads in the same way. Eat hot.

VARIATION: For appam with egg, break an egg into the center of the bread after it has cooked for 2 minutes, then cover and cook for another minute. Remove from the pan and eat immediately.

*You can use 2 teaspoons rapid-rise active dry yeast instead of the fresh yeast. Add the dry yeast to the food processor with the drained rice and coconut. Pulse to mix, then add the water and continue with the recipe.

Ajith Kumar, chef at Rasa Samudra, ladles the appam batter into the hot quad. For a delicious variation, you can break an egg into the center of the appam before the final minute of cooking (far right).

The dosas at Rasa Samudra (right) are like thin crêpes.

Chef Ajith Kumar deftly spreads the dosa batter onto the hot griddle using the back of the spoon.

Th1s *is probably one of the most famous South Indian flatbreads, but you can find it now all over India. Das's recipe is for the basic dosa flavored with fenugreek. It can be filled with many varieties of stuffing, but the most common is potato and ginger. It can also be eaten plain for breakfast with some fresh coconut or chili chutney. Das advised: "Don't be put off by what seems a lengthy process. Although the soaking and grinding will take a bit of time, it is really an easy dish to make. It might take a few attempts before you make the perfect dosa, but do keep trying." My second attempt was delicious — the dosa had the earthy flavor of a spicy blini.*

Chef Ajith Kumar makes large, paper-thin dosas for the restaurant, but Das explained that the unrolled home-style ones are smaller and thicker — there's no real correct size. It is best to cook the dosas on a heavy iron griddle, if you have one, or you can use a large, thick-based crêpe pan or griddle, non-stick for preference.

Dosa

MAKES ABOUT TEN 5-INCH BREADS

$^2/_3$ cup (125g) basmati rice

$^1/_2$ cup 85g urad dal (Indian split peas), washed

$^1/_2$ teaspoon fenugreek seeds

fine sea salt to taste

oil for greasing

a heavy griddle or heavy-based frying pan

Parboil the rice — it should still be firm in the center. Drain and cool. Measure the rice in a measuring cup, then put it into a large bowl and add twice its volume of water. Leave to soak for 8 hours or overnight.

Put the urad dal and fenugreek seeds into another bowl and cover with 1 cup (230ml) cold water. Leave to soak overnight too.

Next day, drain both the rice and dal, but keep them separate. Put the rice into a blender or food processor and process for a few minutes, slowly adding about ½ cup (125ml) fresh water until you have a smooth paste. Transfer to a large bowl (the mixture will increase in volume during fermentation). Rinse the blender and add the drained dal mixture. Process as before, slowly adding about 4 tablespoons fresh water to make a smooth paste. Add to the rice batter and mix well with a spoon. Add a little salt, then mix again and cover the bowl. Leave to ferment for 12 hours — the batter is well fermented when it has become a mass of small bubbles.

When ready to cook, stir in enough water to make a thick pouring consistency.

Heat the griddle or pan until very hot. Lightly grease using a cloth, paper towel, or onion half dipped in oil. (Do this between cooking the breads, too.) Pour a ladle of batter onto the hot surface, then use the base of the ladle or the back of a spoon to spread the batter thinly in a spiral motion. Brush or drizzle a little extra oil onto the edges of the dosa and cook until the bottom becomes crisp and golden. If very thin, lift off the dosa using a large spatula; turn over thicker ones and cook for a few minutes more until golden. Serve as soon as they are made.

3 Working and shaping the dough

MOST BREAD RECIPES start with the same simple ingredients – flour, water, salt, and yeast – but they produce an enormous variety of loaves. So how those ingredients are used – in particular, how they are worked together to make a smooth, supple, and elastic dough – largely determines the result.

Kneading is vital for an even-textured, well-risen loaf, as it develops the gluten in the flour (gluten is formed when the protein in wheat flour is dissolved in water). The strands of well-developed gluten enable the dough to stretch as the bubbles of gas produced by the yeast expand. Kneading also ensures the yeast is evenly distributed, so the loaf will rise and cook evenly. Here are some tips for kneading:

• The best dough is slightly soft rather than stiff – a stiff dough will be hard to knead and won't rise as well. The result will be a tough, dense loaf.

• Only sprinkle the work surface with flour if the dough feels too soft and sticky.

The hands of master chef Pierre Koffmann (see page 88)
shape smooth balls of dough.

• First stretch the dough away from you using the heel of your hand, then gather the dough back into a ball and give it a quarter turn. Continue with this kneading action energetically, stretching and turning the dough. As the dough is kneaded, it gradually changes texture, becoming smoother, firmer, pliable, and elastic.

• If the dough starts to feel tough and hard to work, shape it into a ball, cover it with a sheet of plastic wrap, and let it relax for 10 minutes. Or, you can raise it with one hand to shoulder height and throw it down onto the work surface with a resounding slap. Repeat as necessary. This shock treatment works wonders for both parties.

• You can also knead the dough in a large electric mixer fitted with a dough hook. But a machine can easily overknead – something impossible by hand. Use low to medium speed, don't overload the machine, and reduce the kneading time. Just for the record, I have never been able to knead dough satisfactorily in a food processor.

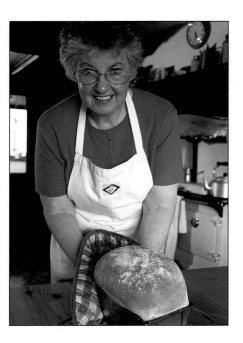

ROSEMARY ROWSON *is a natural teacher — she intuitively instills confidence and ability, so that she is in heavy demand at Denham College, the Women's Institute residential adult education college in Oxfordshire, England. Having cooked her first Sunday lunch at the age of seven, she eventually took over cooking the family meals on weekends before training as a Home Economics teacher. She and her husband and children moved to their farm in Dunsford, Devon, 20 years ago, first keeping a dairy herd, then beef cattle.*

"It has been my life, teaching home economics and cooking. I really enjoy demonstrating. I find people are interested in why you have to do things a certain way, and why this and why that happens. It's chemistry really." She never fails to get a kick of satisfaction when her students produce their first loaves of bread: "They are so thrilled, so proud of the results. Women who don't turn a hair at running a farm or producing a meal for 20 can be nervous about making bread, so I just show them how easy it is."

This handsome loaf, which Rosemary makes from locally milled top-quality organic white flour, emerges from the oven twice as big as its pan. It has a good crunchy crust and slightly chewy crumb. Rosemary says that the oldest members of Dunsford W. I. remember their grandmothers making this bread, as there wasn't a local bakery. She says it tastes like the bread of her childhood. It slices well and is excellent for sandwiches and toast.

Rosemary Rowson's farmhouse loaf

MAKES 1 LARGE LOAF

6¹/₂ cups (750g) unbleached white bread
    flour

2 teaspoons fine sea salt

2 tablespoons (30g) unsalted butter, diced

2 teaspoons sugar

1¹/₂ 0.6-oz cakes fresh yeast (23g)*

1³/₄ cups (450ml) lukewarm water

a loaf pan, about 10 x 5 x 3 inches, greased

Gently warm the flour before you start — leave it beside a heater, or in an airing cupboard or a low oven, for a few minutes, or give it 15 seconds on high in the microwave. (The warmth will encourage the yeast to grow well.)

Mix the salt with the flour, then rub in the butter using the tips of your fingers until the mixture resembles fine crumbs. Stir in the sugar, then make a well in the center. Crumble the yeast into a bowl or cup and stir in some of the water. When the yeast is thoroughly dispersed, pour the liquid into the well in the flour. Using a wooden spoon, start mixing in the flour, gradually adding the rest of the water. The mixture should come together as a soft but not sticky dough. If the dough seems dry and there are crumbs in the bottom of the bowl, add a little more warm water.

Turn the dough out onto a lightly floured work surface — don't worry if it looks an unpromising mess at this point. Using floured hands, knead the dough thoroughly for 5 minutes — the dough will feel firmer, very smooth, and pliable. Return the dough to the floured mixing bowl and cover tightly with plastic wrap. Leave to rise in a warm but not hot spot until doubled in size — about 1 hour.

Remove the dough from the bowl and knead gently on a lightly floured work surface to expel all the bubbles of air. Using plenty of flour on your hands and the work surface, flatten out the dough to a rectangle with the short end the same size as the length of the pan. Roll up tightly and put into the prepared pan, seam-side down. Lightly dust with flour. Put the pan into a large plastic bag and leave to rise as before

At the beginning of kneading, the dough is soft and very rough-looking.

Rosemary pushes and stretches the dough away, then folds it back on itself.

She gives the dough a quarter turn and repeats the stretching and folding.

After 5 minutes of this kneading, the dough is left to rise for 1 hour and then shaped.

Once in the loaf pan, Rosemary puts the bread to rise in a large plastic bag.

Having risen to almost double its original size, the bread is ready for baking.

until almost doubled in size – the time will depend on the temperature of the dough and the room and on the vigor of the yeast, but allow 40–60 minutes. Do not let the loaf get any larger or it may collapse in the oven.

Toward the end of the rising time, preheat the oven to 450°C.

Remove the pan from the bag and bake for 30–35 minutes until the bread is a dark golden brown and sounds hollow when unmolded and tapped underneath (if it sticks to the pan, dislodge gently with a round-bladed knife). Return the unmolded loaf to the oven, putting it straight on the shelf, and bake for a further 5–10 minutes until the crust is really crisp and golden. Cool on a wire rack.

The bread is best eaten within 4 days, or toasted. Once thoroughly cooled, it can be frozen for up to a month.

*You can use 4 teaspoons rapid-rise active dry yeast instead of the fresh yeast. Mix the dry yeast into the warm flour with the sugar, then add the water and continue with the recipe.

M Y 6-year-old son, Daniel, loves making things. He belongs to a craft club and has come home with two clocks, a puppet, and a shadow theater. He also loves food and cooking, and his ambition is to have his own Chinese restaurant. Dan makes this amazing loaf for tea on Sunday. The saffron is put in the milk on Saturday and left overnight to infuse, then the dough is mixed at breakfast time. Dan kneads the dough for 5 minutes in our large electric mixer fitted with the dough hook, as it is too heavy and sticky for him to knead thoroughly by hand. The dough is then scooped out, pressed into a loaf pan, and left to rise while he has a swimming lesson. It is baked alongside the Sunday lunch. The final loaf has an excellent buttery flavor and cake-like crumb even though it does not contain eggs and is only risen once. It really does taste like a slowly made, luxurious brioche.

Daniel's saffron bread

MAKES 1 MEDIUM LOAF

¹/₂ teaspoon saffron strands

1¹/₄ cups (300ml) hot milk

4 cups (500g) unbleached white bread flour

1 teaspoon fine sea salt

²/₃ cup (150g) unsalted butter, diced

¹/₄ cup (50g) firmly packed light brown sugar

1 0.6-oz cake fresh yeast (15g)*

²/₃ cup (100g) mixed dried fruit

a loaf pan, about 8¹/₂ x 4¹/₂ x 2¹/₂ inches, well greased

Daniel rubs the diced butter into the flour using his fingers — a messy job!

Crumble the saffron into the hot milk and stir well, then cover and leave to infuse overnight in a cool spot (in warm weather, leave to cool and then put into the fridge).

Combine the flour and salt in a large mixing bowl. Add the diced butter and rub in with the tips of your fingers until the mixture resembles fine crumbs. Stir in the sugar, then make a well in the center of the mixture. Gently warm the saffron milk — it should just feel comfortable to touch. Crumble the yeast into the milk and whisk or stir until dispersed, then pour into the mixing bowl. Mix with your hands until the dough comes together to make a heavy, sticky dough.

Turn out onto a work surface and knead thoroughly for 10 minutes (or knead in an electric mixer fitted with a dough hook for 5 minutes on low speed). The dough should be firmer and very smooth and pliable. Add the dried fruit, and knead for another minute until it is thoroughly and evenly mixed in. Press the mixture into the prepared pan — it should be half full — then put the pan into a large plastic bag and close tightly. Leave until the dough has risen to the top of the pan — about 1 hour in a warm room, 2 hours at room temperature, 3 hours in a cool room.

Toward the end of the rising time, preheat the oven to 350°F.

Uncover the loaf and bake for about 1 hour until it is a good golden brown and sounds hollow when unmolded and tapped underneath. Cool on a wire rack. Eat thickly sliced, with or without butter.

The bread is best eaten within 4 days, or toasted (it can also be used to make a luxurious bread pudding). Once thoroughly cooled, it can be frozen for up to a month.

*You can use 1 envelope (2¹/₂ table-spoons) rapid-rise active dry yeast instead of the fresh yeast. Mix the dry yeast into the flour with the salt, then continue with the recipe.

T HIS *is a simple and attractive way to shape bread rolls for a special meal. The buttermilk adds a subtle and pleasant tang to a white flour dough. If the mixing liquid is cold, it will retard the yeast action, so remove the buttermilk from the fridge a couple of hours before you start, to bring it to room temperature. If you prefer, the rolls can also be baked, spaced well apart, on a floured baking sheet.*

Buttermilk cluster

MAKES 16 ROLLS

6^1/$_2$ cups (750g) unbleached white bread flour

^{1}/$_2$ tablespoon fine sea salt

1 0.6-oz cake fresh yeast (15g)*

1 tablespoon lukewarm water

about 1^3/$_4$ cups (450ml) buttermilk, at room temperature

1 egg, beaten with 1 teaspoon water

1–2 tablespoons coarsely ground oats, poppy seeds, sesame seeds, or wheat or rye flakes

a round baking pan about 12 inches diameter, well greased

Shape neat balls by cupping portions of dough under your hand.

Combine the flour and salt in a large mixing bowl and make a well in the center. Crumble the fresh yeast into a small bowl and cream it to a smooth paste with the lukewarm water. Stir in the buttermilk. Pour the liquid into the well in the flour and gradually work the flour into the liquid to make a fairly soft dough. If it sticks to your fingers or the bowl, add a little more flour. If there are dry crumbs at the bottom of the bowl, work in a little extra buttermilk or lukewarm water.

Turn the dough onto a lightly floured work surface and knead it thoroughly for 10 minutes until very smooth and elastic. Return the dough to the bowl and cover with a damp dish towel, or place the bowl in a large plastic bag and close tightly. Leave until the dough has doubled in size – about 1^1/$_2$ hours at room temperature.

Punch down the dough to deflate it, then divide it into 16 equal pieces (you can do this by weight or by eye). Shape each piece into a neat ball and arrange in the pan, spaced slightly apart. Cover as before and leave to rise until almost doubled in size – about 30 minutes.

Meanwhile, preheat the oven to 425°F.

Uncover the rolls and brush very lightly with the beaten egg glaze. Try to avoid glueing the dough to the sides of the pan with the glaze, as this will prevent the dough from rising in the oven. Sprinkle with the oat meal, seeds, or flakes, then bake for about 30 minutes until firm and golden. Carefully unmold either by unclipping the pan or by inverting the rolls onto a wire rack and then turning them back again the right way up. Serve warm or on the same day.

Once thoroughly cooled, the rolls can be frozen for up to a month.

* You can use 1 envelope (2^1/$_2$ teaspoons) rapid-rise active dry yeast instead of the fresh yeast. Mix the dry yeast with the flour and salt, then continue with the recipe.

"IT'S PERFECTLY POSSIBLE TO MAKE GOOD BAGUETTES at home with a domestic oven," claimed Pierre Koffmann. To prove it, he left La Tante Claire, his Michelin-starred restaurant at The Berkeley Hotel in London, for the quieter, more confined setting of Anthony's studio kitchen.

A chef's secrets

Kneading changes bread dough in a vital way. The more it is worked, the more elastic and strong the strands of gluten become. When the dough has been thoroughly kneaded and the gluten is fully developed, you should be able to stretch the dough so thinly – without it tearing – that you can see through it.

Everything served at Pierre's restaurant is treated with the same importance – the butter, bread, and cheese are all chosen and handled with as much care as the *poulets de Bresse* and the lobsters. Pierre buys in *pain complet* from Patrick LePort (see page 102), but he also bakes a 20–pound batch of bread every day. He has even designed a trolley to display the bread and cheese. "It's important to realize that the bread has to go with the food. It's hard to compare French bread with Italian or German, as it depends on what you are eating. Deeply flavored German rye complements their food; it would not be so good with another cuisine. My bread goes with French cooking. My grandmother used to buy bread once a week, and it was always better the next day. That's how it should be, and with Patrick's, it is. These days in France, a baguette is stale after three hours – that's not good bread."

Pierre has some excellent guidelines for baking impressive (old-style) French baguettes and other breads at home:

• "The best flavor and texture comes from French flour." French varieties of wheat have individual characteristics quite different from North American ones. Look out for French-style bread flour in specialist food stores (also available from King Arthur Flour, see Directory, page 172).

• "For deep flavor and a loaf that stays fresh for longer, give the dough two fermentations." The first (for baguettes) should be a "poolish" – a soft, batter-like dough made with half the flour, all the water, and a little yeast – which is left to rise, overnight if possible, until doubled in size and very bubbly. The second fermentation, when all the ingredients have been incorporated, goes quickly because the poolish has enabled the yeast to have a head start and become very vigorous.

• "Temperature is crucial. If you work like this, you will never make mistakes." To calculate the correct temperature for the water, everything for the bread should add up to 192°F, so if your kitchen is 68°F, and your flour is 64°F, then the water must be 60°F. In hot weather you may need to used chilled water.

• "Knead energetically for a good 10 minutes." As the dough is pushed out and stretched with the heel of the hand, the gluten in the flour develops into strands. The gluten can then make a kind of scaffolding for the bread during baking. As the bubbles of gas produced by the yeast expand in number and size, the elastic strands of gluten stretch to accommodate the extra volume. In an unkneaded dough, the gas bubbles cannot expand, and the resulting bread is heavy and dense.

• "Rise the dough in a warm, humid atmosphere." A large plastic bag, slightly inflated and securely closed, is ideal.

• "Use a razor-sharp knife for slashing the dough." Anything else will tear it.

• "If possible, bake in a conventional oven." An oven with top and bottom elements will give a better result than a convection oven. Whatever you use, get the oven as hot as possible, and put in a sheet of water to make it steamy. Professional ovens add a burst of steam when the loaves go in, to develop the razor-sharp, thin glossy crust; you can use a water-spray mister to get the same effect.

• "For a crisp crust, put the bread right on the oven shelf for the last 5 minutes baking."

*T*HE *length of the loaves depends on the size of your oven. Pierre Koffmann made the baguettes shown in the photographs in a standard domestic oven. If you have an extra wide oven, divide the dough into four, and shape to fit your sheets.*

Baguettes

MAKES 7 SMALL LOAVES

8¼ cups (1kg) French-style white bread flour

1 tablespoon fine sea salt

2 0.6-oz cakes fresh yeast (30g)*

2½ cups (600ml) still spring water (see page 89 for instructions about water temperature)

several baking sheets

Make the "poolish" using half the flour, half the salt, and a quarter of the yeast dispersed in all the water. Put all these ingredients into a large mixing bowl (choose one with a lid, if possible) and beat with your hand to make a smooth, thick, batter-like dough. Cover with a lid or plastic wrap and leave at about 68°F until doubled in size and very bubbly – 8 hours or overnight.

The next day, work in the rest of the yeast dispersed in 1 tablespoon of water, the rest of the salt, and enough of the remaining flour to make a firm dough. Knead thoroughly for 10 minutes until very elastic. Return the dough to the cleaned and dried bowl, cover, and leave as before until doubled in size – about 1 hour.

Gently turn out the dough onto the work surface. Do not punch it down. Cut into seven equal pieces and gently shape each into a ball. Cover with a piece of plastic wrap and leave to relax for 10–15 minutes.

Roll out each ball to a rectangle about 8 x 9 inches. Roll up tightly, like a jelly roll, folding in the sides before you finish. Pinch together the seam to secure it thoroughly. On an unfloured work surface, roll the dough sausage with your hands as follows: Put one hand on each end of the roll, then move your right hand forward so the dough at that end is rolled forward; at the same time move your left hand back to roll the dough backward. Repeat in the opposite direction. The dough should be rolled to and fro on a slight diagonal like this until you have a neat loaf with tapering ends the length of your baking sheet.

Lightly flour a clean, dry cloth and set it on a large sheet or board. Gently arrange the shaped loaves on the cloth, pleating the cloth to make a light support for each loaf and a barrier between it and the next. When all the loaves have been shaped and arranged on the cloth, put the sheet into a large plastic bag. Leave to rise at 68°F until doubled in size – about 45 minutes.

Toward the end of the rising time, preheat the oven to its hottest setting. Put a dish of water on the oven floor to create a steamy atmosphere.

Uncover the risen baguettes and very gently roll, rather than lift, them

Pierre carefully lifts the risen dough onto the work surface.

Left: He rolls out each piece of dough to a 8 x 9½cm rectangle.

Right: He rolls up the rectangle tightly, tucking in the sides.

Then he rolls the dough to and fro to make a thin sausage to fit the sheet.

The shaped loaves are left to rise on a floured cloth, pleated to give support.

Just before they are baked, Pierre slashes the loaves with a razor-sharp knife.

onto the baking sheets (turning them upside down, if necessary, to get a flat surface). Using a razor-sharp knife, make four curved slashes along the length of each loaf. Put the sheets into the oven and either spray or sprinkle the inside with water to create a burst of steam. Quickly close the oven door and bake for about 20 minutes until the loaves are crisp and golden. Tip them off the sheets straight onto the oven shelf and bake for 5 minutes more. Cool on a wire rack.

The baguettes are best eaten within 24 hours. They do not freeze very well.

*You can use 2 envelopes (5 teaspoons) rapid-rise active dry yeast instead of the fresh yeast. Combine the dry yeast with the flour, in the proportions given.

The freshly baked rolls and baguettes are best eaten within 24 hours.

T HE *firm dough for these rolls is made like that for baguettes (see page 90), except that the "poolish" stage is omitted. As a variation, for extra flavor, Pierre often adds a piece of dough saved from the previous day's baking – about 8 ounces (250g).*

Pierre Koffmann's bread rolls

MAKES ABOUT 36 ROLLS, DEPENDING ON SIZE

8¼ cups (1kg) French-style white bread flour

1 tablespoon fine sea salt

2 0.6-oz cakes fresh yeast (30g)*

2½ cups (600ml) still spring water (see page 89 for instructions about water temperature)

several baking sheets

Put the flour and salt into a large mixing bowl. Disperse the yeast in the water, add to the bowl, and mix to make a firm dough. (Work in a piece of saved dough, if using.) Turn out onto a work surface and knead thoroughly for 10 minutes until very elastic. Return the dough to the cleaned and dried bowl, cover with plastic wrap, and leave at about 68°F until doubled in size – about 1 hour.

To make *triangles*: Roll out the dough to a square ¼ inch thick. Cut the square into two rectangles, then cut each rectangle into triangles with sides about 1¼ inches long. Arrange on floured baking sheets, and cover with plastic bags. Leave to rise at 68°F until doubled in size – about 45 minutes. Before baking, slash with a sharp knife.

To make *purses*: Set aside ¹/₁₀ of the dough. Roll the remaining dough into a thick cylinder, then slice into thick disks. Mold the disks into golfball shapes. Roll out the reserved dough fairly thinly, then cut out disks the same diameter as the balls. Set a ball on each thin disk of dough and push a thin wooden spoon handle through both to

For triangular rolls, Pierre cuts neat shapes from a rectangular strip of dough.

secure. Leave to rise on a baking sheet as for the triangles. For baking, gently turn upside down on a floured baking sheet.

An alternative way to make purses is to divide the dough into pieces and shape each into a small ball, slightly larger than a golfball. Using plenty of flour, roll out one side of each ball to make a flap. Fold the ball of dough over the flap. Leave to rise on a baking sheet as above. For baking, gently turn over onto a floured baking sheet.

To make *ears of wheat*: Shape the dough into a cylinder, then cut into thick disks and mold each into a golfball shape. Roll each ball with your hands to make a sausage shape with tapering ends. Leave to rise on a floured baking sheet as for the triangles. Before baking, make four cuts with kitchen scissors, almost but not quite through the dough, along the length of each roll. Fold or flip over the cut sections alternately to resemble an ear of wheat.

Toward the end of the rising time, preheat the oven to its hottest setting.

Put a dish of water on the oven floor to create a steamy atmosphere.

For purses, he rolls pieces of dough between his palms to make golfball shapes.

He sets each ball on a disk of dough, then pushes a spoon handle through the two.

After rising, the shaped purses are turned upside down on a floured sheet for baking.

For ears of wheat, Pierre rolls small pieces of dough into sausages with tapering ends.

Using sharp scissors, he snips the dough sausages, then flips the cut sections over.

Put the rolls into the oven and either spray or sprinkle the inside with water to create a burst of steam. Quickly close the door and bake for about 15 minutes until the rolls are crisp and golden. Tip them off the sheets straight onto the oven shelf and bake for 2 minutes more. Cool on a wire rack.

The rolls are best eaten within 24 hours. They do not freeze very well.

*You can use 2 envelopes (5 teaspoons) rapid-rise active dry yeast instead of the fresh yeast. Combine the dry yeast with the flour, then add the water and continue with the recipe.

Lechlade in Gloucestershire is where you'll find The Flour Bag. Look for the larger-than-life statue of a baker outside the shop.

WALKING INTO THE FLOUR BAG in Lechlade, Gloucestershire, England, makes my heart give a little skip. Every space is occupied with an edible delight, an eclectic mix obviously chosen by someone with a love of the good things in life and an eye for detail. The deli counter has homemade pâtés and terrines, as well as the largest variety of marinated olives in the county. Thirty-odd different olive oils in bottles, cans, and pots stand hugger-mugger with serving boards sliced from ancient olive trees struck down by lightning. Think of a pasta – it's there, along with books to help you cook it almost as well as Marcella Hazan. There are exotic spices and jars of esoteric coffee beans, as well as an excellent stock of basics – organic flours and grains, legumes, seeds, and sugars.

The best of everything

Then, of course, there are the breads – 19 different kinds, baked each morning in the oven behind the shop. The breads look great, and they taste even better. There's a chewy ciabatta made with 100% virgin olive oil; Jewish white – a light rye and white sourdough flavored with caraway and fennel seeds (my husband said the taste took him right back to his family in New York); a seeded loaf with poppy, sesame, and sunflower plus millet, malted oats, and wheat flakes; an Italian bread so rich in cheese, tomatoes, and nuts it can be eaten just as it is; and so many more.

Maurice Chaplais takes great pride in his hand-crafted loaves: "When we first saw the bakery 14 years ago, it was an anachronism, and the old baker had been working in the same artisanal way for the last 40 years, with the same few pieces of equipment." There was a massive oil-fired brick oven, and two archaic mixers for kneading the dough. "Until then I wanted a modern state-of-the-art bakery, but we fell in love with this one. The oven takes eight hours to heat up, so I put it on at bedtime. The mixers are almost 50 years old, but they are excellent as they work very slowly with small quantities of dough."

Maurice, who is half-French, came to baking after a career that ranged from making cocktails in the West Indies and cooking on a yacht, to running a hotel and restaurant in Corsica, the Bahnhopf Buffet in Berne, Switzerland, and Wrens in Oxford, England (*the* Oxford restaurant of the Seventies), where he met his wife Nanette. Then, by chance, he found himself volunteering to run a large French bakery for friends: "I didn't know a thing at first, but we ended up selling filled croissants to British Rail outlets and a supermarket. We developed the system of supplying frozen raw dough for baking on site." This led to work with oven manufacturers, selling the latest technology to large-scale bakeries and factories, but being a sales manager wasn't for him. "I wanted to take a step back. I've always liked cooking, but I love making bread – it's a living thing, and you have to respond to it, respect it."

Maurice and Nanette work incredibly hard, and the working day is long. "The bakery and shop have to fit in with family life – we have four young children – but it's still a twelve-hour day." The bread cycle begins at 5p.m. when Maurice makes a sponge dough using white bread flour from Shipton Mill and a very little yeast. This will form the basis for many of the breads made next morning. "This makes my favorite basic bread; the flavor speaks for itself – it needs nothing else." The flour is at its best when used to make an overnight sponge: "Rather like wine, the best bread is not rushed. The same chemicals occur in bread fermentation as they do in wine, so it's like comparing a beaujolais nouveau and a well-made, properly matured beaujolais, and I know which I prefer." The amount of yeast for this overnight sponge has to be calculated to take the ambient temperature into account. The mixed dough is left to rise overnight in a large plastic tub – in the coolest spot in summer, and a sheltered one in cold, frosty weather.

Maurice then weighs out the rest of the ingredients for each of the 19 different breads. Everything is prepared so it can just be added to the sponge in the morning. "Some of my breads are complex and I want to have everything at hand so I can work at speed, otherwise the bread would never get into the oven." Maurice uses the best of everything – free-range eggs, raw molasses sugar and unrefined cane sugar, slow-acting fresh yeast rather than rapid-rise, pure vanilla and almond extracts, locally smoked bacon, pine nuts, expensive walnut oil, and extra virgin olive oil for the ciabatta (10% of the total dough weight). "I don't worry about the cost of the ingredients. I made up the recipes for all my breads and I like to use the best available ingredients – but I charge for it too."

He keeps a light rye sourdough starter to add flavor to yeasted white loaves, such as the baguettes and Jewish bread, and a dark rye starter for his pumpernickel and dark rye loaves. "I'm not a purist, and I'm not very keen on very dense breads, so I use both yeast and sourdough. In my dark rye breads I add a little wheat flour just to lighten the texture. The intense flavor comes from dark rye flour from Shipton Mill." The sourdough starters are refreshed once a week.

Nanette and Maurice start work on the dough at the large wooden table just before 6a.m. Nanette puts in an hour and a half before the children wake up. An accomplished cook and baker herself, she worked in the bakery full-time before the children came along, and now does the paper work and deliveries and helps in the shop, all on very little sleep. At 8a.m. Valerie Watson takes over from Nanette, shaping the risen dough, loading the ovens, turning out the hot loaves. The bread fills the shop in waves, and the smells intensify. The large statue of a baker outside beckons to customers, and quickly a line forms.

So how does Maurice recognize a perfect loaf? "It's finding I want to eat the whole thing – a totally piggish answer."

Both Nanette (below) and Maurice Chaplais (bottom) work incredibly hard in their bakery, producing 19 different kinds of hand-crafted bread.

THE *very attractive shape of this loaf from Maurice Chaplais is the result of baking it in a garden flowerpot. The bread, full of sunflower seeds, pistachios, and hazelnuts, has a delicious flavor, moist crumb, and crunchy texture.*

Sunflower-seed bread

MAKES 2 MEDIUM LOAVES

DOUGH:

3 cups (350g) unbleached white bread flour

scant 1 cup (100g) whole-wheat flour,
    preferably stoneground

1 teaspoon fine sea salt

1 tablespoon (15g) lard or white vegetable fat

1 0.6-oz cake fresh yeast (15g)*

1¹⁄₃ cups (330ml) lukewarm water

TO FINISH:

¹⁄₃ cup (50g) sunflower seeds

¹⁄₃ cup (50g) raw (unroasted) pistachio kernels

1 heaped teaspoon fennel seeds

2 tablespoons (15g) hazelnuts, toasted and
    chopped quite fine

extra sunflower seeds for the top

2 unused clay flowerpots, 6 inches wide and
    5¹⁄₂ inches high, very well greased

Combine the flours and salt in a large mixing bowl. Rub in the lard using the tips of your fingers until there are no visible lumps. Crumble the yeast into the water and stir until thoroughly dispersed, then add to the flour mixture. Mix until thoroughly combined to make a slightly soft but not sticky dough. If the dough seems dry or stiff, add a little more water; if the dough is sticky add a little more flour.

Turn out onto a work surface and knead very thoroughly – about 10 minutes. Combine all the remaining ingredients (except the sunflower seeds for the top) and knead into the dough until evenly distributed. Return the dough to the bowl, cover with a dish towel, and leave in a warm place for about 30 minutes.

Turn out the dough onto a work surface and punch down to deflate. Divide the dough into two equal pieces. Knead each piece for a minute, then shape into a neat ball. Dip each ball into sunflower seeds spread on a plate, then place in the greased flowerpots, seed-side up. Leave in a warm place until the dough has risen just above the rim of the flowerpots – about 1 hour.

Toward the end of the rising time, preheat the oven to 400°F.

Bake the loaves for 25–30 minutes until a good golden brown. Using a round-bladed knife, scrape off the dough that has escaped through the hole in the base of the flowerpot, then ease the bread out (it usually sticks the first time, but gets easier the more the flowerpot is used). Cool on a wire rack.

The bread is best eaten within 4 days, or toasted. Once thoroughly cooled it can be frozen for up to a month.

*You can use 1 envelope (2¹⁄₂ tespoons) rapid-rise active dry yeast instead of the fresh yeast. Mix the dry yeast with the flours and salt, then continue with the recipe.

Maurice feels that baking the dough in flowerpots adds to the appeal of moist and crunchy Sunflower-Seed Bread.

"THIS *is a very tasty, somewhat extravagant bread, ideal for a dinner party or for eating with antipasto or salads," is Maurice's advice. He came up with this recipe for a smart local restaurant, and it has proved a popular special-occasion bread in his shop.*

Maurice Chaplais's Italian bread

MAKES 2 MEDIUM LOAVES

DOUGH:

4 cups (450g) unbleached white bread flour

1 teaspoon fine sea salt

1 tablespoon (15g) lard or white vegetable fat

1 0.6-oz cake fresh yeast (15g)*

1¹/₄ cups (330ml) lukewarm water

TO FINISH:

¹/₄ cup(30g) dry-packed sun-dried tomatoes

2 tablespoons (15g) pine nuts

1 cup (100g) grated sharp Cheddar cheese

1¹/₂ teaspoons dried herbes de Provence

1 large or 2 small baking sheets, greased

Combine the flour and salt in a mixing bowl. Rub in the fat using the tips of your fingers, until there are no visible lumps. Make a well in the center of the mixture. Crumble the yeast into the water and stir until thoroughly dispersed, then add to the flour mixture. Combine to make a soft but not sticky dough. If the dough is dry and stiff, work in a little extra water; if it is sticky work in extra flour.

Turn out onto a work surface and knead thoroughly until very pliable – about 10 minutes. Return to the bowl, cover with plastic wrap or a dish towel, and leave in a warm place for about 30 minutes.

Meanwhile, soak the sun-dried tomatoes in boiling water for 30 minutes until softened, then drain and chop roughly. Combine with the pine nuts, cheese, and herbs.

Turn out the dough and punch down to deflate. Add the tomato mixture, and cut and fold the dough over, rather than kneading, until thoroughly distributed. Divide into two equal pieces and shape each into a neat oval about 10¹/₂ inches long. Place on the prepared baking sheet and leave in a warm place until doubled in size.

Toward the end of the rising time, preheat the oven to 400°F.

Bake the loaves for 25–30 minutes until they turn golden brown and sound hollow when tapped underneath. Cool on a wire rack.

The bread is best eaten warm, but will keep well for up to 3 days. Once thoroughly cooled, it can be frozen for up to a month.

* You can use 1 envelope (2¹/₂ teaspoons) rapid-rise active dry yeast instead of the fresh yeast. Combine the dry yeast with the flour and salt, then continue with the recipe.

T HIS *loaf, full of oats, has a dense, nutty texture and a rich brown color. It is one of Maurice Chaplais's most popular loaves: "As well as being a delicious treat, it always makes my cus- tomers smile when I tell them the only liquid used in this recipe is Murphy's stout — none of that boring old water." The dough is mixed and then left to rise slowly overnight. It is a good bread to eat with soup or salad as well as cheese.*

Stout and oat bread

MAKES 2 MEDIUM LOAVES

¹/₃ 0.6-oz cake fresh yeast (5g)*

2 tablespoons (30g) firmly packed molasses
   sugar or dark brown sugar

1¹/₃ cups (325ml) Murphy's stout

3¹/₂ cups (400g) unbleached white bread flour

²/₃ cup (100g) steel-cut oats, coarsely ground
   in a food processor to the texture of fine
   bulghur wheat

1 cup (100g) toasted oat flakes

1 teaspoon fine sea salt

1 tablespoon (15g) lard or white vegetable fat

jumbo oat flakes to finish

1 large or 2 smaller baking sheets, greased

Crumble the yeast into a bowl, add the sugar and stout, and stir well until the yeast has dispersed and the sugar dissolved. Combine the flour, ground oats, toasted oat flakes, and salt in a large mixing bowl. Rub in the fat with your fingertips, then make a well in the center of the mixture. Pour in the stout mixture. Work all the ingredients together to make a slightly soft dough.

Turn out onto a work surface and knead thoroughly — about 10 minutes. Put the dough into a container with a lid, or a large bowl tightly covered with plastic wrap, and leave to rise for at least 8 hours — or overnight — in a cool place. (In very warm weather, leave the dough in the fridge or reduce the quan-tity of yeast to prevent over-rising.)

Next day, turn out the dough onto a work surface. Punch down to deflate the dough, then divide it into two equal pieces. Knead each piece for a minute to disperse the bubbles of air, then shape into a neat ball. Dip the top-side of each ball into the jumbo oats, then place on the prepared baking sheet with the oat-covered side upper-most. Leave to rise in a warm place until the balls of dough are doubled in size — about 1 hour.

Toward the end of the rising time, preheat the oven to 400°F.

Bake the loaves for about 25 minutes until they sound hollow when tapped underneath. Cool on a wire rack.

The bread is best eaten within 5 days — the flavor deepens the longer the bread is kept — or toasted. Once thoroughly cooled it can be frozen for up to a month.

* You can use ¹/₄ teaspoon rapid-rise active dry yeast instead of the fresh yeast. Mix the dry yeast with the flour, coarsely ground oats, oat flakes, and salt, then continue with the recipe.

"You are going to have a recipe for quark bread, aren't you?" demanded our German friends. I was then given several slightly different recipes, which I used to create my own version. My thanks to Gill and Gaby for their efforts and translations.

I used a mixture of stone-ground whole-wheat flour, very coarsely ground whole-wheat

flour, and cracked wheat berries to replace the German coarse wheaten flour traditional for this loaf. The dough is bound with quark, a German skim-milk soft cheese. The combination is excellent — a richly flavored, tangy bread with a rough but moist texture. I like it best with honey and preserves, but my German friends eat it for brunch with cheese.

Quark wheaten bread

MAKES 1 MEDIUM LOAF

2¹/₂ cups (300g) whole-wheat bread flour, preferably stoneground

1¹/₂ cups (200g) coarse whole-wheat flour

scant 1 cup (100g) cracked wheat

¹/₂ tablespoon fine sea salt

2 0.6-oz cakes fresh yeast (30g)*

¹/₂ cup (100ml) lukewarm water

1 tablespoon clear honey

2 cups (500g) low-fat quark, at room temperature

1 tablespoon sunflower oil

a baking sheet, floured

Mix together the flours, cracked wheat, and salt in a large bowl, and make a well in the center. Crumble the yeast into another bowl and stir in the water and honey to make a smooth liquid. Pour into the well in the flour and mix in enough of the flour to make a thick batter. Cover the bowl with a damp dish towel and leave until the batter is puffy and spongy – about 30 minutes.

Mix the quark and oil into the spongy batter, then work in the rest of the flour. This will not feel like a normal whole-wheat bread dough, and I find squeezing the dough together easier than stirring or mixing in the usual way. The dough should come together to make a slightly sticky rather than firm or hard dough. Add a little extra water if there are dry crumbs or the dough feels very stiff.

Turn out onto a work surface and knead thoroughly for 10 minutes – the consistency of the dough will change as you work it and will become elastic, cohesive, and pliable. Return the dough to the bowl, cover with a damp dish towel, and leave to rise until doubled in size – 1–2 hours, depending on kitchen temperature.

Punch down the dough, then turn out onto the work surface and shape into a round loaf. Put onto the prepared baking sheet. Score the top of the loaf with a cross (otherwise the surface will tear during rising), then put the sheet into a large plastic bag. Slightly inflate the bag, then tuck the ends under the sheet to secure them. Leave the loaf to rise until almost doubled in size – 30 minutes to 1 hour.

Toward the end of the rising time, preheat the oven to 425°F.

Remove the loaf from the bag and bake for 35–40 minutes until it is a good brown and sounds hollow when tapped underneath. Cool on a wire rack.

The bread is best eaten within 5 days, or toasted. It does not freeze very well.

*You can use 2 envelopes (5 teaspoons) rapid-rise active dry yeast instead of the fresh yeast. Omit the sponge stage. Mix the dry yeast with the flour mixture, make a well in the center, add the water, honey, quark, and oil, and mix together as given, then continue with the recipe.

For the best results, the quark should be at room temperature when it is added to the spongy batter.

The easiest way to mix this dough is to squeeze the ingredients together with your hand.

THIS early-twentieth-century recipe is based on the overnight sponge dough favored by Clive Mellum (see page 16). Although the tea cakes were traditionally enriched with lard, these days many bakers prefer a hard white vegetable fat. Unlike those from the South and West of England, Yorkshire tea cakes, the size of a decent saucer, are flavored with currants alone. No spice, saffron, or candied fruit peel is added, so the quality of the dough is important.

Yorkshire tea cakes are really wonderful when split and toasted by an open fire, then lavishly buttered, and enjoyed with a pot of freshly brewed tea.

Yorkshire tea cakes

MAKES 12 CAKES

SPONGE:

$^2/_3$ 0.6-oz cake fresh yeast (10g)

2$^1/_4$ cups (560ml) lukewarm water

8$^1/_4$ cups (1kg) unbleached white bread flour

1 tablespoon fine sea salt

TO FINISH:

4 cups (500g) unbleached white bread flour

$^1/_2$ cup (100g) lard or other white fat, diced

$^1/_2$ cup (100g) sugar

$^1/_2$ tablespoon fine sea salt

$^2/_3$ cup (100g) currants

1$^2/_3$ 0.6-oz cakes fresh yeast (25g)

1$^1/_4$ cups (300ml) lukewarm milk

several baking sheets, greased

To make the sponge, crumble the yeast into the water, then stir or whisk well until smooth. Combine the flour and salt in a mixing bowl, add the yeast liquid, and work in to make a soft but not sticky dough. Turn out onto a work surface and knead thoroughly for 10 minutes. Return the sponge dough to the bowl, cover tightly with plastic wrap, and leave to rise at room temperature overnight or for up to 12 hours.

Next day, put the second quantity of flour into a large mixing bowl, and rub in the diced fat with your fingertips until the mixture resembles fine crumbs. Stir in the sugar, salt, and currants. Crumble the fresh yeast into the milk and whisk until smoothly dispersed, then pour into the flour mixture. Work the ingredients until they come together into a dough.

Punch down the risen sponge dough to deflate it, then add to the fruit dough. Work the two doughs together, then turn out of the bowl onto the work surface and

Tip the risen sponge mixture on top of the fruit dough.

Work the two mixtures together until thoroughly combined, then knead well.

After resting, divide the dough into equal pieces with a cleaver or large sharp knife.

Prick the buns all over with a fork so they will rise evenly in the oven.

knead thoroughly for 10 minutes — the dough should look sleek and be without streaks. Cover the dough with the upturned bowl or a sheet of plastic wrap and leave to rest for 15 minutes.

Divide the dough into 12 equal pieces and shape each into a ball. Press or roll each ball to a round 5 inches across (use a saucer as a guide), then arrange, spaced well apart, on the prepared baking sheets. Cover with plastic wrap or place the sheets in large plastic bags. Leave to rise for 30–40 minutes until nearly doubled in size.

Meanwhile, preheat the oven to 425°F.

Uncover the buns and prick them well with a fork. Bake for about 15 minutes until chestnut brown and firm.

Eat warm with butter, straight from the oven. Or cool on a wire rack, then split and toast. The cooled buns can be frozen for up to a month.

Yorkshire Tea Cakes are delicious split and toasted, then liberally buttered.

"ONCE TASTED, NEVER FORGOTTEN" – a principle that has served Patrick LePort well: "Word of mouth sells my bread. It's the finest sort of advertising." His bakery, La Boulangerie Savoyarde, in a hamlet called Ecole en Bauges, hidden in the picturesque Col du Frene in France, doesn't attract passing trade: "It seems isolated here, but it's easy to reach Geneva, Annecy, or Grenoble – once you get back on the main road." Patrick says this without irony: he supplies bread to Michelin-starred restaurants like La Tante Claire in London and Pierre Orsi in Lyon, France.

Simplicity is the key

So why do chefs like Pierre Koffmann and gourmet-store owner Ernest Hilton, of the Montignac Boutique in London, take such trouble to buy Patrick's bread? "I've been baking with only organic ingredients, sea salt, and spring water here for 25 years, and in that time there hasn't been one gram of yeast on the premises. All my breads are made with a sourdough *levain* started 25 years ago." He adds that, of course, he doesn't use apple or raisin juices or powdered cultures to enhance his *levain*.

Patrick comes from Brittany, and has an English mother. He was studying organic vegetable and food production when he visited Lionel Poilâne's bakery in the rue du Cherche-Midi in Paris. "I was inspired. I decided I had to make bread, and I wanted to make organic sourdough breads." With some friends he opened an organic vegetarian restaurant in Holland, and learned how to cook and bake from scratch. "Our customers then encouraged us to buy a bakery and helped us by giving subscriptions. So I had to learn very quickly." After three years he returned to France: "I wanted to live in the countryside, and I found this house with bakery attached. It's perfect here."

For the first five years in Ecole en Bauges he had trouble getting the dough to rise: "I was looking for a loaf with a light, open texture and a distinct but not aggressive flavor. Eventually I realized it had to be the quality of the flour. In Holland, I had been baking with stoneground flour from a windmill, and had never had any problem with my sourdoughs, so it was clear that the best flour comes from high-quality wheat milled on large stones. This ensures the wheat grains are thoroughly cracked open, not crushed, and you get a more active, better tasting dough." Patrick now buys his flour from Moulin Pichard near Gap: "I need 35 tons a month, and that makes 50 tons of bread. I work hand in glove with the miller there, and I respect him like a father – I can tell immediately if there is a difference in the flour."

Patrick's breads are wonderfully good and utterly distinctive, yet they are all made to one basic recipe: "Be simple when you make bread. Also, be happy or the bread won't be quite as good."

Patrick LePort made a special pain complet *for Anthony and me when we visited him. For all his breads, including his wonderful olive* fougasse *(below right), he uses flour milled from organic French wheat.*

THE *best-selling loaf at La Boulangerie Savoyarde, pain complet is made in several sizes — the 3-kilo and 5-kilo loaves are the most popular as they keep the longest. Patrick uses white flour with an 80% extraction rate. It has a beautiful, creamy white color, as some of the bran and wheat germ have been left in. The nearest American equivalent is 90% organic white bread flour plus 10% white whole-wheat flour. Patrick's sourdough starter, or* levain, *is very vigorous, and quite mild. He says it should have a milky aroma; a whiff of acid means it is too sour. His tip: "You want a very vigorous* levain *that gives the bread an open light texture plus a pleasant mild flavor. It has to be very lively and vigorous or the dough will sag and flop. If you have a problem with your* levain — it smells sour or seems weak — then just keep dividing and feeding it every 12 hours." Patrick feeds his levain (using an equal weight of flour and enough water to make a very soft and sticky dough, not a liquid batter) 6 hours before he needs it, and keeps it at room temperature. If you store yours in the fridge, as I do when I travel, bring it back to room temperature before feeding.*

This basic recipe can be used to make one large loaf, several smaller ones, rolls, Fougasse des Olives, Kamut, and other breads using spelt, rye, or mixed grain flours. One last tip from Patrick: handle the dough as little as possible after kneading.

Patrick LePort's pain complet

MAKES 1 LARGE LOAF

7oz (200g) soft-dough sourdough starter (see page 49), at room temperature

4 cups (450g) organic bread flour (see recipe introduction), at room temperature

1¹/₂ cups (350ml) lukewarm still spring water

¹/₂ tablespoon fine sea salt

a baking sheet or pizza baking stone

The ideal temperature of the mixed dough should be 79°F, so gently warm the flour in winter or if your kitchen is cold. Mix the four ingredients in a large bowl until thoroughly combined. The dough should be soft but not sticky — you may have to add a little more flour or water, depending on the consistency of your sourdough starter.

Turn the dough out onto the work surface and knead for 4 minutes. Let the dough rest for 2 minutes, then knead again for a further 4 minutes. Return the dough to the bowl and cover with a sheet of plastic wrap, or put the bowl into a plastic bag and close tightly. Leave to rise until doubled in size — about 1¹/₂ hours, depending on the warmth of your kitchen.

Gently punch down the risen dough, and gently fold and shape it into a round or oval loaf. Do not work the dough or handle it roughly. Leave to rise in a linen-lined

At La Boulangerie Savoyarde, Patrick LePort and his bakers make 50 tons of bread every month, and the massive oven is fired continuously from Sunday evening to Friday night. Pain complet (right and far right) is the best selling loaf, but Patrick is very proud of his Kamut bread (top right).

dough-rising basket, or a bread basket or colander lined with a floured cloth, until doubled in size – about 2¹/₂ hours at 79°F. (In winter Patrick recommends using a cardboard box filled with hot water bottles as a rising chamber.)

Toward the end of the rising time, preheat the oven to 450°F. Put the baking sheet or baking stone into the oven to heat.

Turn out the loaf onto the hot sheet or stone, and slash the top with a razor. Bake until the loaf turns a dark golden brown and sounds hollow when tapped underneath – about 35 minutes. Cool on a wire rack.

The bread is best eaten the day after baking and keeps well for up to a week. Once thoroughly cooled, it can be frozen for up to a month.

VARIATION: *Kamut*

"This is our second best seller," says Patrick. "I'm very proud to have it on our list. I was one of the first bakers in France to use kamut flour. If you think spelt has a good flavor, you'll really like this. It has a taste all of its own and gives a golden crumb. The flour I use comes from an organic farm in Montana. I believe the original grains came from a pharaoh's tomb in Egypt, and were taken back to America for cultivation. For me it was an exciting discovery – a whole new taste in bread."

Make up the Pain Complet as given, using kamut flour instead of the bread flour. If you find that varying the flour means the dough rises faster or slower than with your usual flour, Patrick recommends changing the temperature of the water and the room rather than changing the proportions of the recipe.

For Kamut, the dough is made with the flour of the ancients.

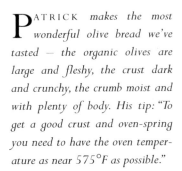

PATRICK *makes the most wonderful olive bread we've tasted – the organic olives are large and fleshy, the crust dark and crunchy, the crumb moist and with plenty of body. His tip: "To get a good crust and oven-spring you need to have the oven temperature as near 575°F as possible."*

Fougasse des olives

MAKES 1 FLAT LOAF

530g Pain Complet dough (half the quantity given opposite)

¹/₂ cup (70g) pitted organic olives

a baking sheet or pizza baking stone

Make up the dough and leave to rise, then gently punch down.

Put the dough onto a well-floured work surface, and gently flatten with your hands. Put the olives on top, then fold the dough over like an envelope to enclose the olives. Cover with a sheet of plastic wrap and leave to rest for 15 minutes.

Gently press and flatten the dough to a round about 9 inches across. Turn it over onto a floured dish towel, cover with a sheet of plastic wrap or another floured cloth, and leave to rise until doubled in size – about 2¹/₂ hours.

Toward the end of the rising time, preheat the oven to its hottest possible setting, and put the baking sheet or pizza baking stone in to heat.

Quickly invert the risen dough onto the hot sheet or stone. Very carefully cut five slits and gently open them up to make holes. Bake for 6–12 minutes (depending on the heat of the oven) until crisp and a good brown. Transfer to a wire rack.

Eat the *fougasse* warm or within 24 hours. Once thoroughly cooled, it can be frozen for up to a month. Serve warm.

WALKING THROUGH A GARAGE under a small modern house in the village of Gergei, in Sardinia, at three in the morning, we were not awake enough to realize we were about to watch the most spectacular bread baking of our lives. Next to the garage was a small, low-ceilinged room with a strip light, a tiny window, a couple of trestle tables, a gas stove, and an unusual brick oven. There Signora Speranza Carai and her husband, Guiseppe Scintu, a shepherd, spend eight hours early each Saturday making *pane carasau*, huge paper-thin disks of very crisp bread.

A traditional Sardinian crispbread

Speranza – her name means hope – explained that *pane carasau*, known outside the area as *carta da musica*, is a specialty of the rugged and mountainous Nuorese region and Logudoro in the north of Sardinia. "It's very light, with little moisture, and keeps almost forever." It has traditionally been made for shepherds, who spend a week at a time on the hills and even longer during the bi-annual transhumance. They eat sections of the bread with fresh ewe's or goat's milk cheese, or drizzled with olive oil. At home, *pane carasau* is used rather like lasagne to make a quick hot meal (see *pane frattau*, page 109).

When Speranza and Guiseppe put up their house 17 years ago, they had to get a builder down from Barbagia, where Speranza comes from, to construct the oven: "*Pane carasau* needs a very specific sort of oven, with a low roof. You can't use it to make any other kind of bread. The oven is fired in a special way using small sticks, and it's ready after about 45 minutes."

The cloths used to interleave the dough circles are hung to dry at the end of each night's baking.

The unique oven used for baking pane carasau *has a low roof, and Guiseppe has to fire it with twigs.*

As a tiny girl Speranza helped her mother make bread, and then at 15 she worked in the local bakery. For the last 20 years, she has been making *pane carasau* at home. Each batch uses 22 pounds of flour (a mixture of 90% durum wheat semolina flour and 10% fine white flour) plus a minute quantity of fresh yeast. This makes 70 disks that are then split to make 140 sheets of crispbread. The night's baking has already been sold to local shepherds.

In the early hours of Saturday, Speranza starts the first of her two batches of dough. Mixed in plastic dishwashing bowls, the dough is slightly soft and a creamy-beige color that reminds me of pasta. This idea is reinforced when an electric pasta machine is plugged in. The dough is not kneaded by hand, but put through the giant rollers time and again until it comes away in one long, pliable piece, which is divided by eye into pieces the size of dinner rolls.

Guiseppe rolls out each ball of dough to a round about 12 inches across using a rolling pin, then Speranza puts each round through the pasta machine rollers until the dough has stretched paper-thin to almost 2 feet across. The disks are interleaved with a floured cloth, covered in plastic and then with plenty of blankets, and left to relax in the hot smoky room.

Meanwhile, the couple make up the second batch of dough, light the fire, clean up, make breakfast, and prepare for the second stage. The long trestle tables are pushed to one side, and two very low chairs and small tables are set around the fire. Guiseppe checks that the inside of the oven is white-hot, then pushes the smoldering sticks to the back and wipes clean the front section.

Speranza unwraps the top disk of dough and flops it onto the floor of the oven. It instantly balloons up, and she flips it over and holds it close to the fire. She then tosses the inflated bread across to the table by her husband who deflates it by gently pressing down with a large basket. He deftly splits the bread in half horizontally and stacks the sheets on either side of him to cool.

The entire process of baking and splitting takes no more than a minute. It is very hot work, and the pair need to concentrate. The slightest hole or tear in the dough means it won't inflate and can't be split, and they need every piece to make up the orders. When all the disks are cooked, they are briefly returned to the cooling oven to crisp the cut surface. Once cold, the stacks of *pane carasau* are wrapped in tissue paper ready for the shepherds. (My version of *pane carasau* is given overleaf.)

I F Y O U *have a pasta machine, you can make small disks or larger rectangles; otherwise a bit of effort with a rolling pin will make the dough thin enough. It took me a couple of attempts to learn the tricks of this recipe: use plenty of flour when rolling out, and when layering up the thin sheets; don't overcook or allow brown spots to appear or the disks will be hard to split; split as soon as the bread comes out of the oven. Any disasters — bread that doesn't puff or won't split — will still taste good. Just return them to the oven and bake again for 2 or 3 minutes until crisp.*

Pane carasau

MAKES 6 CRISPBREADS

2 cups (225g) Italian-style flour

3 tablespoons (25g) unbleached white bread flour

a pinch of fresh or active dry yeast

a pinch of fine sea salt

about $2/3$ cup (150ml) lukewarm water

several baking sheets

Mix the flours and warm gently (add the dry yeast, if using). Dissolve the salt in half of the water. Add the fresh yeast and stir until dispersed. Add the liquid to the flour mixture and mix together, adding enough of the rest of the water to make a slightly soft but not sticky dough.

Put the dough through the rollers of a pasta machine, on the widest setting, about 20 times until the dough comes away in one piece and seems elastic and pliable. Otherwise, knead by hand for 10 minutes. Divide the dough into six equal pieces and shape each into a neat ball. Cover with a sheet of plastic wrap and leave to relax in a warm kitchen for 20 minutes.

Using plenty of flour, roll out the balls of dough as thinly as possible to make disks about 10 inches across. Or put each ball through the pasta machine several times, using finer and finer settings, until you have a paper-thin sheet that does not tear (it is better to have a slightly thicker piece of dough than one that is likely to get a hole). Stack the pieces of dough, interleaving them with well-floured squares of wax paper or plastic wrap, then cover the whole stack with plastic wrap and then several cloths — the idea is to keep the dough warm and prevent it from drying out rather than to make it sticky. Leave to rest for $1^1/2$ hours in a warm kitchen.

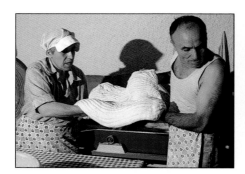

Speranza and Guiseppe work the rough dough through a pasta machine (top right), then lift it onto the table ready for dividing.

Once Guiseppe has rolled out the dough into disks, Speranza takes each one and puts it through a series of rollers to stretch it thinly.

She then places each ultra-thin disk of dough between floured cloths and leaves it to relax while the fire is prepared.

Speranza cooks one disk at a time. The dough instantly balloons in the heat of the oven. Immediately after baking, the bread is split in two and, after cooling, is given a final crisping in the oven.

Toward the end of the resting time, pre-heat the oven to the hottest possible setting (make sure it is clean or it will smoke when it gets very hot). Put several baking sheets into the oven to heat.

Uncover one piece of dough at a time and quickly put onto a hot sheet, without stretching or wrinkling the dough. Bake for about 1 minute until the dough balloons. Tip the cooked bread onto a wooden board and gently deflate by pressing with a clean dry cloth. With a sharp pointed knife, slit the bread in half horizontally as if opening a pitta bread. Leave to cool, cut side uppermost. Cook the rest of the breads in the same way.

Turn off the oven. Return the bread sheets to the oven, a few at a time, to crisp for a couple of minutes. Cool thoroughly before storing in a dry place.

The bread is best eaten within a week and is not suitable for freezing.

VARIATION: *Pane frattau*

Dip sections of *pane carasau* into boiling stock (mutton is traditional, vegetable the most common today) – after just one second the bread will feel soft and pasta-like. Cover the bottom of a warmed soup dish with the moistened bread, spoon a little warm tomato sauce over the top, and sprinkle with grated pecorino sardo (Sardinian ewe's milk cheese). Repeat the layers twice more. Put a just-poached egg in the center, cover with more tomato sauce and cheese, and eat immediately.

"THE SADNESS REACHED AS FAR AS CAGLIARI when our mother retired as a baker." For Fedgrico, Luigi, and Roberto Matta, it took years of industry to reach their mother's standard and win back her customers, and several more to gain wholesale contracts to supply shops and bakeries all the way from their own village of Gergei to the Sardinian capital, Cagliari.

Keeping it in the family

Olinda, aged 89, and Tia Benigna Casu, 75, ran the family bakery to great acclaim before Tia Benigna's sons took over.

"Baking is a woman's business. Our grandmother, Francesca Basili, and great aunt Olinda (now 89) were famous in this area for their bread. Then our mother, Tia Benigna Casu, took over, and she carried on the good name. But her daughters, our sisters, preferred to sell bread in the shop rather than to bake all night, as they had families, so when the time came for her to retire, the bakery had to close."

Apparently the local protest was so loud that Signora Casu was persuaded out of retirement and, with a bit of arm-twisting, broke with Sardinian tradition to train her three sons as bakers. She retired again, but customers complained that the bread was not like it used to be. The mayor of Gergei said there was a near riot outside the shop, and Signora Casu had to return to supervise things until the bread was perfect. Now everyone is happy: the family honor has been upheld and once again the bread is celebrated as far as the capital.

The bakery makes just two breads: *civraxiu* and *coccoi*. Fedgrico explained that they were really peasant breads: "The Campidano plain [in the south of Sardinia, and north of Cagliari] has been renowned for its durum wheat since long before the Roman invasion." Perfect soil and growing conditions mean excellent quality as well as quantity. "Bread, pasta, sheep and goat meat, and dairy products plus olive oil have been our staples since the earliest times. Sardinia was called the granary of Rome." Today the main industry is sheep cheese, followed closely by olive oil and wheat for pastamaking.

"'Cibaria' was the term the Romans used for our flour, from which comes *civraxiu*, our large round or oval loaf. It's made from a soft dough, or *spongiau*, and has a crisp crust and soft crumb. We use white flour, but some bakers add a bit of whole-wheat." The bread is put on every table at each meal, thickly sliced. "It's good with lamb dishes – try dipping it into the juices at the bottom of a dish of roast lamb."

Coccoi is now an everyday bread, but until recently it was kept for festivals and high days. "The dough is much heavier – it needs to keep its shape as it is always highly decorated (snipped with scissors) before baking." There are two kinds: *pane 'e scetti*, made from the purest white flour, and *pane 'e simbule*, which uses whole-wheat flour. The breads can be shaped into snails, crowns, cockscombs, and even more fanciful designs for weddings (see page 168).

Right: Ground-up olive pits are used for firing the bakery oven, as local health inspectors frown on the traditional brushwood. Far right: Loading the breads into the oven is a two-man job.

THE *Matta bakery uses a mixture of local flours — 60% white bread flour, 20% fine durum wheat semolina flour, and 20% coarser, slightly granular in texture, semolina flour. The fine semolina is the Italian '00' flour for pastamaking. You can get close to the right texture for the coarser semolina flour by grinding semolina in a spice mill or heavy-duty blender or food processor to a fine powder. Alternatively, replace all of the semolina flour — both fine*

and coarse — with Italian-style flour from King Arthur Flour (see Directory, page 172), which has a slightly granular texture. The Matta brothers save a small piece of dough from each night's baking and then add it to the next batch for extra flavor. You can use a soft-dough (not liquid) sourdough starter (see page 49) instead.

Civraxiu and Coccoi

MAKES 2 MEDIUM LOAVES

8¹/₄ cups (1kg) flour (see recipe introduction)

¹/₂ tablespoon fine sea salt

about 2 cups (500ml) lukewarm water

²/₃ 0.6oz cake fresh yeast (10g)*

1¹/₂-oz (35g) saved-dough starter (see recipe introduction)

extra coarse semolina flour for shaping

2 baking sheets

Top right: The Matta brothers put the shaped loaves to bed in wooden trays lined with sheets and blankets.

Above: Just before baking the coccoi *loaves, they are snipped with scissors for a well-defined shape.*

Combine the flours in a large mixing bowl. Dissolve the salt in a little of the water, and add to the bowl. Disperse the yeast in a tablespoon of the rest of the water and set aside. Add the piece of saved dough and almost all the remaining water to the flour and work the ingredients together to make a firm, but not dry dough, working in more water as needed.

Turn out onto a work surface and knead thoroughly for 10 minutes (or knead in a heavy-duty electric mixer fitted with the dough hook for 6 minutes on medium-low speed). Gradually knead in the yeast mixture, and knead for a further 5 minutes (3 minutes in the mixer). This firm dough is now ready for *coccoi* bread. To make *civraxiu*, knead in a little extra water to make a fairly soft but not sticky dough. Cover the dough with several dry cloths and leave for 15 minutes before shaping.

Divide the dough in half and shape each piece into a round (*civraxiu*) or oval (*coccoi*) loaf. Drop or roll the round *civraxiu* loaves in semolina flour to coat; leave the *coccoi* loaves plain. Cover the loaves with dry cloths. (The Matta brothers literally put the bread to bed — in special wooden trays lined with old blankets and then with a clean sheet sprinkled with semolina flour. The loaves are arranged in the folds of the sheet to keep them separate, and covered with another sheet and then blankets and a quilt.) Leave the loaves to rise until they are doubled in size — 1–3 hours, depending on room temperature.

Toward the end of the rising time, preheat the oven to 425°F. Put the baking sheets into the oven to heat.

Uncover the loaves. Snip the top of each *coccoi* with kitchen scissors so it resembles a crown or cockscomb. Set the loaves on the heated baking sheets and bake for about 40 minutes until a good brown, and the loaves sound hollow when tapped underneath. Cool on a wire rack.

The bread is best eaten within 4 days, or toasted. The crust gradually softens and the flavor deepens as the bread ages. Once thoroughly cooled, the bread can be frozen for up to a month.

* You can use 2 teaspoons rapid-rise active dry yeast instead of the fresh yeast. Combine the dry yeast with the flour, then add the salt water and continue with the recipe.

4 Baking bread

BAKING IS THE SECOND HALF of the metamorphosis of flour into bread, whether it be in a thermostatically-controlled domestic gas, electric, or solid fuel oven; on a solid iron griddle, girdle, *kadai,* or *tawa* set over a flame; in a *tandoor* set into the ground and heated by coals; or in a traditional wood-fired brick bread oven.

Cooking on a flat stone set over hot embers was the first method used to transform soft, gruel-like dough into appetizing, easily digestible food. It is still the way millions bake their daily bread. The simple beehive oven, now a popular backyard accessory in Britain, has been used to bake bread for 3000 years in small communities from Egypt and Turkey through the Balkans and the Mediterranean.

Until ovens could be controlled thermostatically – a recent development – baking was a hit or miss affair. Successful baking was as much about knowing the oven and reading its moods as having the perfect dough. Even with modern ovens, it's worth using an oven thermometer to double-check the thermostat.

Dr. Maurice Bichard (see page 62) bakes his bread in an eighteenth-century brick oven.

You can improve the baking performance of a standard domestic oven very simply. Thorough heating is vital – putting the risen dough into an oven that's cold or not up to temperature will not do it any favors. Get the oven as hot as possible, then reduce the heat to the one given in the recipe – most bread bakes best in a slowly cooling oven. A baking or pizza stone will ensure a crisp crust on the underside of a loaf. Simply heat up the stone in the oven, then turn the risen loaf directly onto the hot stone and bake. You can also use a heated metal baking sheet.

A steamy atmosphere in the oven when the bread goes in to bake helps to develop a crisp crust (vital to baguettes) and helps with oven-spring, which is the expansion of the loaf in the heat of the oven. You can easily create steam by putting a dish of hot water on the floor of the oven or spritzing the loaves with a fine mist of water (from a spray gun or plant mister).

A final important point: never undercook bread. Slight overcooking is always better.

ANDREW WHITLEY is the man who changed the taste of supermarket bread in Britain. Alongside the shelves of sliced white, you can now find his artisanal sourdough loaves, large *boules* of *pain de campagne*, authentic no-holds-barred Russian rye breads – all made with organic flour and baked in wood-fired ovens. He is an unlikely hero, quiet, self-effacing,

mild-mannered. "Today bread is seen as a commodity that people put into their shopping carts almost without thought. I hope my artisanal bread will go someway toward changing that."

An environmental crusader

The road signs to The Village Bakery appear as soon as you turn off the main road going north from Penrith. Eventually you arrive in Melmerby, a small village in the north-west of England, bleakly beautiful. The bakery and restaurant, the largest business in the area, with 60 local employees, attract visitors even on a miserably damp Monday.

A linguist and Russian scholar, Andrew was a producer with the B.B.C.'s Russian service when he became seriously interested in E. F. Schumacher and his "small is beautiful" theories. Andrew started making bread from scratch, even growing his own rye, and contemplated setting up a self-supporting commune. Then he met Nick Jones, who was restoring an old watermill, Little Salkeld, in Cumbria (see Directory, page 172), and was looking for a baker to use his organic stoneground flour. In 1975, Andrew gave up his job, and he and his wife moved north. "We started with a tea shop at the back of the mill, and I soon knew I could make decent bread."

Andrew Whitley (top right and below) fires his massive brick oven with wood briquettes.

After 18 months he had enough confidence in his skills to buy an eighteenth-century stone barn next to his home in Melmerby, which he converted to a bakehouse and small restaurant. He decided to farm organically the five acres of land that came with the barn, and to install a wood-fired bread oven for environmental reasons. "It's a renewable fuel. I use wood briquettes, but we are surrounded by woodland that could be managed ecologically." At first he produced an organic stoneground whole-wheat loaf: "It is hard to believe now, but then you couldn't buy one in Penrith."

By 1991, the bakery was doing enough business to expand again, and Andrew installed a 100-ton purpose-built wood oven, the first of its type in Britain. "It is a simple low-cost way to bake. It cooks through retained heat, and is easily refired during baking. It also warms the water for the restaurant and for making the dough. The radiant heat is recycled through the greenhouse next door to benefit the tomatoes, and even the ashes are used as an organic fertilizer." He is determined to demonstrate that the way to produce good bread is to combine artisan techniques with a caring approach to the environment.

Andrew was keen to get to grips with a real Russian rye sourdough, and, on one of his many trips to Russia, achieved his dream: "I baked bread with an old Russian lady, and slept above the stove in her kitchen while the snow fell outside." He returned with a scrap of her sourdough starter hidden in a sock. It thrived, and is the basis of his Rossisky rye bread.

Today he produces 20,000 organic loaves and buns a week, getting all his flour from Shipton Mill (see page 13). Each batch can take up to 24 hours, depending on the weather – in comparison, a standard sliced white loaf takes a large commercial bakery 3 hours. He has had more than his fair share of problems, but still sticks to his original guiding principles. "I started out with the idea that if I made something good, people would buy it. I had to want to eat the bread myself. I had to be sure that there was nothing in it that was for the benefit of the baker rather than the consumer. I always wanted to live my life as an artisan, not an intellectual, and I think I've achieved that, even if I'm now a businessman, too."

Andrew's breads are a revelation, much better than any I found in Russia. He also makes a great organic chocolate cake, and is keen to promote other organic producers. It is hard not to warm to a man who declares, like a true amateur, "I still get a kick when I take the bread out of the oven."

The Village Bakery (below), in peaceful Melmerby in the Cumbrian hills, is situated in a converted eighteenth-century stone barn.

*Rossisky and Borodinsky
loaves take the best part of
a day to rise.*

ANDREW WHITLEY *tells the history of this bread: "I spent 2 wonderful weeks in Kostroma, in Russia, in 1990 — everywhere I went I was given bread, often specially baked to traditional recipes by country grandmothers. The highlight was a weekend in the village of Tererinskoye. An old lady invited me back to her wooden izba to make real rye bread, and as it fermented I got to fulfil one of my student ambitions — to sleep on the pechka (the wooden seating surrounding the kitchen stove) as the snow fell outside. It was one of the most uncomfortable nights of my life, but the bread we baked next morning was memorable and I came home not just with recipes but a piece of sourdough. Carefully refreshed with rye flour and water at various stages of its journey back to Cumbria, it has played 'mother' to the many thousands of sourdough rye loaves I've since made."*

This Russian sourdough rye is a yeast-free, wheat-free bread that is much more like "normal" bread than many rye breads. Andrew says he has been contacted by people, both those allergic to wheat and to yeast, as well as those with no food allergies, to say what a delicious, different bread it is. It can be made into sandwiches, makes great toast, and goes well with soups and salads.

Initially there are three stages, although you don't have to go through the whole rigmarole once you've made a sourdough starter — it keeps indefinitely if you look after it. The first stage takes 3 or 4 days; the second stage takes 24 hours to bring your sourdough to life; and the third stage is the 24-hour wait after you have made the bread — it has to rest a day before you eat it.

Rossisky

MAKES 2 LARGE OR 4 SMALLER
LOAVES

STARTER:
scant ¹/₂ cup (45g) organic wholegrain rye
    flour
6 tablespoons lukewarm water

FIRST REFRESHMENT:
4¹/₂ tablespoons (30g) organic wholegrain rye
    flour
¹/₄ cup lukewarm water

SECOND REFRESHMENT:
3¹/₄ cups (340g) organic wholegrain rye
    flour
2¹/₂ cups (560ml) lukewarm water

TO MAKE THE BREAD:
5³/₄ cups (600g) organic wholegrain rye
    flour
2 teaspoons fine sea salt
1¹/₄–1¹/₂ cups (300–350ml) lukewarm water

two loaf pans, about 10 x 5 x 3 inches or four
    loaf pans, about 8¹/₂ x 4¹/₂ x 2¹/₂ inches,
    greased

First make the starter. Mix together the flour and water in a small bowl or cup to make a smooth batter. Cover with plastic wrap and leave to ferment in a warm but not hot place for 2 days. It will start to bubble and have a sweet apple-like smell.

Stir in the flour and water for the first refreshment and leave overnight, covered.

The next day, add the ingredients for the second refreshment and mix to make a smooth, thick, sloppy batter. Leave to ferment, covered, in the kitchen for 24 hours. This is now your sourdough starter.

You will need almost all of the starter to make your first batch of bread; keep the rest in the fridge for your next batch — it will need to be "fed" every 2 or 3 days with equal parts of rye flour and water to an equal weight of starter, to keep it going (you will need to build up the quantity gradually in order to make the next batch of bread). About 24 hours before using, give it a final "feed," and bring to room temperature.

Measure 2 pounds (900g) sourdough starter and combine with the flour, salt, and enough water to make a very sticky, wet dough — the amount of water you need will depend on the thickness of your starter. Mix thoroughly in the bowl for 10 minutes — conventional kneading will be difficult. The mixture is too sloppy to shape a loaf, so wet your hands with cold water and just scoop the dough into the pans. Cover with a sheet of plastic wrap and leave to rise until the dough is level with the top of the pans — anything from 1 to 8 hours, depending on the vigor of your starter and the temperature.

Toward the end of the rising time, preheat the oven 450°F.

Uncover the loaves and bake large ones for about 1 hour, the smaller ones for 45–50 minutes, or until the bread sounds hollow when unmolded and tapped underneath. Turn out onto a wire rack and leave to cool completely, then wrap the loaves and leave to rest for a day before slicing.

The bread will keep for almost a week and can be frozen for up to a month.

Note: With a new and not yet very vigorous starter, give the dough at least 2 hours to rise in the mixing bowl, covered, before punching it down and transferring it to the baking pans for a second rise. A warm room is a definite advantage.

Every week, Andrew and his team of bakers produce 20,000 loaves, including the wheat-free, yeast-free Borodinsky.

THE *doyen of Russian breads, this is a yeast-free, wheat-free loaf flavored with malt and molasses plus whole and ground coriander. It makes the best smoked salmon and cream cheese sandwiches, and also goes well with hearty soups. Hunting down the recipe turned out to be hard work. While on a trip to St. Petersburg in 1996, Andrew Whitley visited the bread museum, but, amazingly, they had no information about it. He tracked down some loaves in a shop, and eventually heard the colorful and probably apocryphal story of its origins — a general's wife inspired the troops before the battle of Borodino by baking loaves perfumed with the native coriander.*

Andrew told me he baked a batch for a party of children from Chernobyl, who were staying nearby. When they saw the loaves on the table ready for their supper, they shouted in glee: "You've brought us our own bread." A modest man, he says it was his greatest compliment.

Borodinsky

MAKES 2 LARGE OR 4 SMALLER LOAVES

1³/₄ lb (800g) rye-flour sourdough starter (see Rossisky, opposite), at room temperature

6¹/₂ cups (680g) organic light rye flour

1¹/₄ cups (280ml) lukewarm water

2 teaspoons fine sea salt

3 tablespoons (60g) molasses

1¹/₂ tablespoons (30g) malt extract syrup

1 heaped teaspoon ground coriander, plus extra for sprinkling

about ¹/₂ teaspoon whole coriander seeds

two loaf pans, about 10 x 5 x 3 inches, or four loaf pans, about 8¹/₂ x 4¹/₂ x 2¹/₂ inches, greased

Combine all the ingredients apart from the whole coriander seeds in a large mixing bowl. Mix thoroughly and work in the bowl for 10 minutes — the dough will be too soft and sticky to knead in the usual way. Sprinkle a few whole coriander seeds into the bottom of each loaf pan. As the dough is too sloppy to shape into loaves, wet your hands with cold water and just scoop the dough into the pans to fill evenly. Cover the pans loosely with a sheet of plastic wrap and leave the dough to rise until level with the top of the pans — 1–8 hours, depending on the warmth of your kitchen and the vigor of the sourdough.

Toward the end of the rising time, preheat the oven to 450°F.

Uncover the loaves, spray with a little water, and sprinkle with a little ground coriander. Immediately put into the oven and bake for 15 minutes. Then reduce the oven temperature to 400°F and bake the large loaves for a further 45 minutes and the smaller ones for 30–35 minutes, or until the unmolded bread sounds hollow when tapped underneath. Turn out onto wire racks and leave to cool completely, then wrap the loaves and keep for a day before slicing.

This bread keeps well for almost a week, and the flavor mellows and deepens. It can also be frozen for up to a month.

M ELMERBY, *in northwest England, is only 20 miles from the Roman wall, and the discoveries of the Roman granaries, drying kilns, and bakehouses prompted Andrew Whitley to research what they wouing wateld have made to feed the troops. The Romans are credited with introducing watermills, spelt flour, and improved ovens to Britain around 50 B.C. Andrew's classicist brother found a reference in Pliny to a bread made with spelt flour and raisin juice. Since spelt would have been the grain used by the local population, and it would have been easy to transport dried fruit, Andrew set to work. He came up with a naturally leavened bread made with wholegrain spelt flour (though probably less coarse than the Roman version), a spelt sourdough starter, and raisin juice, which adds vigor to the natural yeasts in the sourdough and sweetness to the tang of the spelt.*

As a re-creation of a bread eaten 2000 years ago it is remarkable, but it is not merely an academic exercise — the loaf is extremely popular with even my least historical friends and family. I like this bread with strong cheese or soup. The first batch will taste fine, but subsequent batches will have a greater depth of flavor and will rise better as the sourdough starter becomes more vigorous.

Hadrian's bread

MAKES 1 LARGE OR 2 SMALLER LOAVES

STARTER:

6 tablespoons (45g) organic wholegrain spelt flour

6 tablespoons lukewarm water

FIRST REFRESHMENT:

$^1/_4$ cup (30g) organic wholegrain spelt flour

2 tablespoons lukewarm water

SECOND REFRESHMENT:

$1^2/_3$ cups (200g) organic wholegrain spelt flour

$^1/_2$ cup (100ml) lukewarm water

RAISIN MUSH:

$^1/_3$ cup (50g) organic raisins

3 tablespoons boiling water

TO MAKE THE BREAD:

$3^1/_3$ cups (410g) organic wholegrain spelt flour

$^3/_4$ teaspoon fine sea salt

about 1 cup (200ml) lukewarm water (see recipe)

a baking sheet, lightly floured

First make the starter. Mix the flour and water together in a cup or small bowl. Cover with plastic wrap and leave for 2 days in a warm, but not hot, place. The mixture will start to ferment and bubble and will develop a sweet apple-like smell.

Stir in the flour and water for the first refreshment. Cover and leave overnight.

Measure $3^1/_2$ ounces (100g) of the starter (discard any excess) and mix with the flour and water for the second refreshment to make a soft dough. Leave to ferment, covered, in the kitchen for 4 hours. This is now your sourdough starter.

Most of this starter will be used in the first batch of bread. Keep what is left in the fridge for your next batch, refreshing it as above for the second refreshment, in the same proportions every couple of days. Give it a final refreshment 4 hours before making bread and leave it to return to room temperature, so that it is vigorous.

For the mush, steep the raisins in the boiling water for 30 minutes. Then put into a blender or food processor and whiz into a fine mush or purée. Measure 10 ounces (300g) of the starter and put into a bowl with the raisin mush, flour, salt, and lukewarm water. Mix all the ingredients together to make a soft but not sticky dough — the amount of water you need to bind the dough will depend on the thickness of your starter and, of course, the flour you use.

Turn out onto a floured work surface and knead thoroughly for 10 minutes. Shape the dough into either one large round or 2 smaller rounds, then dip the shaped bread into a little extra spelt flour to coat all over. Place on the prepared baking sheet, or in a bowl-shaped basket lined with a floured dish towel. Cover loosely with a sheet of plastic wrap and leave to rise in a warm place until doubled in size — allow up to 5 hours.

Toward the end of the rising time, preheat the oven to 450°F.

If you have risen your bread in a basket, tip gently onto the floured baking sheet. Slash an "H" across the top of the loaf with a sharp knife, then bake for 1 hour for a large loaf, 40–50 minutes for a smaller one, or until the bread sounds hollow when tapped underneath. Cool on a wire rack. The bread will keep for a week. Once it has thoroughly cooled, it can be frozen for up to a month.

CREATING THE CONSIDERABLE HEAT needed to bake bread is crucial to success. According to Tom Jaine (see page 134), the beehive oven has done this for 3000 years, "give or take a decade. It evolved in Egypt and around the Mediterranean, but was also quite independently developed by the Turkic peoples of the Balkans." The oven also became common in western Europe, particularly in Ireland and the West of England.

The ancient beehive oven

Anthony spent a jolly week at his house in Devon, England, testing a modern version. It was made in Portugal, completely by hand, and consists of two terracotta ovens stacked one on top of the other, surrounded by insulation. "When we got it home and set it in place on a sturdy plinth, we couldn't use it right away," he said. "First we had to get a small fire going to dry it out without cracking it. We did this by adding a few small sticks at a time for a couple of increasingly impatient hours.

"Then, to fire it properly for baking, we needed to allow an hour to an hour and a half, not more, for the heat to build up. We used wood from the garden and builders' offcuts – first small sticks, then larger bits. The inside went very black, and when this burned off it turned white. At this point we started checking the temperature with an oven thermometer. Of course, it's often too hot to start baking, and we had to wait a bit. We've learned that it's best to have an adaptable dough that can stand uncertainty.

"When the oven was ready, the embers and ashes had to be raked and swept out – I didn't use a damp cloth for fear of cracking. Then the loaf was turned out onto a homemade peel (a smooth piece of planking well dusted with flour), slashed, and gently slid onto the oven floor. The door was put in place, and we sat and and awaited the result. The baking time depends on the heat of the oven, and how quickly the temperature drops – though that was not a problem for me this time – and the size of the loaf, so it can take a little bit longer than in a conventional oven. My first few loaves were overcooked and charred on the outside, but the insides tasted delicious. I discovered that after re-firing the oven for 30 minutes, I was able to bake a second batch."

Anthony says he cooked the best leg of lamb he has ever made in this oven, and numerous casseroles. "As long as you remember to cover the oven each night once it has cooled, to prevent it from absorbing rain and water from the atmosphere, it's a really great way to cook."

Anthony uses a homemade peel to slide the loaf into the oven (far left). The door is set in place (left center), and after 40 minutes he checks to see if the loaf is thoroughly cooked.

"THE UNIQUE FEATURE that makes a brick oven the unrivaled king among ovens is retained heat," Paul Merry told me. For years I had believed that it was the particular flavor of the smoke from each type of wood used – rather like the exotic sticks thrown on to enhance barbecues.

Building and baking

Wood-fired masonry ovens are Paul's specialty, and his expertise is unrivaled. He has built and installed ovens in several prestigious restaurants in Europe, including Villandry and Moro in London. So, over many hours of discussion, we learned exactly how a bread oven should be built. "A brick oven really challenges the user to develop true craftsmanship, while the oven itself seems to develop its own personality." In other words, it is not for the faint-hearted. Paul's smallest ovens are designed to fit into a wall or bench top – the fire on the floor of the oven, a cast-iron door, and a chimney sited in the most suitable place. The next size up is a one-meter oven, in a traditional dome. The fire is now in a separate furnace made of fire-brick, beneath the floor. The flames gush into the baking chamber through a vent at the back. This is easier to use than the simple oven – there is no need to sweep out the ashes and embers before use, and the oven can be fed as needed to maintain a high temperature. All Paul's ovens are fitted with a temperature gauge – something every baker quickly learns to value. Incredibly, an oven of this size can bake up to 15 loaves in pans, or around 8 pizzas, at one time.

Like many of the craft-bakers we met in writing this book, baking was not in Paul's blood: "As a young man I showed no inclination to begin the career for which I had studied in Australia. Instead I was drawn to rustic crafts, and had a deep fascination with the precarious position of the craftsman in our modern industrial society." After several years as a hippy back-packer he fell into breadmaking, working part-time in bakeries in England and Scotland, then returning home to Melbourne. "I wanted to find a plot of land to build my own bakery. A few years went by while I learned the necessary building skills and, more importantly, how to build a traditional wood-fired bread oven." In 1980, he opened a small bakery, St. Andrew's, in the dry hills just outside the city. He had built not only the oven, which filled an entire corner of the bakery, but also the building itself. He spent 10 years as a local village baker, gradually acquiring the skills that earned him a reputation as a master craftsman. "I enjoyed teaching the apprentices, passing on the knowledge I had gained. I see it as my duty to help put the clock back. Small craft bakeries are an endangered species. The keys are hand-making and shaping, and allowing time for proper fermentation of the dough."

Paul became fascinated by the farm courtyard ovens in Italy, as well as brick pizza ovens, and decided to design the perfect small wood-fired oven. This led him to England and Andrew Whitley, who wanted help setting up and running his majestic wood-fired oven at The Village Bakery (see page 114). "It was an exciting time, and from Andrew I gained a depth of knowledge about sourdoughs and natural leavens." Paul developed the "Leaven's Above" breadmaking course at The Village Bakery, which is aimed at professional as well as home bakers.

He has now installed the prototype for his small brick oven at The Nunnery, a former Benedictine nunnery, now a hotel, near Kirkoswald in Cumbria, England. From here he runs courses for serious craft-bakers, restaurateurs, and amateurs – and he plans the designs for more bread ovens.

Paul Merry is justifiably proud of his beautifully constructed oven. The advantage it has is that he can add more wood during the baking process, and can check the temperature on the outside gauge.

PAUL MERRY *calls this The Nunnery's everyday bread. He makes it with a good-quality organic bread flour, spring water, and a soft-dough white sourdough starter. Paul prefers to refresh his starter every day to keep it in shape, even if he is not baking. He stores it, tightly covered, in the fridge, but allows it to come back to room temperature before use.*

The recipe makes a great loaf, both in looks and taste. The high proportion of sourdough starter used helps the dough to puff up quite fast and gives a slightly open texture and mildly sour tang.

Paul Merry's French country bread

MAKES 1 LARGE LOAF

SOURDOUGH STARTER:
2 cups (225g) unbleached white bread flour
$^2/_3$ cup (150ml) lukewarm water

FIRST REFRESHMENT:
3$^1/_4$ cups (375g) unbleached white bread flour
1 cup (250ml) lukewarm water

SECOND REFRESHMENT:
2$^1/_2$ cups (300g) unbleached white bread flour
scant 1 cup (200ml) lukewarm water

TO FINISH:
4 cups (450g) bread flour (unbleached white,
    whole-wheat, spelt, or a combination)
1$^1/_2$ teaspoons fine sea salt
about 1$^1/_4$ cups (300ml) lukewarm water

a baking sheet, greased

Make the sourdough starter: Mix together the flour and water to a soft dough. Keep, covered with a damp dish towel (moistening as necessary), at room temperature for about 3 days until small bubbles appear, and there is a cidery whiff.

For the first refreshment, mix the flour and water with the starter and leave, covered as before, until sponge-like – about 24 hours.

Measure 10 ounces (300g) of the starter (discard the rest). Mix with the flour and water for the second refreshment to make a soft dough. If you are ready to make a loaf, cover the starter as before and keep at normal to warm room temperature until puffed up – 3–4 hours. If you are not going to bake, cover the bowl tightly and store it in the fridge. Then, when you wish to bake, remove the starter from the fridge, bring it back to room temperature, and refresh as given for the second refreshment.

To bake a loaf, measure 1 pound (450g) of the refreshed puffed-up starter (keep the rest in the fridge for the next loaf). Mix the flour with the salt on a work surface and make a large well in the middle. Pour the water into the well and gradually draw some of the flour into the water to make a rough dough. Add the starter and work in, along with the rest of the flour; use your hands to gather up the floury mass to bring the ingredients together until you have a soft but not sticky dough, adding a little more water or flour as necessary.

Knead the dough very thoroughly for 10 minutes, pressing and stretching it on the work surface with the heel of your hand. Put the dough into a bowl, cover with a damp dish towel, and leave to rise until doubled in size. The time this takes will depend on the vigor of your starter and the room temperature, so allow 4–12 hours.

Punch down the risen dough with your knuckles to deflate, then shape into a round or oval loaf. Put onto the prepared baking sheet (or into a basket or colander lined with a floured linen cloth) and cover as before, or slip the sheet or basket into a large plastic bag, tucking the ends under. Leave to rise once more until doubled in size 2– 4 hours.

Toward the end of the rising time, preheat the oven to 425°F.

If the dough has been risen in a basket, turn it out onto the baking sheet. Slash the top of the loaf with a serrated knife or razor blade, then bake for about 35 minutes until the loaf turns a good brown and sounds hollow when tapped underneath. Cool on a wire rack.

The bread is best eaten within 5 days, or toasted. Once thoroughly cooled, it can be frozen for up to a month.

*A*LTHOUGH *one of his pet hates is "things in bread" — he would rather teach the principles and craft of a well-fermented loaf — Paul Merry developed this recipe to please his students and is justifiably keen on the result. The flavor is gentle rather than aggressive, the texture is light rather than stodgy, moist rather than oily, and the bread is altogether more-ish. It makes a great accompaniment to soups.*

Pesto-Parmesan bread

MAKES 2 MEDIUM LOAVES

4 cups (500g) unbleached white bread flour

$^1/_2$ tablespoon fine sea salt

$^2/_3$ 0.6-oz cake fresh yeast (10g)*

$1^1/_3$ cups (325ml) lukewarm water

$^1/_2$ cup (50g) freshly grated Parmesan cheese

PESTO SAUCE:

1 large bunch of fresh basil – you need
2oz (60g) leaves (stems removed)

a pinch of fine sea salt

1–2 cloves garlic

$^1/_4$ cup (35g) fresh pine nuts or walnut pieces

$^1/_3$ cup (35g) freshly grated Parmesan cheese

4 tablespoons virgin olive oil

two loaf pans, about $8^1/_2$ x $4^1/_2$ x $2^1/_2$ inches,
well greased

Paul flattens and folds the dough to a rectangle the length of the pan, then rolls it tightly like a jelly roll.

To make the pesto sauce, put the basil leaves, salt, peeled garlic, and nuts into a mortar or food processor. Pound or blend until a coarse purée is formed. Work in the cheese, then add the oil in a thin stream, as if making mayonnaise, to make a thick, creamy purée. Spoon into glass jars, cover with a layer of olive oil, and close tightly. Store in the fridge (this makes about twice as much as you need for the bread).

Combine the flour and salt in a large mixing bowl, and make a well in the center. Crumble the yeast into a cup and stir in the water until smooth. Pour the liquid into the well in the flour and mix to make a fairly firm dough.

Turn out onto a work surface and knead thoroughly for 10 minutes until the dough is firm — because the pesto is rich and oily, the dough should not be soft and sticky at this stage. Spoon half of the pesto (75g) onto the dough and gently knead it in. When there are no streaks of pesto or patches of oil visible, sprinkle the grated Parmesan over and gently work into the dough. The finished mixture should look very evenly colored, with the pesto and cheese well distributed. Return the dough to the bowl and cover with plastic wrap or a damp dish towel. Leave to rise in a slightly warm, but not hot, place until doubled in size – about 1 hour.

Punch down the risen dough with your knuckles to deflate it, then turn out onto a work surface. Divide into two equal pieces. Flatten each piece with your hands to a rectangle the length of your pan, then roll up tightly like a jelly roll. Put the shaped dough into the pans, tucking the ends under — they should be slightly more than half full. Cover and leave to rise as before until almost doubled in size.

Toward the end of the rising time, preheat the oven to 425°F.

Uncover the loaves and bake for about 30 minutes until they are golden brown and sound hollow when unmolded and tapped underneath. Cool on a wire rack.

Serve thickly sliced, warm or toasted, within 5 days. The cooled loaves can be frozen for up to 2 weeks only.

* You can use 1 envelope ($2^1/_2$ teaspoons) rapid-rise active dry yeast instead of the fresh yeast. Combine the dry yeast with the flour and salt, then continue with the recipe.

VARIATION: If you are making a batch of your favorite white bread, cut a 1–pound (500g) piece from the dough and knead in 2 ounces (50g) pesto and $6^1/_2$ tablespoons (40g) grated Parmesan, then rise as above. Punch down the risen dough and shape into a round loaf. Put onto a greased baking sheet, leave to rise, and bake as above.

THE *bakehouse at Skansen, the vast open-air museum in Stockholm (see page 158), dates from the beginning of the eighteenth century, and comes from the very north of Sweden, close to the border with Norway. To concentrate the heat in a cold climate, the oven has a narrow entrance and low ceiling. Ulf Edlund explained that until the twentieth century, to avoid the danger of fire, each big farm or village would have a separate bakehouse and oven. Since streams froze, milling was not a year-round activity, so baking depended on the availability of flour as well as grain; this explains the development of crispbreads, which keep all winter.*

This is the large flatbread we watched Ulf making at Skansen. Until quite recently tunnbrød, or thin bread, was the everyday bread eaten in the whole of northern Sweden. Ulf's recipe uses very little yeast; other bakers omit it altogether, which enables the bread to be kept almost indefinitely. After the short initial baking, the bread is soft and pliable, and can be eaten folded or wrapped around a hot filling. If the bread is baked again for longer at a lower temperature, it becomes dry and very crisp, and will keep for much longer. This recipe contains the most common combination of flours. You can alter the taste and texture by varying the proportions.

Tunnbrød

MAKES 12 MEDIUM CRISPBREADS

1¹⁄₂ cups (350ml) milk

2 tablespoons (25g) slightly salted butter

²⁄₃ 0.6-oz cake fresh yeast (10g)*

1 cup (100g) rye flour

1¹⁄₂ teaspoons sugar

1¹⁄₂ teaspoons fine sea salt

scant 1 cup (100g) whole-wheat flour

scant 1 cup (100g) barley flour

2¹⁄₂ cups (300g) unbleached white bread flour

several baking sheets or a pizza stone

Gently warm the milk and butter until the butter has just melted. Crumble the yeast into a large mixing bowl and mix with the lukewarm milk mixture until smooth. Combine the rye flour with the sugar and salt, then work into the liquid, followed by the other flours. Mix thoroughly to make a soft dough.

Turn out onto a floured work surface and knead thoroughly for 10 minutes. Return the dough to the bowl and cover with a damp dish towel or put the bowl into an oiled plastic bag. Leave for 8–12 hours at cool room temperature.

Turn the risen dough onto a floured work surface. Knead gently for a couple of minutes, then divide into 12 equal pieces. Shape each into a ball. Cover lightly with a dry dish towel and leave to rest for 1 hour.

Meanwhile, preheat the oven to 450°F. Put several baking sheets or a pizza stone into the oven to heat.

Roll out each piece of dough to a round about 8 inches across (a grooved rolling pin will help to stretch the dough). Dust off the excess flour, then prick the dough round well with a fork or roll it with a hob-nail bumpy wooden rolling pin. This will prevent the dough from puffing up like pita bread.

At Skansen, a wooden pole is used to put the bread rounds into the oven and take them out, rather than a peel.

Ulf's assistant brushes the soft and pliable baked sheets of dough to remove any scorched flour or ashes.

Put the dough rounds, in batches, onto the very hot baking sheets or pizza stone and bake for 2–3 minutes until lightly colored. Stack the breads on a wire rack as they are cooked. Eat while soft and warm. Or, lower the oven temperature to 350°F and bake the breads for a further 15–20 minutes until there are no soggy or soft patches, and they are speckled with spots of golden brown. Cool thoroughly on wire racks, then store in an airtight container.

The double-baked breads are best within a week of baking, and are not suitable for freezing.

* You can use 2 teaspoons rapid-rise active dry yeast instead of the fresh yeast. Add the dry yeast to the rye flour with the sugar and salt. Mix in the other flours and make a well in the center, then pour in the milk mixture and gradually mix to a soft dough. Continue with the recipe.

THIS *coarse, dark Swedish bread owes its deep, peculiar, yet exquisite flavor to stoneground rye flour, which is developed by scalding with boiling water and then soaking for a day. The final loaf is moist and not nearly as dense as the recipe suggests. It tastes even better if left to mature for a day or two before slicing.*

Skallat brød

MAKES 4 SMALL LOAVES

STAGE ONE:

1 cup (75g) coarse wheat bran

1³/₄ cups (200g) coarse stoneground rye flour

3 cups (700ml) boiling water

STAGE TWO:

3 0.6-oz cakes fresh yeast (50g)*

2 cups (500ml) lukewarm water

1 tablespoon vegetable oil, olive oil, or melted butter

4 cups (500g) coarse stoneground whole-wheat bread flour

2²/₃ cups (300g) coarse stoneground rye flour

1¹/₂ tablespoons fine sea salt

about 2¹/₂ cups (300g) stoneground unbleached white bread flour

oil for brushing

a large roasting pan, about 14 x 10 inches, well greased

For stage one, mix the bran and rye flour in a large heatproof bowl. Leave the boiling water to cool for a minute before pouring it into the bowl. Stir well, then cover the bowl with a damp dish towel and leave at normal room temperature for 24 hours, or 18 hours in hot weather.

For stage two, crumble the yeast into a cup, add the water and oil or butter, and mix until smooth. Stir into the stage-one mixture, then work in the whole-wheat and rye flours and the salt. When thoroughly combined, gradually work in the white flour to make a soft, slightly sticky dough that leaves the sides of the bowl clean. Knead the dough gently in the bowl for a couple of minutes, then cover the bowl with a damp dish towel and leave until the dough has doubled in size – about 2 hours.

Turn out the dough onto a floured work surface and gently knead for 5 minutes only. Divide the dough into four equal pieces, and shape each into a rectangular loaf about 6¹/₂ x 4 inches. Lightly brush the sides of the loaves with oil, then arrange in the prepared pan so they are not quite touching. Cover as before and leave to rise until the loaves have almost doubled in size – about 1 hour.

Toward the end of the rising time, preheat the oven to 425°F.

Uncover the loaves and put the roasting pan into the oven. Immediately reduce the temperature to 375°F and bake for 45 minutes to 1 hour until the loaves are lightly browned and sound hollow when tapped underneath. Remove them from the pan, separate gently, and leave to cool on a wire rack, covered by a clean, dry dish towel to give a soft crust.

Wrap the thoroughly cooled loaves in wax paper or a dry dish towel and leave for a day before slicing. They can also be frozen for up to a month.

* You can use 3 envelopes (7¹/₂ teaspoons) rapid-rise active dry yeast instead of the fresh yeast. Mix the dry yeast with the whole-wheat and rye flours, then add to the stage-one mixture after adding the water, oil or butter, and salt.

"DID YOU KNOW that the Shakers invented and patented the first revolving bread oven?" Our editor Norma MacMillan, who has written a book inspired by the Shakers (see bibliography, page 172), sent us to Canterbury, New Hampshire, a living museum of Shaker life, and then to Sabbathday Lake, Maine, the last Shaker haven on earth.

Baking with a loving hand

Sister Frances Carr is the Eldress of the thriving Shaker community at Sabbathday Lake, Maine. Buildings in Shaker villages were painted different colors according to their function; white was reserved for spiritual buildings, such as the Meeting House at Sabbathday Lake (below).

Over the last 200 years, the Shakers have developed a vast range of highly innovative, time-saving household and agricultural tools, as well as the furniture, crafts, and architecture so highly praised today for their simple beauty. But the Shakers are not just quaint history and elegant furniture; they are people pledging their hands to work and hearts to God, striving to make their small community an early heaven on earth.

The Shaker movement broke away from the Quakers in Manchester, England, in the mid-eighteenth century. The name, originally Shaking Quakers, refers to the way members once trembled and danced in ecstatic worship. Their charismatic leader, "Mother"Ann Lee, thought to be a prophet and the Second Coming of Christ, took her small band of followers to America in 1774, to avoid persecution, only to discover they were as much feared and persecuted in the New World as the Old.

The Shaker settlers founded self-sufficient "family" communities, but their way of life is very different from that of the Amish and Mennonites. The Shakers believe in the equal status of men and women (with the communities run by an Elder and Eldress), racial equality (as soon as they became prosperous they bought slaves to set them free), common ownership of goods, confession, pacifism, and celibacy. New members came to the community as converts; later they took in orphans. By the mid-nineteenth century, there were more than 6000 members living in two dozen communities all over the United States. They became prosperous through strenuous work, careful and creative farming, making furniture and handicrafts, patenting time-saving devices, producing candies, foodstuffs, preserves and medicines. But membership dwindled, and all the Shaker communities, apart from Sabbathday Lake, closed as the last members died.

Sabbathday Lake, Maine

The community at Sabbathday Lake, in south-central Maine, was founded in 1794, 10 years after the death of Ann Lee. The early white wooden Meeting House, the Library (the former school house), Trustees' House, and barns are all immediately recognizable as New England Shaker architecture. The large red-brick dwelling house that dominates the site, and where the eight remaining Sisters and Brothers live, was built much later, when the community was at its peak. The dozen or so old buildings are surrounded by almost 2000 acres of good farmland and orchards, much of it leased out, some of it heavily wooded, running down to the shores of the most attractive lake.

It was not the best day to visit: at the height of the summer season, the lay guides and helpers were fully stretched leading tours and running the shop and museum, and the Family were about to host their annual Friends Weekend. A marquee was being erected on the lawn outside for the hundred or so guests; there were menus to be decided, duties to be allocated. But the Eldress, Sister Frances Carr, greeted us with a warm, welcoming smile.

That the community is thriving and even increasing is largely due to Sister Frances. Called "the most powerful person in the Shaker realm" by religious writer Suzanne Skees, Sister Frances is anything but intimidating, chatting gaily, recommending the

The rosewater made at Sabbathday Lake is regarded by cooks as the finest available in New England.

nearby wildlife park for my children, asking after my parents-in-law, telling us about her trips away. She came to the community 60 years ago as a small child, along with her sister Ruth, and became a fully covenanted Shaker at 21. She led us straight into the kitchen where she was cooking the noon dinner, as she has done for 50 years, and introduced us to Sister Marie – "my right hand, I couldn't work without her" – who was making that day's batch of bread.

As Sister Frances scrubbed the freshly harvested carrots, the Elder, Brother Arnold, told us about the buildings and the community, and showed us Sister Frances's book, *Shaker your Plate* (see bibliography, page 172). It contains her favorite recipes, some learned as a child, others developed over the years using newly available ingredients and equipment, like the microwave. "Most of my recipes originated here or at Alfred [another Maine community, which eventually moved to Sabbathday Lake]. Neither of the communities has ever had a reputation for the style of food found in other Shaker cookbooks. Ours is rather the simple, down-to-earth cooking of rural Maine." And here at Sabbathday Lake, they grow most of what they eat.

Sister Frances kindly let me read some of the old notebooks, diaries, and recipe books in their library: "After all, Sabbathday Lake is in its third century of feeding the hungry." As you would expect, they were fascinating. The recipes were recorded in minute handwriting by many different hands, and were faded and marked with use. One 1856 notebook, unsigned, gives a recipe for "pan bread," which calls for 5c flour, 3c sugar, 1c butter, 1c milk, 1c "ferment," 3 eggs, and 1/2 a nutmeg, mixed to a dough and baked in the same large pan. Some of the books had recipes and adverts clipped from newspapers and magazines stuck in. One, thought to be from the end of the nineteenth century, and much splattered, was for French tea rolls. The dough, made with white flour, milk, sugar, lard, and salt plus a quarter of a Clarke's yeast cake, had two 8-hour rises. The same book also contained a recipe for making hop yeast for baking: "…steep a quart of malt and wheat or flour with boiling water. Leave to stand, then add vegetable stock. Leave another 15 hours and bottle." This was followed by several recipes for doughnuts – some similar to Sister Mildred's (page 131) – and gingerbread.

The favorite flavorings for baking were home-manufactured rosewater (acres of roses were raised at the Mount Lebanon, New York, community), lemon, maple syrup and maple sugar, and molasses. Vanilla and sugar were expensive and not often used at first, but the earliest printed recipe for a chocolate cake appears in a Shaker book.

The men's retiring room in the 1883 Dwelling House at Sabbathday Lake.

The recipe books were obviously used by the rota of cooks in the community kitchens, and Sister Mary Ann Hill devotes most of her 1857 Canterbury notebook to passing on her wisdom to the novices. After a large section on the best recipes for wool dyes, some cures for human and animal ailments – several from Indian sources – and a recipe for making coffee from rye grains (apparently it went down well if flavored with plenty of sugar and cream), she writes about breadmaking:

In order to have good bread, there are three things very essential – good flour, good risings, and a careful hand. Now, if any lady friends will comply with the following directions, I will guarantee them as good bread as was ever broken by mortal hand.

– For wheat bread, milk is the best wetting.

– The sponge should not be permitted to get too light. It is ready when bubbles just break on the surface.

– Bread should never be cut until it is twelve hours old, and then only what is to be eaten immediately.

The large buildings indicate the size of the community in years gone by — there were once over 50 buildings at Sabbathday Lake.

Canterbury, New Hampshire

In 1992, the last Canterbury Sister, Ethel Hudson, died aged 96. It was the end of a community founded in 1782 by missionaries sent by Mother Ann. Although there were never more than 300 members, the Canterbury Shakers became known for the high quality of their agricultural produce and livestock. In the 1870s, they invented a washing machine capable of dealing with the laundry of hundreds of farm workers: the first machines were horse-powered, the later ones, sold to hotels, used steam. By selling sweaters, cloaks, and herbal remedies, including syrup of sarsaparilla, the community became wealthy enough to put up over 100 buildings and to increase its holdings to 4000 acres.

The dwelling house, built in 1793, housed the dining hall, kitchen, and bakery. Two sisters worked from 4:30a.m. to 2p.m. baking breads, pies, and pastries for the community. The oven was then used to prepare the evening supper; afterward, stone jars of beans were left to bake overnight. In the 1930s and '40s, there was a good market for the beans and brown bread in the nearby town of Concord.

The Shaker Village at Canterbury is now a living museum, and Daryl Thompson, the last child raised by the Shakers there, is one of the guides. Volunteers demonstrate traditional Shaker crafts: making wooden boxes and flat brooms, woodworking, printing, and taping chairs. The dwelling house has become a tearoom; there is a fine restaurant in the old Creamery, and a bakery in the former power house opposite. The chef, Jeff Paige, is lucky to be able to use the organic fruit and vegetables produced at the Shaker Village. He spent time learning about Shaker food with the last Canterbury sisters: "The Eldress Bertha Lindsay told me to take the ordinary and make it extraordinary in everything you do." His team served us a memorable meal of corn chowder, maple baked beans, and local ham. My daughter had a cold strawberry soup, which she said was the best thing she had tasted in her entire life (she is three, but has lived well). This is one restaurant that really is worth a detour.

"SISTER MARIE BURGESS *began to work in the community kitchen later than most —
she came to Sabbathday Lake at 19 and started work in the Trustees' office kitchen helping
with the busy and profitable candy industry,"* Sister Frances Carr told me. *"By the time she came
into the community kitchen, there were just the two of us working here. When I was learning,
there were always four working in the kitchen, with 60 or more people to cook for. Well, she soon
mastered the art of bread and pastry making, and her breads, pies, and biscuits have become great
favorites with all who know them here. Her excellence as a breadmaker attests to her dedication
and patience in a trade which is so essential to the happiness of the family. Truly bread is the staff
of life and this community has long been sustained by Sister Marie's good breads."*

Sister Marie's whole-wheat bread

MAKES 2 LARGE LOAVES

1 cup (230ml) milk

2 tablespoons sugar

2 teaspoons fine sea salt

4 tablespoons (50g) butter or margarine

1/2 cup (120g) molasses

2 0.6-oz cakes fresh yeast (30g)*

1 1/2 cups (350ml) lukewarm water

2 1/2 cups (370g) unbleached all-purpose flour

about 5 cups (650g) organic whole-wheat
    flour

2 tablespoons melted butter or margarine for
    greasing bowl

two loaf pans, about 9 x 5 x 3 inches, greased

*Sister Frances says that whole-wheat loaves
made by Sister Marie (below) sell by the
dozen at their Christmas Fair.*

Heat the milk until bubbles form around the edge of the pan, then remove from the
heat and add the sugar, salt, butter or margarine, and molasses. Stir until the butter melts.

Crumble the yeast into a cup, add a little of the water, and stir until dispersed.
Stir in the rest of the water and the lukewarm milk mixture.

Put the white flour and half of the whole-wheat flour into a large mixing bowl
and add the just warm liquid. Beat with a wooden spoon until smooth — about 4 minutes. Gradually add the remaining whole-wheat flour, mixing in the last of it with
your hand, until the dough will leave the sides of the bowl. It should feel soft and
slightly sticky.

Turn the dough onto a lightly floured work surface and allow to rest for 10 minutes, after which it will feel firmer. Then knead the dough for 10 minutes. ("Kneading
is very important, so do not neglect it," instructs Sister Frances.) Put the dough into a
large greased mixing bowl, and turn the dough over so as to bring the greased side up.
Cover with a light towel and leave to rise in a warm place away from drafts until the
dough doubles in size — about 1 1/4 hours. Another tip from Sister Frances: "A good
test is to poke two fingers into the dough; if the indentation remains [when you pull
out your fingers], the dough is ready."

Punch down the dough with your hands, then turn it out onto a lightly floured
work surface. Divide it in half and shape each portion into a neat ball. Leave to rest for
10 minutes.

Shape each portion into a loaf to fit your pans, then place in the pans and cover
with a towel. Leave to rise in a warm place until the dough has doubled in size and
reached the top of the pans — allow 1 1/2 hours.

Toward the end of the rising time, preheat the oven to
400°F.

Uncover the loaves and bake for about 40 minutes until
browned and they sound hollow when unmolded and tapped
underneath. Remove the bread from the
pans immediately and leave to cool on a
wire rack.

Wrap the cooled bread and keep
until the next day before slicing, or
freeze for up to a month. The bread
makes great toast.

*You can use 2 envelopes (5 teaspoons)
rapid-rise active dry yeast instead of the fresh yeast. Mix the dry
yeast with the white flour, and continue with the recipe.

In the dining room at Sabbathday Lake, we shared noon dinner with the community: home-produced and organic pot roast of beef in a rich gravy, organic carrots and the much-prized Maine potatoes in their skins, cucumber salad, and whole-wheat bread, followed by one-dish apple pudding and coffee.

SISTER MILDRED, *a former Eldress at Sabbathday Lake, also managed the candy business. These doughnuts were served on Sundays after Worship and were also made for sale. Adding ginger to the dough cuts down on the amount of grease the doughnuts take up during frying. There is no added taste of ginger in the final product. Plain yogurt can be used in place of the buttermilk, if needs be.*

Sister Mildred's doughnuts

MAKES 18 DOUGHNUTS

1 cup (175g) sugar

2 tablespoons melted lard

1 extra large egg, beaten

1 teaspoon baking soda

1 cup (230ml) buttermilk

3 cups (450g) unbleached all-purpose flour

1 teaspoon grated nutmeg

1/2 teaspoon ground ginger

a pinch of fine sea salt

vegetable oil for deep-frying

sugar, or sugar and cinnamon, for dusting

Cream the sugar, lard, and egg together with a wooden spoon until light. Stir the soda into the buttermilk and add to the creamed mixture. Gradually work in the flour, spices, and salt to make a firm dough.

Roll out on a floured work surface using a lightly floured rolling pin to about 1/4 inch thick. Cut out rounds using a 3–inch biscuit cutter. Stamp out the center of each round with a 3/8-inch cutter. Re-roll the trimmings to make more rings.

Heat oil in a deep fryer to 375°F. Fry the doughnuts, in batches, for about 3 minutes until golden and puffed up, turning frequently. Make sure the oil does not become any hotter or drop below 350°F. Drain the doughnuts on paper towels and dust with granulated or confectioners' sugar, or a mixture of sugar and cinnamon. Eat the same day.

The organic squashes grown by volunteers at Canterbury Shaker Village are used for breads, soups, and pies.

J EFF PAIGE, *the chef at Canterbury Shaker Village, spent time learning about Shaker food with the last Canterbury sisters:"In the Shaker kitchens, meals were planned and cooked to satisfy both bodily and, in a sense, spiritual hunger. This quote from Kitchen Sister Lisset sums up my own approach to cooking: 'No cook is really good without a lively imagination and the will to use it.'*

"This was Eldress Bertha Lindsay's favorite bread. We feature it daily at the restaurant and sell out of it every day at the bakery."

To make the butternut squash or pumpkin purée, you will need to start with about 1³/₄ pounds (800g) of the vegetable. Peel the squash or pumpkin, remove the seeds, and dice the flesh. Without adding water, cook the cubes in a steamer or microwave until they soften, then purée until smooth in a food processor. If using pumpkin, you may need to sieve the purée, to remove any fibers.

Shaker squash bread

MAKES LARGE LOAF

1 cup (225ml) milk

4 tablespoons (50g) unsalted butter

¹/₂ cup (100g) sugar

1 teaspoon fine sea salt

1 0.6-oz cake fresh yeast (15g)*

about 8 cups (1kg) unbleached all-purpose
    flour

1¹/₂ cups (450g) fresh butternut squash or
    pumpkin purée, at room temperature

2 large eggs, at room temperature, beaten

melted butter for brushing

a loaf pan, about 9 x 5 x 3 inches, well greased

Heat the milk and butter until the butter has melted, then remove from the heat. Combine the sugar and salt in a large bowl, and pour in the milk mixture. Stir well, then leave to cool, uncovered, until lukewarm.

Crumble the yeast into the milk mixture and stir until dispersed. Work in half the flour and beat with your hand, or using a heavy duty electric mixer on medium-low speed, for 2 minutes. Add the squash purée and the eggs, and mix well. Continue to work in the remaining flour, a bit at a time, until you have a firm dough that begins to leave the sides of the bowl.

Turn out the dough onto a lightly floured work surface and knead thoroughly for 7–8 minutes, adding a little extra flour if necessary to prevent the dough from sticking to your hands or the surface. Put the dough into a clean, lightly greased bowl and turn the dough over so it is coated. Cover the bowl with a damp dish towel and leave the dough to rise in a warm place until doubled in size – about 1¹/₂ hours.

Punch down the dough, divide it in half, and shape each piece into a loaf to fit your pans. Place in the pans, cover and leave to rise until doubled in size – about 1 hour.

Toward the end of the rising time, preheat the oven to 400°F.

Uncover the loaves and bake for 35 minutes until a good golden brown, and the loaves sound hollow when unmolded and tapped underneath. Turn out onto a wire rack and brush with melted butter. Leave to cool.

The bread is best eaten within 4 days, or toasted. Once thoroughly cooled, it can be frozen for up to a month.

* You can use 1 envelope (2¹/₂ teaspoons) rapid-rise active dry yeast instead of the fresh yeast. Combine the dry yeast with half of the flour in a mixing bowl, then work in the milk mixture followed by the purée and eggs. Continue with the recipe.

VARIATION : *Squash biscuits*
Roll out the dough ¹/₂-inch thick and cut out rounds using a 2¹/₂-inch biscuit cutter. Arrange the rounds in a greased 8-inch-square baking pan so they almost touch, or, for golden sides, arrange the biscuits spaced well apart on a greased baking sheet. Bake for about 20 minutes. These are best served warm.

"FRESHLY *baked bread is my downfall," Jeff Paige admitted. "Within minutes of removing it from the oven, I'm smothering steaming slices with butter. This recipe relies on the quality of the stoneground organic whole-wheat flour we use from Gray's Grist Mill." (See page 24 and Directory, page 172.)*

Honey-wheat bread

MAKES 2 MEDIUM LOAVES

2¹⁄₄ cups (500ml) milk

1 tablespoon molasses

2 tablespoons honey

1¹⁄₂ 0.6-oz cakes fresh yeast (25g)*

¹⁄₄ cup sunflower oil

1 tablespoon fine sea salt

3 cups (400g) organic unbleached white bread flour

about 3 cups (450g) organic coarse whole-wheat flour, preferably stoneground

2 loaf pans, about 8¹⁄₂ x 4¹⁄₂ x 2¹⁄₂ inches, well greased

Heat the milk in a large pan or flameproof casserole over medium heat until scalding hot, then remove from the heat and leave until lukewarm.

Add the molasses and honey, then crumble in the yeast and stir until thoroughly dispersed. Stir in the oil and salt. Combine the flours and add a handful at a time, mixing well after each addition. You should have a slightly soft but not sticky dough – add more whole-wheat flour if necessary. (The dough can be mixed in a bowl rather than in the pan.)

Turn out the dough onto a lightly floured work surface and knead until it becomes firmer, and very smooth and elastic – 7–8 minutes. Put the dough into a lightly oiled bowl and turn the dough over so it is completely covered in a thin layer of oil. Cover the bowl with a damp dish towel and leave the dough to rise in a warm place until it has doubled in size – about 1¹⁄₂ hours.

Punch down the dough to deflate, then divide it into two equal pieces. Shape each piece into a loaf to fit your pans. Place the loaves in the prepared pans, then cover and leave to rise as before until doubled in size – about 1 hour.

Toward the end of the rising time, preheat the oven to 350°F.

Uncover the loaves and bake for 45 minutes until golden brown and they sound hollow when unmolded and tapped underneath. Cool on a wire rack. The bread is best eaten within 4 days, or toasted. Once cooled, it can be frozen for up to a month.

* You can use 1 tablespoon rapid-rise active dry yeast instead of the fresh yeast. Combine the dry yeast with the flours in a large bowl, make a well in the center, and pour in the milk, molasses, honey, oil, and salt mixture. Gradually work the flour into the liquid to make a soft but not sticky dough, and continue with the recipe.

In 1878, the revolving bread oven (left), designed by Sister Emeline Hart, was installed at Canterbury. Its four revolving shelves enabled the Shaker Sisters to bake a great quantity at one time – up to 60 loaves or pies could be loaded and baked with relative ease. A heat indicator (far left) was made for the door in 1909. (Photographs by kind permission of Canterbury Shaker Village.)

I F YOU HANKER AFTER your own wood-fired oven and want something larger than a portable beehive oven (see page 119), but not as high-tech as Paul Merry's (page 120), then the best place to start is with Tom Jaine. Former editor of *The Good Food Guide* in Britain and restaurateur, Tom is the publisher of Prospect Books and author of *Building a Wood-Fired Oven* (see bibliography, page 172), which is a most useful and practical guide. As Tom says, "It describes the construction of a brick oven in your garden – no fire hazards, no major construction problems, no planning difficulties. It's the ultimate project for the D.I.Y. cook and novice builder."

The D.I.Y. baker

The design is based on the oven in the yard outside his house near Totnes in Devon, England. "We built it 8 years ago now, with the help of a very enthusiastic breadmaking friend from Germany, Rolf Peter Weichold, who has an old mill and bakery. I suppose it would cost about £600 [almost $1000] now, but I explain how to keep the cost down." The book also gives an excellent history of the bread oven: "Ovens were invented in the ancient world for one thing only – baking bread. Their design, materials, and methods of firing haven't changed."

Tom's oven takes 4–6 hours' firing to reach the right temperature for baking bread – about 450°F. Tom says he is not fussy and will burn almost any wood he can get hold of – old gate posts and wood from building sites. "It does need firing three or four times a week to maintain it; otherwise it takes ages to get it going well. Only baking bread in brick gives the bread that crackling-deep crust and smell of wheat and burnt flour. I adore it. "

When the oven has reached the correct temperature, Tom rakes out the ashes, wearing thick gardening gloves as it is a hot messy business.

It's almost a full day's work for Tom Jaine to fire his brick oven, prepare the dough, and then bake the bread.

Hens roost in the cosy roof of the oven overlooking the river at the end of the garden.

The wind is always a problem. He then cleans the floor, or sole, of the oven with a wet rag on the end of a broomstick: "Give it a good swoosh out or it will be disgusting. The steam is useful too." The logic of steam in breadmaking is another theme running through his book. "Early on in the eighteenth century, the French introduced a sloping floor to the oven. When the oven is loaded, and sealed hermetically, the moisture is recycled, rather than allowed to escape, and this develops the bread's crust. Later in the century, they added the Viennese techniques for dripping water down the back of the oven. Then they could produce the baguettes, *bâtards,* and *ficelles* which we all now eat." Tom explained that the tradition of eating yeasted bread in Britain, rather than the sourdough-based loaves of our neighbors, is because "we have been brewing since the year dot, and bakers and brewers traditionally worked together. Our bread must have always been yeasted."

The loading of the oven has to be carefully worked out if you are baking a large batch of bread: start at the back and sides, then fill the center and the front. Tom says that it is possible to bake a second batch 40 minutes or so after the first is removed.

"Experience is the main factor in successful baking. The things that make me maddest, when I'm baking at home, are the ones that are hardest to get right. It's essential to provide the right conditions for the dough – it's what divides a professional from a non-professional result. To prevent a skin from forming on delicate loaves, and to encourage and develop whole-wheat and rye doughs, you need a moist, slightly rising temperature for rising. My ideal would be a purpose-built dough-rising cabinet. I do worry, though, about becoming an obsessed perfectionist. After all, I'm only making bread to put on the table for breakfast."

*"**T**HIS is an absolute standard recipe, but we do like yeasted white bread," Tom Jaine said. "I like bread that I'm used to, as with coffee and tea, not 'road to Damascus' stuff. I'm quite happy to eat the same bread every day."*

Tom Jaine's white bread

MAKES 2 MEDIUM LOAVES

6¹/₂ cups (800g) unbleached white bread flour

2 teaspoons fine sea salt

2 0.6-oz cakes fresh yeast (25g)*

2 cups (500ml) lukewarm water

2 baking sheets or two loaf pans, about
    8¹/₂ x 4¹/₂ x 2¹/₂ inches, well greased

Tom likes to shape the dough into smaller pieces and then to rise them in pairs. This produces attractive loaves that can be divided easily.

If you are using a wood-fired bread oven, you need to start the fire before you begin making the bread dough.

Mix the flour and salt in a large bowl. Disperse the yeast in the water, then add to the flour. Mix well to make a slightly soft but not sticky dough. If the dough sticks to your fingers or the bowl, work in a little extra flour; if there are dry crumbs in the bottom of the bowl add a little extra water.

Turn the dough onto a work surface and knead thoroughly for 10 minutes until the dough feels smooth and very pliable. Return the dough to the bowl and cover with a damp dish towel. Leave to rise in a warm spot until doubled in size – allow a couple of hours.

Punch down the risen dough to its original size with your knuckles, then turn out onto a lightly floured work surface. Cut into two equal pieces. Knead each piece for a minute, then flatten to a large rectangle. Fold the short sides into the center, press the dough flat, and roll up tightly like a jelly roll. If using pans, roll the shaped dough with your hand to make a sausage to fit. Put the shaped loaves, seam-side uppermost, in heavily floured cloth-lined baskets, or seam-side down in the greased loaf pans. (Alternatively, to give a more interesting shape, and to make a loaf that divides easily, cut the dough into four pieces. Shape each as above and put two shaped pieces of dough into each basket or pan.) Cover with plastic wrap and leave to rise in a warm spot until doubled in size – allow 1 hour.

Toward the end of the rising time, preheat a conventional oven to 425°F. If the loaves have been risen in baskets, put the ungreased baking sheets into the oven to heat. A wood-fired oven needs to be at 450°F for baking, and loaves will be baked directly on the oven floor.

Uncover the loaves and dust with flour. For a wood-fired oven, turn the loaves out of their rising baskets onto a floured baking peel. Quickly slash the top of each with a serrated knife, then thrust the peel into the oven so the loaves shoot off onto the oven floor. For a conventional oven, turn out basket-risen loaves onto the heated baking sheets, then slash the tops of the loaves before baking. If baking in loaf pans, slash the loaves, then place the pans in the oven. Bake for 25–35 minutes, depending on the heat of the oven and the shape of the loaves. They are done when they have turned a good brown and sound hollow when tapped underneath. Cool on a wire rack.

The bread is best eaten within 4 days, or toasted. Once thoroughly cooled, it can be frozen for up to a month.

*You can use 2 envelopes (5 teaspoons) rapid-rise active dry yeast instead of the fresh yeast. Mix the dry yeast with the flour and salt, then add the water.

Above: Use a large metal spatula or pancake turner to transfer the potato bread to the hot griddle.
Left: Warm Potato–Apple Bread goes well with ham, salad, and a glass of cider.

THIS *recipe comes from County Armagh, Ireland, which has good apple orchards. Two circles of potato dough are filled with tart eating apples (the sharper the better) and cooked on a griddle on top of the stove. I like this bread with hot ham or cold cuts.*

Potato-apple bread

SERVES 4–6

1 lb (500g) floury potatoes, cooked (see recipe)

1 teaspoon fine sea salt

1/2 teaspoon baking powder

3 tablespoons (40g) unsalted butter, diced

3–5 tablespoons unbleached all-purpose flour

2 medium-sized tart apples, peeled, cored, and thinly sliced

a pat of butter

a griddle or heavy frying pan, lightly greased

The potatoes can either be baked or boiled in their skins until tender. When cool enough to handle, peel off the skins, then put the hot flesh through a potato ricer or mash it – do not put into a food processor or you will end up with wallpaper paste. Stir in the salt, baking powder, and diced butter, then work in enough flour to make a firm dough – the exact amount will depend on the type of potato you use and how it was cooked.

Divide the dough into two equal pieces. On a well-floured work surface, roll out each piece to a round about 7 inches diameter. Cover one round with the apple slices and add the pat of butter, then cover with the other round of dough. Crimp or pinch the edges together to seal.

Heat the greased griddle or pan over medium heat. Add the potato bread. Turn the heat to low and cook gently until golden brown on the underside – about 5 minutes. Using a large spatula, lift the bread onto a flat plate, then quickly invert it back onto the griddle so the bread can cook on the other side. Cook for a further 4–5 minutes until browned. Cut into wedges and eat immediately.

137

A T teatime or a late evening supper, British dropped scones can take the place of bread. Eat them warm with butter, homemade jam, honey, or golden syrup (which was my favorite childhood topping). The scones can be cooked on a hot griddle or girdle, in a frying pan, or directly on the (cleaned) top of a solid-top stove such as an Aga.

This is my favorite of the very many recipes for dropped scones I have tasted and made over the last 30 years. It comes from an old colleague in Caithness, Scotland, who used to entertain us, on our afternoons off, to the most wonderful teas I have ever eaten. Other recipes use golden syrup instead of the sugar, or add butter or buttermilk, even evaporated milk. But I think you can't better this version of dropped scones.

Helen's dropped scones

MAKES ABOUT 18 SCONES

1¹/₃ cups (200g) unbleached all-purpose flour

¹/₈ teaspoon fine sea salt

1¹/₂ teaspoons cream of tartar

³/₄ teaspoon baking soda

2 tablespoons sugar

1 extra large egg, beaten

1 cup (250ml) whole milk

a griddle, girdle, or heavy-based frying pan,
    lightly greased

Set the greased griddle, girdle, or pan over low to medium heat.

Sift the flour, salt, cream of tartar, baking soda, and sugar into a mixing bowl. Make a well in the center. Beat the egg with the milk, and pour into the well. Using a whisk or wooden spoon, draw the dry ingredients into the liquid to make a smooth batter.

Make a test scone first just to check the griddle is the right temperature and the batter the right consistency: Drop a tablespoonful of batter onto the hot griddle — it should hold its shape and small bubbles should form on the surface and then burst after a couple of minutes or so. Loosen gently underneath using a small, flexible metal spatula, then flip over when the underside is a nice golden color. Cook for 1–2 minutes more until the other side is lightly colored. If necessary, adjust the heat under the griddle. If the cooked sample seems too solid and heavy, the batter is too thick, so add a little more milk.

Cook the rest of the batter in the same way, three or four dropped scones at a time, then wrap in a clean cloth until ready to serve. Eat warm as soon as possible, or toasted the following day.

Drop spoonfuls of batter onto the hot griddle, spacing them so they have room to spread.

As soon as bubbles appear and burst on the surface, flip the scones using a palette spatula.

Cook until the scones are golden on both sides, then remove from the griddle.

Left: Spoon the fluffy batter onto the hot griddle.

Cook until the pancakes are well risen and golden on each side. Eat right away, with thin-cut crisp bacon and real maple syrup.

EATEN *for breakfast with crisp bacon, eggs, and maple syrup, these are large, thick pancakes given their fluffy texture with stiffly beaten egg whites rather than chemical leavening agents. Three generations of my husband's family have started the day on these pancakes, layered with peanut butter and maple syrup. They are quick and easy to make — indeed, my little ones have been helping with the batter since they were both 18 months old.*

Griddle pancakes

MAKES ABOUT 16 LARGE PANCAKES, TO SERVE 4–6

1¹/₃ cups (200g) unbleached all-purpose flour

¹/₈ teaspoon fine sea salt

2 tablespoons sugar

4 extra large eggs, separated

2 tablespoons (30g) unsalted butter, melted

1 cup (250ml) milk

butter for greasing

a griddle or heavy-based frying pan

Put the griddle or frying pan onto a low to medium heat.

Sift the flour, salt, and sugar into a mixing bowl, and make a well in the center. Add the egg yolks, melted butter, and milk to the well, then whisk in the dry ingredients to make a thick, smooth batter. Beat the egg whites until stiff, then fold into the batter with a large metal spoon.

When the griddle is medium hot, grease it very lightly with butter. Cook the pancakes in batches of three, using a large heaped spoonful of batter for each one. Cook for 1–2 minutes until golden underneath, then turn over with a metal spatula and cook for another minute. Eat right away.

VARIATION: For a traditional New England breakfast, add ³/₄ cup (100g) fresh blueberries to the batter before cooking the pancakes.

Udit Sarkhel turns away several dozen diners each night from his restaurant in Southfields, west London. Since he opened Sarkhel's a couple of years ago, he has been able to decorate a wall with framed prestigious awards – other chefs would sweat blood for just one. Yet he likes to say his is a family restaurant rather than a fashionable destination, even though many customers regularly travel across town for one of his dinners.

Udit gained a reputation for authentic home–style as well as grand and exotic cooking at the Bombay Brasserie, for many years the most celebrated Indian restaurant in London. He was head chef for 10 years. "It was a big gamble opening my own place, but I knew I could get another good job if I had to."

Traditional Indian baking

From a Bengali fishing family, Udit switched from studying medicine to catering, because, he says, the catering college in Bombay was in such a beautiful building. He then spent 22 years with the Taj group, working all over India. Everywhere he went, he explored local ingredients and cooking methods – now he uses the Internet to pursue his research. When we met he had just come back from a day cooking with John Lister (see page 13), making breads with kamut flour, an ancient grain found in the tombs of Egyptian pharaohs. Udit said it resembled a very old variety of wheat found in the north of India. "It's a very long grain, with a good ratio of bran to endosperm. You can really taste the wheat when it's cooked."

The traditional Indian oven, called a *tandoor*, is a well-insulated clay shell, heated by charcoal or gas, with the temperature controlled by the air inflow. While a gas oven takes a mere 1^1/$_2$ hours to reach the optimum baking temperature, a charcoal-fired *tandoor* needs an entire day. To test if the oven is hot enough, it is splashed with water, which should disappear instantly, steam and all. "The *tandoor* grills and bakes at the same time," Udit told me, "but it's different from a barbecue, as the moisture given off by the food is kept within the shell. With the lid on, the result is dry heat from the charcoal plus steam from the food, and it's like a pressure cooker. Food – particularly meat and vegetables – can be both moist and well-cooked."

The first *tandoors* in India were set into the ground, in a communal part of a village, and baking was a social part of the daily routine. "The women would take the dough down to the ovens, then sit and chat while each shaped, then baked, 30 or 40 naans to feed her extended family. The cooked breads would be tied in a cloth for the walk home." Today, larger and more affluent households have their own oven in the backyard. Udit showed us the portable *tandoor* he stores in his garden shed and wheels out for weekend parties.

Indian breads are also baked on a *tawa*, which is a heavy, flat griddle. Set directly on the heat, it is used for chapatis and stuffed breads, as well as marinated fish and meat. "A *tawa* can be bought easily, and for a reasonable sum, from most Indian food shops, and, of course, you can use them for other things, not just breads."

For chef Udit Sarkhel (above), no Indian meal is complete without bread. At home, he cooks naan in his backyard using a portable tandoor *(right).*

N AA N *comes from the Northwest Frontier in India, the Punjab region, where the best wheat is grown. It is a leavened bread, made from white flour with a very low bran content and medium to strong gluten. Udit likes to use ordinary rather than bread flour and adds very little salt; he uses baking powder as the leavening agent, as it is more controllable when cooking for large numbers. The dough is quick to make, but must rest several times or the result will be tough. "Naan is versatile — you can eat it with semi-dry meat dishes, or dip it into vegetable or chicken dishes with plenty of gravy. This recipe makes glistening, aromatic bread: a magical combination of taste and scent."*

Udit says it's impossible to cook authentic naan without a tandoor. The rolled-out dough is stuck onto the wall of the oven using a thick cloth pad and then, a couple of minutes later, removed with long skewers. "At home, the best alternative is to use a baking stone or terracotta tile — the kind sold for pizza. Put it into the oven when you switch it on, then get it and the oven as hot as possible." A word of warning: whichever method you choose, remove all rings and other jewelry before you start.

At Udit's restaurant, the naan is shaped by hand (below right) and baked in a charcoal-fired tandoor.

Garlic naan with chilies and cilantro

MAKES 14 BREADS

DOUGH:

6 cups (900g) unbleached all-purpose flour

1 tablespoon baking powder

1 teaspoon sugar

1 teaspoon fine sea salt, or to taste

1 large egg, lightly beaten

1 1/4 cups (300ml) milk, boiled and then cooled to about 120°F

about 1 1/4 cups (300ml) lukewarm water

4 tablespoons vegetable oil

TO FINISH:

2 tablespoons chopped garlic

2 tablespoons chopped fresh cilantro

1/2 teaspoon finely sliced green chili peppers (as mild or hot as you choose)

melted butter for brushing (optional)

a *tandoor* or a pizza stone or large baking sheet

Sift the flour, baking powder, sugar, and salt into a large mixing bowl. Make a well in the center, and pour in the egg and milk. Gradually work the dry ingredients into the liquid, adding the water a little at a time, until all the flour has been incorporated and the dough is firm but supple, not dry or hard — you may need to add a little more water. There is no need to knead the dough. Cover the bowl with a clean, warm, wet cloth and leave to rise for 30 minutes.

Punch down the dough, then work in the oil, kneading lightly in the bowl until it is thoroughly incorporated. Cover as before and leave to rise again for 1 hour.

Divide the dough into 14 pieces and shape each one into a neat ball. Place these on a sheet lightly dusted with flour, cover as before, and leave to rise for 30 minutes.

If using a *tandoor*, preheat according to the manufacturer's instructions. If using a conventional oven, preheat it to 475°F, and put the pizza stone or large baking sheet in to heat.

The dough balls are traditionally beaten out flat using the palms of both hands, but it is simpler to roll them out to rounds 1/4 inch thick, using plenty of flour to prevent sticking. Scatter the garlic, cilantro, and chilies over the dough and pat in with damp fingers. If using a *tandoor*, stick the flattened dough onto the side of the oven using a thick pad and cook for 2–3 minutes, then remove with long skewers. Alternatively, put the naans, in batches, on the hot pizza stone or baking sheet and bake for 5–6 minutes until puffed and golden brown. Brush the hot naans with melted butter, if liked, and serve at once. Reheating and freezing is not recommended.

THESE *unleavened whole-wheat breads stuffed with a spicy potato mixture are loved by North Indians. "They are robust eaters, and like their breads thick," says Udit Sarkhel. "Aloo paratha is very popular for breakfast with chilled yogurt, or eaten straight off the* tawa *as a snack, or with a main dish. You can use leftover mashed potatoes for the filling, and save uneaten parathas to eat cold for a packed school or picnic lunch."*

Parathas are traditionally cooked on a tawa, *which is a heavy griddle. Alternatively you could use a standard griddle or a heavy-based frying pan.*

Aloo paratha

MAKES 8 BREADS

DOUGH:

4 cups (450g) fine white whole-wheat
    flour

1 teaspoon fine sea salt, or to taste

about 1 cup (225ml) water

9–10 tablespoons vegetable oil

FILLING:

1 tablespoon vegetable oil

$1/2$ teaspoon cumin seeds

2–3 fresh green chili peppers (as mild or hot as
    you like), minced

$1/4$-inch piece peeled fresh ginger, minced

2 medium-sized potatoes, boiled, peeled, and
    mashed

2 teaspoons *chaat masala* (a spice mixture
    available at Indian groceries)

fine sea salt to taste

2 tablespoons chopped fresh cilantro

a *tawa* or griddle

To make the dough, mix the flour with the salt in a bowl. Gradually stir in the water to make a firm but supple dough — add extra water if the dough feels hard or dry. Cover the bowl with a warm, damp dish towel and leave to rest for 20 minutes.

Divide the dough into eight equal pieces and shape each one into a neat ball. Cover as before and leave to rest while making the filling.

Heat the oil in a frying pan and fry the cumin seeds until they crackle. Add the chilies and ginger, and continue cooking, stirring frequently, until lightly browned. Remove from the heat and stir in the potatoes, *chaat masala,* and salt. Lastly, stir in the chopped cilantro to make a moist, well-flavored filling.

Lightly pat out a ball of dough to flatten. Put about a tablespoon or so of filling (you may want to start with a little less until you get the hang of it) into the center, then draw up the edges of the dough to enclose the filling completely. Turn over so the gathered seam is underneath, then gently roll out to a round about $1/4$ inch thick and 6 inches across. Repeat with the rest of the dough balls and filling.

Heat the *tawa* or griddle until it is medium hot, and lightly oil if necessary. Add one paratha and cook it for about 50 seconds, then flip it over and cook for a further minute. Spoon about 1 tablespoon of oil over and cook until it starts to sizzle, then flip the paratha over. Continue cooking, flipping over the paratha every 30 seconds, until it is golden and crisp on both sides. Keep warm in a tightly covered warm dish, or casserole lined with a napkin, while cooking the rest. Eat warm or cold, with pickles or yogurt.

Udit flattens the dough with his hands (left above), puts the spicy filling in the center, and seals it (left below), then rolls it flat before cooking on the tawa (far left).

NAAN *comes from the Northwest Frontier in India, the Punjab region, where the best wheat is grown. It is a leavened bread, made from white flour with a very low bran content and medium to strong gluten. Udit likes to use ordinary rather than bread flour and adds very little salt; he uses baking powder as the leavening agent, as it is more controllable when cooking for large numbers. The dough is quick to make, but must rest several times or the result will be tough. "Naan is versatile — you can eat it with semi-dry meat dishes, or dip it into vegetable or chicken dishes with plenty of gravy. This recipe makes glistening, aromatic bread: a magical combination of taste and scent."*

Udit says it's impossible to cook authentic naan without a tandoor. The rolled-out dough is stuck onto the wall of the oven using a thick cloth pad and then, a

At Udit's restaurant, the naan is shaped by hand (below right) and baked in a charcoal-fired tandoor.

couple of minutes later, removed with long skewers. "At home, the best alternative is to use a baking stone or terracotta tile — the kind sold for pizza. Put it into the oven when you switch it on, then get it and the oven as hot as possible." A word of warning: whichever method you choose, remove all rings and other jewelry before you start.

Garlic naan with chilies and cilantro

MAKES 14 BREADS

DOUGH:

6 cups (900g) unbleached all-purpose flour

1 tablespoon baking powder

1 teaspoon sugar

1 teaspoon fine sea salt, or to taste

1 large egg, lightly beaten

1¼ cups (300ml) milk, boiled and then cooled to about 120°F

about 1¼ cups (300ml) lukewarm water

4 tablespoons vegetable oil

TO FINISH:

2 tablespoons chopped garlic

2 tablespoons chopped fresh cilantro

½ teaspoon finely sliced green chili peppers (as mild or hot as you choose)

melted butter for brushing (optional)

a *tandoor* or a pizza stone or large baking sheet

Sift the flour, baking powder, sugar, and salt into a large mixing bowl. Make a well in the center, and pour in the egg and milk. Gradually work the dry ingredients into the liquid, adding the water a little at a time, until all the flour has been incorporated and the dough is firm but supple, not dry or hard — you may need to add a little more water. There is no need to knead the dough. Cover the bowl with a clean, warm, wet cloth and leave to rise for 30 minutes.

Punch down the dough, then work in the oil, kneading lightly in the bowl until it is thoroughly incorporated. Cover as before and leave to rise again for 1 hour.

Divide the dough into 14 pieces and shape each one into a neat ball. Place these on a sheet lightly dusted with flour, cover as before, and leave to rise for 30 minutes.

If using a *tandoor*, preheat according to the manufacturer's instructions. If using a conventional oven, preheat it to 475°F, and put the pizza stone or large baking sheet in to heat.

The dough balls are traditionally beaten out flat using the palms of both hands, but it is simpler to roll them out to rounds ¼ inch thick, using plenty of flour to prevent sticking. Scatter the garlic, cilantro, and chilies over the dough and pat in with damp fingers. If using a *tandoor*, stick the flattened dough onto the side of the oven using a thick pad and cook for 2–3 minutes, then remove with long skewers. Alternatively, put the naans, in batches, on the hot pizza stone or baking sheet and bake for 5–6 minutes until puffed and golden brown. Brush the hot naans with melted butter, if liked, and serve at once. Reheating and freezing is not recommended.

5 Celebration breads

THERE WAS A TIME WHEN A TREAT WAS SOMETHING SPECIAL, out of the ordinary. Mincemeat pies, spiked with sherry, were not baked until the week before Christmas. The heavy fruit cake, though made in September, was never cut until Christmas Day. Spicy hot cross buns were only eaten for breakfast on Good Friday. An elaborately decorated or braided loaf was the centerpiece of the Harvest Festival at the end of September.

Today, affluence has made our traditional treats commonplace. Since supermarkets sell them all year for bargain prices, few of us now bother to make them ourselves. But in our travels, meeting bakers both at home and in other parts of the world, Anthony and I have found many celebration breads still made by hand for particular feast days and for special occasions.

In almost every culture, celebratory baking involves using finely ground and sifted white flour instead of the everyday grain. It can also mean adding milk or buttermilk for a soft crust, eggs and butter for a fine golden crumb and rich flavor, sugar or honey

*Gifts of highly decorated breads are blessed during
a traditional Sardinian wedding (see page 168).*

for sweetness, and expensive dried fruits and spices. This is as true for the kulich made to celebrate the holiest day in the Orthodox calendar as for the Easter buns from a tiny village in the West of England. White flour is the basis for the famed decorated breads of Sardinia, where dough is painstakingly turned into edible decorations that are almost too exquisite to eat.

Celebration breads are also usually made to share, because part of the excitement on a special occasion is giving and receiving, eating (and usually drinking) together. Beatrice Grill's friendship bread is typical of this. Until recently, the daily diet in rural Sweden was monotonous, dependent on what was available locally, what you could grow, gather, or catch. The daily bread was hard, coarse, dark, and bitter, so a special loaf had to be different.

Baking with scarce, exotic, or rich ingredients is like decorating the house with leaves and flowers or candles, wearing party clothes, inviting guests – it makes the occasion significant and lifts the bread into another realm.

THE ATMOSPHERE in the Franciscan Brothers' bakery, in Bangor, Maine, is unique – even when crowded, the room, decorated with religious statuary, seems tranquil. Alongside the serving counter, stairs lead up to a small prayer space, open during shop hours for private meditation. All work stops for Mass every morning. The shop is affiliated with St. John's Episcopal Church in Bangor, and the Bishop blessed the bakery and ministry at the opening. The Brothers explained that they are "first order" Franciscans, an open order established to keep members active in their communities while living the rule of St. Francis. They practice obedience, celibacy, and poverty, and are in demand to preach, to take services, and to conduct christenings.

The blessed bakery

At the Franciscan Brothers' bakery and coffee shop in Bangor, Maine, work stops for Mass every morning.

Brother Donald wears tee-shirt and shorts in the heat of a bakery without air conditioning in summer; his colleague Brother Kenneth wears a traditional, heavy woollen habit. Brother Donald, who does all the baking, punches down risen dough to the sound of *All Things Bright and Beautiful* – "a great combination." Then, as he begins to scale and shape the dough, plainsong comes on the stereo. He starts work at 3a.m., putting on the doughs for the breakfast breads, rolls, and muffins for early customers and workers coming off the night shift. Then he works on batches of bread, making 16 loaves at a time in his old mixer. "I make two or three hundred loaves a day – we have 16 types on our list, and I make whatever I fancy, usually 10 kinds a day, plus sourdough and rye on a Saturday."

Although he has a degree in culinary arts and worked as a hotel chef for 15 years, Brother Donald only started making bread five years ago. "I'd had enough of large hotels, so I packed it in to do other things. Then I'd bake all Saturday, working through the night at home, making the dough for six loaves at a time in a plastic bucket and baking them in my old stove." He devised all his own recipes, trying out different ideas until he found bread he liked to eat. "We started selling the bread outside in the Church yard after the service – what wasn't sold was given away. Eventually, one cold, wet Sunday, the Rector invited us inside and things took off from there. The ministry grew at the same time, so one has sustained the other." Brother Donald started baking from the Church kitchens, and they sold the

*Brother Donald (right)
is the most relaxed baker
I've ever met.*

*There is a fine collection of Shaker boxes and other craft items on display (above left), and customers can watch Brother Donald at work
in the open-plan bakery. Above the counter in the coffee shop, where Brother Kenneth serves the customers, is a prayer room open to all.*

bread at roadside stalls (a common sight in Maine is an open car trunk and a sign for corn, blueberries, or tomatoes), as well as other Episcopal churches and local markets.

But the bakery is a big step up. "You could say our prayers were answered, someone stepped in to help us at just the right moment to offer us a lease here. We then had to install ovens and the bare essentials. The premises are perfect for our needs. We are much more than a bakery – we are more of an apostolate."

THE *signature bread of the Franciscan Brothers' bakery, and the most popular, is named for the patron saint of the order. Brother Donald told me: "St. Elizabeth, Queen of Hungary at the very start of the thirteenth century, devoted herself to feeding the poor, against her husband's wishes. One day he stopped her as she made her way out, but miraculously all the loaves of bread hidden in her cloak turned to roses, and she was saved. Because of this I wanted to make a bread flavored with rosewater — I buy it from the Shakers at Sabbathday Lake [see page 126]. But after much trial and error I found it only worked with ginger as a counterbalance. That's fine though, as both rosewater and ginger are very early flavorings." The bread, sliced or made into rolls, is good spread with butter at breakfast or teatime.*

St. Elizabeth bread

MAKES 2 MEDIUM LOAVES

6 cups (700g) unbleached white bread flour

2 teaspoons fine sea salt

6¹/₂ (80g) sugar

3 tablespoons dried milk powder

1¹/₂ tablespoons ground ginger

1 large egg, beaten

¹/₃ cup vegetable oil

1¹/₂ tablespoons rosewater

2 0.6-oz cakes fresh yeast (30g)*

1¹/₂ cups (350ml) lukewarm water

2 loaf pans, about 8¹/₂ x 4¹/₂ x 2¹/₂ inches, greased

Thoroughly combine all the dry ingredients in a large mixing bowl. Mix the egg with the oil and rosewater. Crumble the yeast into the water and stir until dispersed. Pour the egg mixture and the yeast mixture into the flour and work together to make a slightly soft but not sticky dough. If the dough sticks to your fingers or the bowl, work in a little extra flour; if there are dry crumbs and the dough feels stiff, work in a little more lukewarm water.

Turn out onto a work surface and knead thoroughly for 10 minutes. Return the dough to the bowl, cover with plastic wrap and leave until doubled in size — about 1 hour in a warm but not hot spot in the kitchen.

Punch down the dough with your knuckles, then turn out onto a work surface and divide in half. Shape each piece into a sausage about 16 inches long, then fold in half and twist to make a tight figure of eight. Put the shaped loaves neatly into the pans and leave to rise as before (Brother Donald does not cover the dough) until doubled in size — about 45 minutes.

Toward the end of the rising time, preheat the oven to 350°F.

Bake the loaves for about 35 minutes until golden brown and they sound hollow when unmolded and tapped underneath. Cool on a wire rack.

The bread is best eaten within 3 days, or toasted. Once thoroughly cooled, the loaves can be frozen for up to a month.

*You can use 2 envelopes (5 teaspoons) rapid-rise active dry yeast instead of the fresh yeast. Mix the dry yeast with the dry ingredients, then add the water with all the other liquids and continue with the recipe.

St. Elizabeth bread rolls and loaves are flavored with Shaker rosewater.

Note: The dough can also be made into rolls. Divide the mixed but unrisen dough into 2-ounce (60g) pieces. Roll each into a sausage shape and then twist or knot. Arrange on baking sheets and leave to rise until doubled in size. Brush with beaten egg to glaze, if you like, then bake at 400°F for 12–15 minutes.

Brother Kenneth wears the traditional heavy woollen habit of the Franciscan order, even in summer.

"I CREATED *this fancy bread when we were given 60 pounds of cooking dates out of the blue,*" Brother Donald said. "*They work very well with maple syrup, which is very popular in Maine. It's a good bread for brunch and at tea or coffee time.*"

Maple-date wheat bread

MAKES 2 MEDIUM LOAVES

4 cups (500g) unbleached white bread flour

1³/₄ cups (200g) whole-wheat flour

2 teaspoons fine sea salt

¹/₂ cup (75g) chopped dates,

3 tablespoons firmly packed maple sugar or
   light brown sugar

2 0.6-oz cakes fresh yeast (30g)*

1¹/₂ cups (350ml) lukewarm water

1 large egg, beaten

³/₄ cup (170ml) maple syrup

2 loaf pans, about 8¹/₂ x 4¹/₂ x 2¹/₂ inches,
   well greased

Combine the flours, salt, dates, and sugar in a large mixing bowl. Crumble the yeast into the water and stir until dispersed. Pour into the flour mixture followed by the egg and maple syrup. Mix well to make a firm but not stiff dough. If there are dry crumbs, work in a little extra water; if the dough feels sticky work in a little extra white flour.

Turn out onto a work surface and knead thoroughly for 10 minutes. Return the dough to the bowl, cover with plastic wrap, and leave to rise in a warm but not hot spot until doubled in size – about 1¹/₂ hours.

Punch down the dough with your knuckles to deflate, then turn out onto a work surface and divide into two equal pieces. Shape each piece into a loaf to fit the pans. Carefully place the dough in the pans, then leave to rise as before, uncovered, until doubled in size – about 1 hour.

Toward the end of the rising time, preheat the oven to 350°F.

Bake the loaves for about 35 minutes until golden brown and they sound hollow when unmolded and tapped underneath. Cool on a wire rack.

This bread is best eaten within 3 days, or toasted. Once thoroughly cooled, it can be frozen for up to a month.

*You can use 2 envelopes (5 teaspoons) rapid-rise active dry yeast instead of the fresh yeast. Mix the dry yeast with the flours and other dry ingredients, then add all the liquids and continue with the recipe.

149

THE SARDINIAN VILLAGE OF SUELLI celebrates the festival of St. Giorgio, its patron saint, on May 23. The celebration lasts all day, with traditional music, dancing, and elaborately embroidered local costumes, a procession around the village to the church piazza, fair stalls, and demonstrations of local crafts – even the manor house is open to public view.

Around the church, local crafts, including decorated religious bread called pane ceremoniale *(far right), are displayed.*

The village empties at midday as everyone heads for the communal picnic in the cool of the church hall. After enjoying grilled eels from the barbecue set up in the market place, and the local fortified wine, the cool boxes are opened and out come the homemade tarts, pies, and breads of all kinds.

Festival for a patron saint

During the day-long celebrations, dancers and musicians, wearing the highly embroidered traditional costumes of the area, perform in the church piazza, and tractors pull decorated floats in the procession around the village.

GIOVANNA MUCELI, *a teacher, invited us to join her family — she has six children, now all grown up — for the picnic on St. Giorgio's day. Hers was without doubt the most appetizing picnic spread of all. She always makes a couple of stuffed focaccia for this lunch: "It's something you would only get at home — you don't find it in restaurants or shops. For this one I use whatever I have in the fridge, usually salami or prosciutto layered with some cheese — fontina, fresh pecorino, or mozzarella — plus something green like young spinach [you can use bigger, older leaves of spinach or Swiss chard, but they must be blanched] or fresh basil. For the second one I use a* pipérade *or well-drained ratatouille and maybe some cheese or whole roasted garlic cloves. Or I'll use a seafood mixture — mussels, shrimp, and* calamari *flavored with some onions and chili."*

Picnic focaccia

MAKES 1 LARGE FOCACCIA

DOUGH:

1 0.6-oz cake fresh yeast (15g)*

1¹/₄ cups (280ml) lukewarm water

6–7 tablespoons extra virgin olive oil

about 4 cups (500g) unbleached white bread flour

1 teaspoon dried oregano

2 teaspoons fine sea salt

freshly ground black pepper

FILLING:

4–5 oz (100–150g) prosciutto or salami

4–5 oz (100–150g) thinly sliced cheese (see recipe introduction)

1 cup (50g) young spinach leaves or fresh basil, or a combination

coarse sea salt for sprinkling

a baking pan about 9 x 12 inches, lightly oiled

Focaccia stuffed with prosciutto, cheese, and spinach is made for the feast day of this Sardinian village's patron saint.

To make the dough, crumble the yeast into a large mixing bowl. Add half the water, and stir until the yeast is thoroughly dispersed. Pour in the rest of the water and 3 tablespoons of the oil. Add half the flour, the oregano, salt, and a few grinds of pepper, and beat into the liquid. Gradually work in enough of the remaining flour to make a very soft but not sticky dough.

Turn out onto a lightly floured work surface and knead thoroughly for 10 minutes until the dough is smooth and pliable. Return to the bowl, cover with a damp dish towel, and leave to rise until doubled in size – about 1 hour in a warm kitchen, or 2 hours at normal room temperature.

Punch down the risen dough and divide in half. Roll or pat out one piece and press into the prepared baking pan to cover the bottom completely. Cover with the prosciutto or salami, then with the cheese. Grind over a little black pepper (or sprinkle with a few dried red pepper flakes), then cover with an even layer of spinach or basil leaves.

Roll or pat out the second piece of dough to a rectangle the size of the pan and place on top of the spinach, pressing down gently. Press and pinch together the bottom and top edges of the dough to seal in the filling completely. Prick the top layer of dough with a skewer to release any bubbles of air trapped between the filling and the dough. Cover and leave to rise as before until doubled in size.

Toward the end of the rising time, preheat the oven to 425°F.

Uncover the risen focaccia and brush with the remaining olive oil. Sprinkle with salt if wished – the filling may taste salty enough – then bake for 20–25 minutes until crisp and golden.

Turn out of the pan onto a wire rack (don't be tempted to leave the focaccia in the pan as it will turn very soggy). Eat warm or at room temperature, cut in large squares. If not eating immediately, leave to cool completely, then wrap thoroughly and refrigerate for up to 24 hours. Return to room temperature before serving. The focaccia is not suitable for freezing.

*You can use 1 envelope (2¹/₂ teaspoons) rapid-rise active dry yeast instead of the fresh yeast. Add the dry yeast to all of the flour with the seasonings, then add all the liquid at once and continue with the recipe. If the dough feels dry, work in a little more water; if it is very sticky work in a little extra flour.

Paul Merry carefully places the tall Kulich in his oven.

"THIS *tall, rich, and cake-like kulich is a grand sight," says Paul Merry (see also page 120). Few would disagree. Scented with cardamom, enriched with eggs and butter, flavored with honey, fruit, nuts, and saffron soaked in vodka, the dough is suitably extravagant for the main religious festival of the Orthodox church. The baked kulich is often decorated with a thin glacé icing and "XB" (the Russian letters for "Christ is Risen") made from preserved fruit and nuts. In Russia, kulich is traditionally served with a mixture of cream and curd cheese called* pascha *(which literally means Easter).*

Paul spent six weeks in Russia helping Andrew Whitley (see page 114) to set up a small village bakery based on a wood-fired oven. "Andrew went back to Russia to record a program for the B.B.C. Radio 4. There he met a woman who had a large conventional city bakery, but wanted to set up a small commune-type one near her dacha *in the country. It was an exciting project — there were no power tools, and we used the local building materials and soft red terracotta bricks. We had to get the doors from England. But she got her 20-tray wood-fired oven." Paul picked up a few favorite recipes for his collection, and is rightly proud of this one.*

The risen height of the kulich can be up to three times its width. Tall, narrow, cylindrical molds are difficult to find, so look out for 2-pound coffee cans or the large cans of tomatoes used by caterers. You can also use a deep 6-inch round cake pan extended about 5 inches in height with stiff brown paper or a triple thickness of aluminum foil to make a thick collar around the outside.

The dough has four rises, which helps to give the very fine, cake-like crumb, and can be started a day ahead. There is also a slightly faster alternative method.

Russian Easter kulich

MAKES 1 LARGE CAKE

1¹/₂ 0.6-oz cakes fresh yeast (20g)*

²/₃ cup (150ml) milk (see recipe)

4 cups (500g) unbleached white bread flour

¹/₂ teaspoon saffron strands

2 tablespoons vodka, gently warmed

10 cardamom pods

¹/₄ cup (50ml) clear honey

2 extra large eggs

¹/₈ teaspoon fine sea salt

¹/₂ cup (125g) unsalted butter, at room temperature

¹/₄ cup (50g) vanilla-flavored sugar

¹/₂ cup (75g) golden raisins

¹/₃ cup (50g) raisins

2 tablespoons (25g) finely chopped candied citron peel

finely grated rind of 2 lemons

¹/₃ cup (50g) blanched almonds, finely chopped

a tall cylindrical can or deep 6-inch-round cake pan with paper or foil collar (see recipe introduction), lined with brown paper or buttered parchment paper

For a very moist cake that will keep longer, make a sponge starter: In a medium bowl stir one-fourth (5g) of the yeast with ¹/₃ cup (75ml) of the milk, at room temperature, then mix in 1 cup (125g) of the flour to make a firm dough. Cover tightly with plastic wrap and leave at cool room temperature overnight.

Next morning, warm the rest of the milk until lukewarm, crumble in the rest of the yeast, and stir until smooth. Put ¹/₂ cup (50g) of the remaining flour into a large mixing bowl and work in the milk and yeast mixture followed by the sponge starter. You should have a soft dough. Cover and leave for 1 hour until the surface looks bubbly.

An alternative and quicker method is to omit the sponge starter. Instead, put 1¹/₂ cups (175g) of the flour into a mixing bowl. Heat all the milk to lukewarm, crumble in all the yeast, and stir well, then add to the flour. Beat well with your hand to make a smooth, thick batter. Cover with plastic wrap and leave in a warm spot until spongy-looking and doubled in size – about 1 hour.

While the dough is rising, prepare the remaining ingredients. Crumble the saffron into the vodka, cover, and set aside to infuse (the longer the saffron soaks, the deeper the color and flavor will be, so an overnight soak is ideal). Remove the cardamom seeds from the pods and grind the seeds to a fine powder in a mortar and pestle.

Make sure all the ingredients are at warmish room temperature — warm the honey over low heat; beat the eggs and leave in a warm spot; put the rest of the flour, salt, and ground cardamom into a warmed mixing bowl; make sure the butter is pliable but not oily. The dough is so rich that the yeast and gluten need all the help and encouragement they can get, so warmth is important. Also, this is why the fat, which inhibits the gluten, is added as late as possible.

Mix the warm honey with the sugar and the vodka mixture, then add to the risen dough. Start to work the ingredients together, then add the eggs and mix briefly. Gradually work in the flour and cardamom mixture to make a soft but not sticky

Paul showed me how he makes his wonderfully rich and spicy kulich, a perfect bread for a celebration.

dough. Turn onto a work surface and knead thoroughly for 10 minutes. The dough should feel supple and silky. If it seems tough add a little extra warm milk. Using your hands, squeeze and knead in the butter until evenly distributed.

To incorporate the fruit and nuts, Paul showed me a good trick: Flatten the dough to a large rectangle, then sprinkle over the fruit, peel, lemon rind, and nuts. Cut the dough into three pieces, then stack them up to make a layered tower of dough. Flatten gently to a rectangle again, and repeat. In this way the fruit is easily and evenly distributed, and the gluten doesn't tear.

Clean and lightly oil the mixing bowl, then return the dough to it. Cover tightly and leave to rise in a warm spot until doubled in size – about 1 1/2 hours.

Punch down the risen dough with your knuckles to deflate, and turn out onto a work surface. Shape the dough into a cone: Flatten it out into a rectangle, then roll up like a jelly roll and shape one end to a point. Lower the dough into the can or pan, pointed end first, slowly and carefully to avoid dragging down the lining paper. The dough will settle, and the can should be a third to half full. Cover and leave to rise until at least doubled in size – 1–1 1/2 hours.

Toward the end of the rising time, preheat the oven to 350°F – such a rich dough requires only a moderate oven.

Bake the kulich for about 1 hour until a skewer gently inserted into the center

will come out clean. If it seems to be getting too dark, cover the top with a triple thickness of parchment paper. Leave to cool in the can or pan for 15 minutes, then very gently and gingerly ease the soft, delicate cake onto a wire rack. Cool upright, or, if the cake starts to sag, rest it on its side. When thoroughly cooled you can ice the top of the cake with a thin glacé icing, letting it drizzle down the sides in uneven cascades.

The cake is best eaten within a week (or 5 days if made without the sponge starter). If un-iced, it can be frozen for up to a month.

*You can use 2 teaspoons rapid-rise active dry yeast instead of the fresh yeast. Follow the quick method – without the overnight sponge. Mix the dry yeast with the 1 1/2 cups (175g) flour, work in all the luke-warm milk, and continue with the recipe.

THE *uncrowned queen of the creameries in Cornwall, England, is Rachel Roskilly. Rachel and her husband Joe have farmed the luscious pastureland near Porthoustock (or P'r'oust'ck, as the locals spell it) for nearly 40 years, turning the milk from their herd of Jersey and Guernsey cows into clotted cream as well as rich ice cream. It takes almost 6 quarts of milk with 5.8% butterfat to make just 1 pound of clotted cream.*

Everything is done by hand, and Rachel believes the sweet, nutty quality of the cream comes from their method of working. Straight after milking, the milk, still warm, is poured into small, shallow, stainless steel pans, pasteurized, and then gently heated. "The great thing is slow cooking and quick cooling," claims Rachel. This forms the butter-yellow crusted top, which is then spooned off and potted. If correctly stored — at 40°F — the cream will keep for three weeks. It is so thick and rich it can be spread like butter, and is the traditional partner for scones and homemade strawberry or raspberry jam, to make the classic English "cream tea."

For breakfast on Easter Sunday, Rachel makes this popular village recipe for rich fruit and saffron rolls. Eat these aromatic rolls warm with honey and, of course, clotted cream.

P'r'oust'ck Easter rolls

MAKES 12 ROLLS

a very large pinch of saffron strands

2 tablespoons boiling water

about 11 cups (1.35kg) organic unbleached white bread flour, preferably stoneground

1/2 cup (110g) butter, at room temperature, diced

1/2 cup (110g) lard, at room temperature, diced

1 tablespoon fine sea salt

scant 1 cup (175g) sugar

1 heaped cup (175g) currants

4 0.6-oz cakes fresh yeast (55g)*

3 1/2 cups (820ml) lukewarm water

2 egg yolks

GLAZE:

2 egg yolks

2 tablespoons milk

sugar

several baking sheets, greased

Split and filled with honey and clotted cream, these aromatic rolls are a real treat.

Crumble the saffron into a small heatproof bowl and pour in the boiling water. Cover and leave to infuse overnight.

Put the flour into a large mixing bowl and warm gently in a low oven or airing cupboard. Rub the fats into the flour using the tips of your fingers until the mixture looks like fine crumbs. Stir in the salt, sugar, and currants. Make a well in the center.

Crumble the yeast into a measuring cup, and add the saffron liquid and a few tablespoons of lukewarm water. Stir until smooth, then add the rest of the lukewarm water. Pour into the well in the flour mixture together with the egg yolks. Mix the liquids with your fingers, then gradually work in the flour to make a soft but not sticky dough. If the dough sticks to the bowl or your fingers, work in a little extra flour.

Turn onto a lightly floured work surface and knead thoroughly for 10 minutes — the dough should be very smooth and elastic and feel firmer. Return the dough to the bowl and cover with a damp dish towel or put the bowl into a large plastic bag, oiled inside. Leave to rise until the dough is doubled in size. In a warm kitchen this will take about 1 hour; allow 2 hours at normal room temperature, up to 6 hours in a cool room, overnight in the fridge.

Turn the risen dough onto a floured work surface and punch it down with your knuckles. Divide into 12 equal portions. Shape each into a neat ball, then roll or pat out to a disk about the size of a saucer and about 1/2 inch thick (for a neat shape, cut around a saucer with a sharp knife). Arrange the disks, well apart, on the prepared baking sheets. Using a sharp knife, cut a cross into the surface of each disk. Cover as before and leave to rise until doubled in size — the time will depend on the temperature of the dough and of the room, so allow 30 minutes to 1 1/2 hours.

Toward the end of the rising time, preheat the oven to 425°F.

For the glaze, mix the egg yolks and milk, and carefully brush over the top of the risen rolls. Don't let the glaze drip down the sides or the rolls will rise unevenly. Sprinkle with a little sugar. Bake for about 15 minutes until golden and firm. Serve warm, split open and buttered, or with honey and clotted or whipped cream.

The rolls are best eaten within 24 hours, or they can be toasted. Once thoroughly cooled, they can be frozen for up to a month.

*You can use 4 envelopes (3 tablespoons) rapid-rise active dry yeast instead of the fresh. Mix the dry yeast into the warmed flour before the fats, then continue with the recipe.

There is a fair amount of butter in Christine's recipe for this traditional plum bread, and she rubs it into the flour before adding the dried fruit.

CHRISTINE SHERRIFF *(see also page 156) has been making bread since she was nine, and bakes all the bread for the house using her local flour, organic and stoneground, from the Maud Foster mill in Boston, Lincolnshire, England (see page 30). This is her favorite recipe for plum bread — each baker has her own recipe, varying the proportions of fruit to dough, with more or less sugar or fat, adding or omitting spice. She told us that until the Second World War, farmers' wives would each bake a dozen especially rich loaves — representing the 12 days of Christmas — to give as presents.*

The flour should be gently warmed, so leave the bag in a warm spot in the kitchen overnight (or in an airing cupboard) — this helps the rich heavy dough to rise well.

Lincolnshire Christmas plum bread

MAKES 2 MEDIUM LOAVES

1 1/2 0.6-oz cakes fresh yeast (25g)*

1 cup (200g) firmly packed light brown sugar

1 3/4 cups (400ml) mixed lukewarm milk and water

7 cups (800g) organic unbleached white bread flour, warmed

1 teaspoon fine sea salt

1/2 teaspoon freshly grated nutmeg

2/3 cup (150g) butter, diced

1 1/2 cups (225g) currants

1 1/2 cups (225g) golden raisins

2 tablespoons (25g) finely chopped mixed candied peel

1 large egg

2 loaf pans, 8 1/2 x 4 1/2 x 2 1/2 inches, well greased

Crumble the yeast into a bowl, and stir in 1 tablespoon of the sugar and about a third of the milk mixture. Leave in a warm spot while preparing the rest of the mixture.

Mix the warm flour with the salt and nutmeg in a large mixing bowl. Add the diced butter and rub in using the tips of your fingers until the mixture resembles fine crumbs. Stir in the rest of the sugar, the fruit, and the chopped peel. Beat the egg into the rest of the milk mixture and add to the bowl with the yeast liquid. Mix to make a very soft and slightly sticky dough. If the dough is stiff and hard to work, add a little more liquid; if it is very sticky work in a little more flour.

Turn out onto a floured work surface and knead thoroughly for 10 minutes until elastic and silky-textured. Return the dough to the bowl and cover tightly with plastic wrap, or put the bowl into a large plastic bag. Leave to rise in a warm spot until doubled in size — about 2 hours.

Punch down the risen dough to deflate, then turn out onto a work surface and divide into two equal pieces. Gently shape each piece into a neat loaf to fit your pans. Put the dough into the pans, cover, and leave to rise as before until almost doubled in size — about 1 hour.

Toward the end of the rising time, preheat the oven to 375°F.

Uncover the loaves and bake for about 40 minutes until they are golden brown and sound hollow when unmolded and tapped underneath. Turn out of the pans and cool on a wire rack, then wrap and keep for a day before slicing and eating spread with butter.

The bread is best eaten within a week. Once thoroughly cooled, it can be frozen for up to a month.

* You can use 4 teaspoons rapid-rise active dry yeast instead of the fresh yeast. Mix the dry yeast with the flour, salt, and nutmeg. Rub in the butter, then add all the sugar, fruit, and peel, followed by all of the milk mixture combined with the egg. Continue with the recipe.

THIS *intriguing recipe comes from Christine Sherriff, who runs a rural studies center from her farmhouse near Moorby in Lincolnshire, England. She made this recipe for the Lincolnshire Show:"It's a nineteenth-century recipe for a yeasted cake layered with fruit — rather like a giant Eccles cake, but made with a rich bread dough rather than flaky pastry. It doesn't look like much, but it is very good to eat." It was once made to celebrate the season of Pentecost, which starts on Whit Sunday, the seventh Sunday after Easter. Church followers wore white and exchanged gifts of food — this was one for the parish priest.*

Whitsuntide cake

MAKES 1 MEDIUM CAKE

DOUGH:

2 cups (230g) organic unbleached white bread
   flour

$^1/_4$ teaspoon fine sea salt

$^1/_2$ cup (115g) butter

6 tablespoons milk

$^2/_3$ 0.6-oz cake fresh yeast (10g)*

1 tablespoon lukewarm water

lightly beaten egg white for brushing

To make the dough, combine the flour and salt in a mixing bowl, then rub in half of the butter using the tips of your fingers until the mixture resembles fine crumbs. Gently melt the rest of the butter with the milk, and leave to cool until lukewarm. Crumble the yeast into a small bowl and cream to a smooth paste with the water, then combine with the milk mixture. Add the liquid to the flour and work the mixture until it comes together to make a soft and slightly sticky dough.

Knead the dough for 5 minutes – either in the bowl if it is large enough or on a work surface. The dough should feel very pliable. Leave to rise in the bowl, tightly covered with plastic wrap, until doubled in size – about 1 hour in a warm kitchen.

Meanwhile, prepare the filling. Put the currants, sugar, butter, spices, and water into a large, heavy-based pan and cook very gently over low heat for 15–20 minutes until thick, sticky, and aromatic. Remove from the heat and stir in the egg yolk.

Punch down the risen dough to deflate, then divide into four equal pieces. Roll out each piece to a thin rectangle about 9 x 7$^1/_2$ inches. Put one sheet of dough onto the prepared baking sheet and spread with one-third of the fruit filling, leaving a $^3/_4$-inch border of dough all around. Brush the border with beaten egg white, then cover with a second sheet of dough. Gently press down to squeeze out any air bubbles, pressing a little more firmly on the border to seal the dough edges. Add a second layer of filling.

FILLING:

1 cup (150g) currants

³/₄ cup (150g) firmly packed dark brown
    sugar

4 tablespoons (50g) butter

¹/₄ teaspoon freshly grated nutmeg

¹/₄ teaspoon ground allspice

2 teaspoons water

1 egg yolk

GLAZE:

beaten egg

sugar (optional)

a large baking sheet, well greased

Repeat until all the dough and filling have been used, ending with a final covering of dough — you should have four layers of dough and three of fruit. Cover lightly with plastic wrap or a clean, dry dish towel, and leave to rise for about 30 minutes (the cake will only rise slightly).

Meanwhile, preheat the oven to 375°F.

Bake the cake for 25 minutes, then remove from the oven and brush with beaten egg to glaze. Lightly sprinkle with sugar if you wish, though this is not traditional. Return to the oven and bake for a further 15–20 minutes until lightly golden. Gently loosen the cake from the baking sheet and transfer to a wire rack. Eat warm, plain or with cream or ice cream.

The cake is best eaten within 5 days, and the flavor improves on keeping. It doesn't freeze very well.

*You can use 2 teaspoons rapid-rise active dry yeast instead of the fresh yeast. Mix the dry yeast with the flour and salt, then work in the milk and butter liquid. Continue with the recipe.

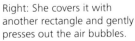

Above: Christine spreads a third of the fruit filling on the first rectangle of dough and brushes the border with egg white.

Right: She covers it with another rectangle and gently presses out the air bubbles.

Above: After the final layer of dough is added, the cake is left to rise.

157

L IKE MANY EMIGRÉS, our friend, Swedish baron Otto Stromfelt, feels most home-sick and nostalgic at Christmas time. This chef and restaurateur waxes lyrical about the feasts of Christmas past in his native Sweden, and when he got onto the subject of bread we were caught up in his enthusiasm – and found ourselves on a plane to Stockholm in time for the festival of St. Lucia, which is on December 13.

Christmas in Sweden

The history of St. Lucia's Day is complex. Over the centuries it has absorbed a pagan winter solstice festival, the feast of St. Nicholas (which was prohibited at the Reformation), preparation for Christmas, and a modern festival of light. Lucia proces-sions – a fair-haired girl wearing a white dress, red sash, and crown of candles, followed by her white-clad young attendants – now wind through most Swedish towns early on the morning. After carols and Christmas songs come coffee and saffron-flavored sweet rolls called Lucia cats (*Lussekatts*). Saffron was once an integral part of Swedish cuisine, because the autumn crocus from which the stamens are taken grew on the island of Gotland, southeast of Stockholm. Today saffron is imported, and is expensive, so it is saved for special occasions such as this one.

Otto told us what country breads to look for. They are usually made with rye and barley flour, plenty of yeast, little salt, and some sugar. The result – well-flavored, light-textured, with a soft crust – is normally served with salted butter.

The recipes that follow come from three bakers we met in Sweden. Pastry chef Beatrice Grill and her partner Per Saletti, also a chef, run a catering business from their home in a remote hamlet north of Uppsala. Beatrice has worked for the Ikea chain of furniture stores for many years, first training their restaurant chefs, now as a traveling troubleshooter, ensuring the restaurants around the world serve authentic Swedish dishes and don't cut corners. She told us baking was an important part of the Christmas celebrations, even for families that don't bake during the rest of the year. She and Per entertain friends and family in the tiny eighteenth-century soldier's hut at the end of their garden. It was inhabited, unmodernized, until the Swedish equivalent of the National Guard was disbanded recently.

Folk music fills the air at the Skansen museum in Stockholm during the St. Lucia fair, and there are scores of tiny stalls selling traditional crafts and foods for the festive season.

The lights in Beatrice and Per's house were very welcoming on a mid-December afternoon.

Baker Magnus Johansson made 4000 Lucia cats for St. Lucia's Day last year, but even so – because they were voted Stockholm's best by a newpaper in a blind tasting – he could not keep up with the demand. He is in charge of the renowned Vete-Katten coffee shop and pâtisserie in Kungsgaten, "the famous old bakery in Sweden," as he put it. It manages to combine old-fashioned charm and Swedish customs with the glamor of a Parisian pâtisserie. His 12 bakers and pastry chefs now bake bread and pastries three times a day so that the evening shopper doesn't have to buy something that was fresh at dawn.

Magnus is proud of the Swedish tradition of baking: "What we have we do very well, and the favorite traditional breads and cakes are still in great demand at Christmas. Not everyone wants international pastries and French bread." He wants to provide his customers with choice and quality – he only uses the finest ingredients available. His outlook reminded me of Jeff Oberweis (see page 52), who also champions the best of traditional, local recipes, giving them equal status with the better-known stars from other countries.

We met our third baker, Ulf Edlund, at Skansen, the vast open-air museum in Stockholm, which celebrates the history of the Swedish people – peasants and ethnic minorities rather than kings. Its collection of original buildings, houses, and farmsteads from all over the country is also the site of the largest, and most charming, Christmas fair, with traditional market stalls selling hand-made Christmas tree decorations and wooden toys, as well as folk music, games, dancing, and enticingly aromatic festive foods including Lucia cats, grilled herrings, braised red cabbage, and a very heady *gluhwein* served with *pepparkakor* (gingersnaps).

Each stall at the Skansen Christmas fair has a painted wooden sign. This one says "Christmas Gifts."

DISCOVERING *this wonderful bread was alone worth the price of the air tickets to Sweden. It is a festival of textures and flavors: crunchy, moist, spicy, fruity, slightly tart, and slightly sweet. Beatrice Grill says it is an old family recipe from the North (I've also heard of this recipe in northern Russia). Her mother and grandmothers would always take along* vanskapsbrød *when they visited friends or family for a special meal — it is also called "friendship bread." The bread is meant for the smörgåsbord, or table of mixed foods, to which each visitor contributes a dish: cured herrings or salmon or meat, cheese, seafood, salami, pickles. Indeed, Beatrice served the bread warm from the oven for a late lunch, with salted butter, a powerful salami, and an 18-month-old Cheddar cheese. This bread really holds its own with strong flavors. If you make nothing else next Christmas, make this.*

The recipe is in two parts and seems a lot of work, as you need to start the mixture the night before, but actual preparation time is short. It calls for lingonberries or cloudberries preserved in a thick, tart, unsweetened conserve, which is available from Swedish food stores, Ikea, and some large supermarkets around Christmas. I have also made the bread very successfully with dried cranberries. A lot of yeast is used: the heavy, sticky dough needs it to prevent the texture of the bread from being dense and heavy. But don't worry — the bread does not taste yeasty.

Vanskapsbrød

MAKES 4 SMALL LOAVES

STAGE ONE:

$^2/_3$ cup (85g) chopped rye berries

$^2/_3$ cup (85g) chopped wheat grains or berries

1 tablespoon fine sea salt

1 tablespoon cumin seeds

scant 1 cup (200ml) lingonberry or cloudberry conserve or $^3/_4$ cup (115g) dried cranberries

$^1/_3$ cup (50g) raisins

scant $^1/_2$ cup (65g) flax seeds

$6^1/_2$ tablespoons (40g) wheatgerm

1 $^3/_4$ cups (400ml) lukewarm water

STAGE TWO:

6 0.6-oz cakes fresh yeast (100g)*

2 cups (500ml) lukewarm water

about $8^1/_2$ cups (1kg) unbleached white bread flour, preferably stoneground

2 large or 4 small baking sheets, well greased or lined with parchment paper

Put all of the ingredients for stage one in a medium-sized mixing bowl and stir gently to mix. Cover the bowl and leave to soak for 5–12 hours, or until you have a thick, porridge-like mush.

For the second stage, crumble the yeast into a very large mixing bowl and mix to a smooth liquid with about a third of the lukewarm water. Stir the remaining water into the soaked mixture from stage one, then add this to the yeast liquid and combine well. Gradually work in enough of the flour – 6 cups (750g) – to make a very soft, sticky, heavy dough that leaves the sides of the bowl.

Turn the dough out onto a heavily floured work surface and knead for a couple of minutes. Cut the dough into four equal pieces. Take one piece at a time, keeping the others lightly covered with a dry dish towel, and knead it gently, gradually working in enough extra flour so the dough just holds its shape – it will still feel soft and slightly sticky. With floured hands, shape the dough into a neat ball about $6^1/_2$ inches across and place on the prepared baking sheet (the loaves can also be risen in cloth-lined baskets or in greased loaf pans, about $8^1/_2$ x $4^1/_2$ x $2^1/_2$ inches). Leave to rise in a warm spot until doubled in size – 30 minutes to 1 hour.

Toward the end of the rising time, preheat the oven to its hottest setting.

Score the top of the risen loaves in a diamond pattern, then put into the oven. Immediately reduce the temperature to 425°F and bake for about 20 minutes until the loaves are lightly browned and sound hollow when tapped underneath. Transfer to a wire rack.

Eat warm the same day, or toasted. Once thoroughly cooled, the loaves can be frozen for up to a month.

* You can use 6 envelopes (5 tablespoons) rapid-rise active dry yeast instead of the fresh yeast. Mix the dry yeast with 4 cups (500g) of the flour. Put all the water into the large bowl with the soaked mixture, and work in the flour and yeast mixture and then the rest of the flour. Continue with the recipe.

In the former soldier's hut she uses for entertaining, Beatrice sets her St. Lucia table. In the foreground is Vanskapsbrød, or friendship bread, behind is saffron cake, and, on the right, in the basket, are Lussekatts (see recipe overleaf).

T HIS *festive cake from Beatrice Grill is colored a beautiful golden-yellow with saffron. Beatrice makes it at Christmas time to serve with good strong coffee.*

Swedish saffron cake

MAKES AN 8 1/2-INCH CAKE

14 tablespoons (200g) slightly salted butter or margarine

2/3 cup (150ml) milk

1 teaspoon saffron strands

2 extra large eggs, at room temperature

1 cup (200g) sugar

1 2/3 cups (230g) unbleached all-purpose flour

2 teaspoons baking powder

confectioners' sugar for dusting

a springform cake pan, about 8 1/2 inches in diameter, buttered, bottom-lined, and sprinkled with dry bread crumbs

Heat the butter or margarine with the milk until melted, then crumble in the saffron and cover the pan. Leave to infuse for 1 hour over very low heat or on a rack above the stove.

Meanwhile, preheat the oven to 350°F.

Using a hand whisk or electric mixer, beat the eggs with the sugar until very thick and light, and the mixture leaves a visible ribbon-like trail on the surface when the whisk is lifted. Gently stir in the just-warm milk mixture. Sift the flour with the baking powder, then sift again into the egg mixture and fold in gently using a large metal spoon until thoroughly combined.

Pour into the prepared pan. Bake for 30–35 minutes until light brown and firm to the touch. Unmold and leave to cool on a wire rack. Serve dusted with confectioners' sugar.

The cake is best eaten within 3 days. It does not freeze very well.

*S*AFFRON *bread — sweet, soft golden, and rich — is traditionally formed into "S"shapes for the Swedish festival of St. Lucia. This version of* **Lussekatts***, or Lucia cats, is based on the Vete-Katten bakery's recipe, which adds raisins to the enriched dough.*

Lussekatts

MAKES 16 CAKES

1 teaspoon saffron strands

scant 1 cup (200ml) light cream or half-and-half

3 0.6-oz cakes fresh yeast (50g)*

2 tablespoons lukewarm water

1/2 cup (100g) slightly salted butter, melted

1 extra large egg, at room temperature, beaten

1/3 cup (60g) sugar

1/2 teaspoon fine sea salt

1/4 cup (40g) raisins

about 4 cups (450g) unbleached white bread flour

beaten egg for glazing

several baking sheets, well greased or lined with parchment paper

At the Skansen fair, the aromatic saffron breads — Lussekatts *and* Karlsbrød *— sell out rapidly.*

Preheat the oven to 350°F.

Crumble the saffron strands into a small ovenproof dish or ramekin and toast in the heated oven for about 10 minutes until darkened but not scorched.

Meanwhile, gently warm the cream in a small pan. Stir in the toasted saffron, cover, and leave to infuse for 1–2 hours.

Crumble the yeast into a large mixing bowl and stir in the water followed by the saffron-flavored cream and the butter, both of which should also be just lukewarm. When thoroughly combined, beat in the egg, sugar, salt, and raisins, using your hand or a wooden spoon. With your hand, gradually work in the flour to make a smooth, soft, slightly sticky dough. Knead the dough in the bowl for 2 minutes, then cover with a damp dish towel, or put the bowl into an oiled plastic bag. Leave until the dough has doubled in size – 30–60 minutes depending on the room temperature.

Turn out the risen dough onto a floured work surface and knead thoroughly for 10 minutes until satiny. Work in extra flour as necessary if the dough is very sticky; it should feel firmer than it did after the first kneading. Cover the dough with the upturned bowl or with a slightly damp dish towel and leave to rest for 15 minutes.

Divide the dough into 16 equal pieces. With your hands, shape and roll each piece into a sausage about 8 inches long, then form into a neat, tight "S" shape. Arrange well apart on the prepared baking sheets. Cover lightly with a dry dish towel and leave to rise until doubled in size – about 1 hour at kitchen temperature.

Toward the end of the rising time, preheat the oven to 400°F.

Carefully brush the shapes with beaten egg, taking care not to glue them to the sheet (this will prevent the dough from rising). Bake for 12–15 minutes until golden brown. Cool on wire racks.

The Lucia cats are best eaten warm the same day. Once thoroughly cooled, they can be frozen for up to a month.

* You can use 3 envelopes (7 1/2 teaspoons) rapid-rise active dry yeast instead of the fresh yeast. Mix the dry yeast with the first cup (100g) of flour you intend to add to the saffron, egg, and raisin mixture. Work in, then continue with the recipe.

Opposite: St Lucia arrives in style at Skansen (far left). The girl chosen to represent the saint wears a white dress, red sash, and a crown of candles.

THE *same saffron dough used for Lucia cats, with an almond filling, is made into a wreath or crown shape for Christmas. It is decorated with sliced almonds and small sugar pearls called* parlsocker; *crushed sugar cubes can be used instead.*

Vetebrod is another sweet bread made from the Lussekatts *saffron dough. For vetebrod the dough is spiced with ground cardamom, rolled around a spicy apple and cardamom filling, and shaped into a long braid.*

Karlsbrød

MAKES 1 LARGE RING

saffron dough as for *Lussekatts* (see opposite), made without raisins
beaten egg for glazing
sugar pearls or crushed sugar
sliced almonds

FILLING:
7 oz (200g) almond paste
1 egg
1 tablespoon sugar
¹/₄ cup (40g) raisins or chopped toasted almonds

a baking sheet, lined with parchment paper

Make the dough, leave to rise, and then knead for 10 minutes as in the *Lussekatts* recipe. Leave to rest for 30 minutes.

Meanwhile, make the filling by combining the almond paste, egg, and sugar in a food processor. Chill until firm.

Roll out the dough to a rectangle 12 x 26 inches and spread with the almond mixture. Sprinkle evenly with the raisins or chopped toasted almonds. Roll up tightly from a long side, like a jelly roll. Pinch the seam to seal, then cut the roll in half along its length using a large sharp knife. Twist the two halves together, then shape into a neat ring, carefully joining the ends by overlapping them. Transfer the ring to the prepared baking sheet. Leave to rise, covered with a dry dish towel, until doubled in size – about 1 hour.

Toward the end of the rising time, preheat the oven to 400°F.

Lightly brush the ring with beaten egg to glaze and sprinkle with sugar pearls or crushed sugar and sliced almonds. Bake for 20 minutes, then reduce the oven temperature to 350°F and bake for a further 10–15 minutes until firm. If the wreath is browning too quickly, cover with wax paper. Cool on a wire rack.

The bread is best eaten within a couple of days of baking, and tastes nicest warm. It does not freeze successfully.

Karlsbrød, filled with almond paste, is traditionally baked in the shape of a Christmas wreath.

THIS *is a spicy, aromatic bread made only at Christmas time in Sweden, when it is served with salted butter, cold ham, and mustard. Some families dip slices of* vortbrød *into the hot stock left from cooking the celebration ham. The rye flour dough was traditionally mixed with* vort — *beer mash from the local brewery — and flavored with the peel of* pomeransskal *(a type of bitter orange). Nowadays a good stout or ale is more often used, and the* pomeransskal *either omitted or replaced by candied citron peel.*

Vortbrød

MAKES 1 LARGE LOAF

1 *pomeransskal* (see recipe introduction) or
   1 oz (25g) candied citron peel

3 0.6-oz cakes fresh yeast (50g)*

1/2 cup (100ml) lukewarm water

1 cup (200ml) stout, gently heated to
   lukewarm

2 cups (200g) rye flour, preferably stoneground

2 1/2 cups (300g) unbleached white bread flour,
   preferably stoneground

4 tablespoons (50g) slightly salted butter

3 tablespoons malt extract syrup

2 teaspoons ground ginger

1 teaspoon ground cloves

1 teaspoon fine sea salt

beaten egg for glazing, if needed

a baking sheet, well greased or lined with
   parchment paper

*You can use 3 envelopes (7 1/2 teaspoons) rapid-rise active dry yeast instead of the fresh yeast. Mix the dry yeast with the rye flour and the third of the white flour, then add the lukewarm liquids. Continue with the recipe.

If using a *pomeransskal*, simmer in water for 10 minutes until soft; drain, saving the cooking liquid. Pare the colored part of the peel off thinly and mince it. If using candied citron peel, rinse it thoroughly, pat dry on paper towels, and mince, using a little flour if necessary to prevent it from sticking together. Set aside.

Crumble the yeast into a large mixing bowl and work in the water and stout until smooth. Work in the rye flour and a third of the white flour to make a thick, sticky paste. Cover and leave for about 1 hour until spongy-looking and doubled in size.

Gently melt the butter with the malt extract and spices, then leave until lukewarm. Mix into the dough with the salt and *pomeransskal* or peel. Gradually work in the rest of the flour to make a soft but not sticky dough.

Turn out onto a floured work surface and knead thoroughly for 10 minutes, adding only enough extra flour to stop the dough from sticking. It should be very smooth and silky, slightly soft, but firm enough to maintain a good shape. Shape into an oval loaf about 12 inches long and put onto the prepared baking sheet. Cover loosely and leave to rise until the loaf is doubled in size — about 1 hour at kitchen temperature.

Toward the end of the rising time, preheat the oven to 425°F.

Brush the loaf with some of the reserved *pomeransskal* cooking liquid (or a little beaten egg), then prick with a fork down the center of the loaf. Bake for 30–35 minutes until a good golden brown and the loaf sounds hollow when tapped underneath. Transfer to a wire rack, cover with a clean, dry dish towel (this will give the characteristic soft crust), and leave to cool.

The bread is best eaten within 4 days. Once thoroughly cooled, it can be frozen for up to a month.

The coffee shop at the Vete-Katten bakery in Stockholm has an old-fashioned Swedish atmosphere.

THIS *very rich bread from Patrick LePort (see also page 103) is made with* fruit confits *(preserved whole fruits), so popular in southern France at Christmas time. Eat on its own, or with cheese. The very long rising time, 12–16 hours, is needed because the butter in the recipe slows down the action of the sourdough starter.*

Christmas bread with fruits confits

MAKES 1 SMALL LOAF

³/₄ cup (90g) organic unbleached white bread flour

3 tablespoons (20g) organic wholegrain flour

¹/₄ cup (60ml) lukewarm still spring water

4 teaspoons lukewarm organic milk

¹/₂ teaspoon fine sea salt

2 oz (60g) soft-dough sourdough starter (see page 49)

1 tablespoon firmly packed organic brown sugar

3 tablespoons (40g) organic unsalted butter

¹/₃ cup (60g) organic raisins

¹/₂ cup (80g) organic *fruits confits*, chopped

2 tablespoons (20g) organic almonds, toasted and chopped, plus sliced almonds to finish

a baking sheet

Mix together the flours, water, milk, salt, and sourdough starter to make a soft but not sticky dough. If necessary, work in a little extra flour as the dough should keep its shape and not stick to your hands or the bowl. Knead the dough thoroughly for 8 minutes until elastic, letting it rest for 2 minutes halfway through, then cover and leave to rise for 1 hour.

Gently work in the remaining ingredients. When thoroughly combined, shape the dough into a ball and dust with rice flour or cake flour. Using a thin rolling pin or the handle of a wooden spoon, flatten one side of the ball and roll out this flap until thin and long enough to fold over the rest of the ball of dough. Roll the loaf in sliced almonds, then place it upside down on a floured cloth. Cover with a sheet of plastic wrap, or put into a large plastic bag, and leave to rise for 12 hours or overnight.

The next day, preheat the oven to 325°F. Put a baking sheet into the oven to heat.

Invert the bread onto the hot sheet and bake for about 1 hour until the loaf turns golden brown and sounds hollow when tapped underneath. Cool on a wire rack.

The bread is best eaten within a week, although it can be kept for up to 2 weeks. Once thoroughly cooled, it can be frozen for up to a month.

Rosemary Barron (above) has put her knowledge of Crete and its history to good use in devising this version of one of the island's traditional breads. It is moist and full of flavor, because cheeses, watercress and other vegetables, and spice are worked into the rich dough.

R OSEMARY BARRON'S *book,* Flavors of Greece, *shows how good Greek food can be. She writes with the authority of a cook who knows and loves her subject. She first went to Crete as a student on an archeological dig in the mid-Sixties. "Halfway up a mountain I realized I was eating the same food — seeds and legumes — we were finding evidence of when we were digging. It was a revelation."*

This recipe is based on a Cretan bread that is traditionally made with khorta, *which is a variety of wild greens, plus the island's distinctive olive oil, fresh sheep's cheese, and the local stoneground flour. "Khorta was a major part of the diet for the Greeks of antiquity. It is still an important food for poorer Greeks, and is used by those who love the flavors of the past. If you want to taste this link with antiquity you have to make it yourself: you can't buy this bread." To remove the natural bitterness and soften the tough fibers, the* khorta *is boiled and thoroughly drained before it is added to the dough. When making the bread in England, Rosemary uses watercress instead of* khorta. *While watercress does not have the bitter flavor or texture of* khorta, *it is very nutritious, and adds its own subtle spicy heat to the bread.*

"On Crete the bread is quite dark and very coarse in texture. Our own stoneground flour is much lighter, so I sometimes add oat bran or chickpea flour to give a coarser texture and more dramatic flavor. In England, I use a mixture of stoneground organic whole-wheat flour and wholegrain spelt flour, an ancient wheat variety."

For a midsummer's night party held in a seventeenth-century barn on a Hampshire farm, Rosemary served her intensely flavored, moist bread with a green salad. "It is best with wild greens, olives, and Mediterranean cheeses or marinated fish. But it is really a meal in itself rather than an everyday, all-purpose bread."

Midsummer watercress bread

MAKES 2 MEDIUM LOAVES

DOUGH:

1 tablespoon strong-flavored Greek honey (try Hymettus)

1/3 cup lukewarm water

1 1/2 0.6-oz cakes fresh yeast (20g)*

4 tablespoons robust extra virgin olive oil (Cretan or Greek)

1 teaspoon fine sea salt

1 large egg

1/2 cup (125ml) lukewarm buttermilk, sheep's milk, or plain yogurt

1 2/3 cups (200g) spelt flour

about 1 3/4 cups (200g) stoneground whole-wheat flour

TO FINISH:

4 tablespoons extra virgin olive oil

1 small celery stalk, finely minced

1 large onion, minced

5 cups (300g) watercress

1 teaspoon freshly ground cumin

1/2 teaspoon fine sea salt

a squeeze of lemon juice

2/3 cup (140g) cottage cheese, rubbed through a sieve

1/4 cup (25g) ewe's milk feta cheese, crumbled

2 loaf pans, about 8 1/2 x 4 1/2 x 2/2 inches, well greased with olive oil

Combine the honey and lukewarm water in a small bowl. Crumble in the yeast and whisk until completely dispersed. In another bowl, whisk together the olive oil, salt, egg, and lukewarm buttermilk (or sheep's milk or yogurt).

Put the spelt flour into a large warmed mixing bowl and make a well in the center. Pour in the yeast mixture and the buttermilk mixture, and work the spelt flour into the liquids. Gradually work in enough of the whole-wheat flour to make a just firm and pliable dough — it should be easy to work, not stiff or dry.

Turn out onto a work surface and knead thoroughly for 10 minutes until elastic. Return to the bowl. Cover with a damp dish towel or plastic wrap and leave to rise in a warm spot until doubled in size – about 2 hours.

Meanwhile, heat half of the olive oil in a sauté pan and gently sauté the celery and onion, stirring occasionally, until a good golden brown — about 20 minutes.

Wash and thoroughly drain the watercress. Pick the leaves and tender sprigs from the stems; set aside. Mince the stems and add to the pan. Sauté for 3 minutes, then add the cumin. Stir and fry for a minute, then add the salt. Coarsely chop the watercress leaves and sprigs, and add to the pan. Sauté for no more than 30 seconds, tossing and stirring the contents. Remove from the heat, sprinkle with the lemon juice, and leave to cool until lukewarm.

Punch down the risen dough. Add the cheeses and the watercress mixture, and very gently squeeze and knead until just mixed — the dough will be soft and slightly sticky. Divide the dough in half and put a piece into each prepared pan. Press down to give an even shape — the pan should be half filled. Cover with a dry dish towel and leave in a warm place until doubled in size — about 1 hour. Do not over-rise.

Toward the end of the rising time, preheat the oven to 375°F.

Bake the risen bread for 10 minutes, then brush lightly with the remaining olive oil and reduce the oven temperature to 350°F. Bake for a further 35–45 minutes until the unmolded bread sounds hollow when tapped underneath. Turn out and cool on a wire rack. The bread will sink on cooling.

Eat warm within 2 days of baking (reheat in the oven preheated to 350°F). Once thoroughly cooled, the bread can be frozen for up to a month, but may be a little solid when thawed.

*You can use 4 teaspoons rapid-rise active dry yeast instead of the fresh yeast. Mix the dry yeast with the spelt flour, then work in the honey mixture and the buttermilk mixture. Continue with the recipe.

A traditional part of the Sardinian wedding ceremony is the blessing of special loaves and ornately decorated breads called pani de sa sposa.

WE HAD AN ADDRESS, but there was no sign in the narrow street to indicate which house was the bakery. We decided to follow our noses.

"*Bello profumo*?" four voices chorus as we open the door and enter the tiny bakery of Tzia Matilda. We sniff appreciatively. The rich smell comes from the oven where fresh walnut shells and almond skins have been added to the fire, next to which is a batch of recently baked amaretti cakes.

A Sardinian wedding

As is the custom on Sardinia, the four bakers are women, three generations of one family. Barbara Ghiani, who admits to being over 80, has been baking bread since she was five years old and had to stand on a chair to reach the table. "As far back as anyone can remember, my grandmothers have been bakers in this village. Our men have all been shepherds. Sometimes we let them help with the fire, but they are not allowed near the dough." Her daughter Mariella and granddaughters Daniele and Simona Contu do the baking. Her son-in-law Giovanni makes the scufflers to sweep out the oven and brings in the olive twigs and scented brushwood.

The women bake bread only on Saturdays, and they bake to order. "Our bread lasts a week. The other days we make small almond cakes and pastries." They make *coccoi*, *ladixedda cun 'erda* (see page 171) – also called *gerda* – for special meals and parties, and their famous wedding breads, the delicate and ornate *pani de sa sposa*.

"We make one dough for all our breads. It's based on a piece of dough saved from last Saturday's batch, which is what gives the bread flavor and helps it to keep for many days. For *coccoi* and *gerda* we add fresh yeast, but we don't want the wedding breads to rise much."

Signora Ghiani always starts the dough on Friday evening. When she arrives 12 hours later, the fire is being lit, and her daughter and granddaughters are hard at work. Unlike many bakeries we have visited there is a lot of laughter and chatting. The women evidently enjoy baking together. They spend several hours shaping and decorating the wedding breads. It is painstaking work. After a lot of instruction I was allowed to help, but I felt I had stumbled into a couturier's *atelier* rather than a bakery.

Some of the wedding breads are blessed in church during the marriage service and some are put onto the wedding table – both as decoration and to eat for luck. The bride also keeps some breads as good luck symbols for the future. Simone explained that in the past people were so poor that they couldn't afford wedding presents, so they made decorations out of bread to give instead.

*S*IGNORA GHIANI *uses a mixture of local flours to achieve the results she is looking for. This recipe is the nearest I could get to her blend. As with the recipe for Sardinian* civraxiu *(page 111), you can mix Italian "00" flour (used for pasta) with fine semolina and white bread flour, or replace the two durum wheat flours with 2¹/₂ cups (300g) Italian-style flour. The quantity of water will vary slightly depending on the flours used — aim for a dough that is firm enough to mold.*

Sardinian wedding breads

MAKES 18–20 SMALL BREADS,
DEPENDING ON SIZE

1³/₄ cups (200g) coarse semolina flour

³/₄ cup (100g) fine semolina flour

7 cups (800g) unbleached white bread flour

3¹/₂ oz (100g) saved-dough starter (see previous page), at room temperature

about 2¹/₂ cups (600ml) lukewarm water

2 teaspoons fine sea salt

many baking sheets

Three generations of women – Signora Ghiani (top right), her daughter Mariella, and granddaughters Daniele and Simona – work an entire day preparing the breads for a wedding. I was allowed to help, but Mariella's husband was only permitted to stoke the fire. The decorative shapes made included a cross, a dove, fish, and anything considered romantic.

Mix the flours together and warm gently. Rinse out a large mixing bowl with warm water, then dry. Put the saved dough into the bowl, add half the water, and work together. Gradually work in enough of the flour to make a slightly soft dough. Knead the dough in the bowl for 5 minutes, using your knuckles to really work the dough. Sprinkle with a little more of the flour, then cover with a clean, dry cloth. Wrap the bowl completely in a thick blanket or plenty of newspaper. Leave overnight for the dough to double in size.

Uncover the dough and add the salt. Gradually work in the rest of the flour and water to make a fairly firm dough. Turn out of the bowl and knead thoroughly for 10 minutes. Take a small quantity of the dough to work with at a time. Keep the rest covered and warm – if the dough cools, it stiffens and is not pliable enough to mold.

The breads can be shaped and decorated any way you wish. You will need a small sharp knife to cut and slit the dough, a pastry wheel or ravioli cutter to give fluted edges, and tiny nail scissors to snip the decorations. Most designs start as a thin rope of dough.

Shape the rope into a heart, pinching the ends together, then make another heart and link with the first. The hearts can be decorated with tiny petals or flowers made from the dough, and with a pattern of snips made with the scissors. Other shapes to make are: interlinked wedding rings with initials, love knots, coronets, bracelets, doves, even a favorite animal.

Arrange the shaped breads on a floured sheet and leave to rise for about 2 hours. They should only rise by about half their original size, not double in volume. If the dough rises too much, the design is lost.

Toward the end of the rising time, preheat the oven to 400°F.

Gently arrange the breads on the baking sheets. If necessary re-define the shapes by snipping with the scissors. Bake for 15–20 minutes, depending on the size and thickness of the shapes. Leave to cool on a wire rack.

The breads are best eaten soon after baking, but can be frozen. As keepsakes, they will last for years, if stored in a cool, dry atmosphere.

L ADIXEDDA CUN 'ERDA *is the local name for white bread rolls flavored with cooked pork and pork fat, elsewhere called* costedda cun gerda. *At Tzia Matilda, they make an exotic version for parties, flavoring the pork mixture with fresh orange and lemon, and plenty of seasoning. It reminded me of a savory lardy cake. Sometimes they add fresh fava beans from the garden, or black olives marinated in herbs and olive oil. This bread is very good warm with salad or soup.*

The pork mixture can be made up to 5 days in advance, and stored in the fridge.

Tzia Matilda's savoury bread rolls

MAKES 12 ROLLS

1 quantity of Sardinian Wedding Breads dough
  (see opposite)
1¹/₂ 0.6-oz cakes fresh yeast (25g)*

PORK MIXTURE:
1 lb (450g) fresh pork side
3 tablespoons olive oil
3 tablespoons water
a strip of orange peel
grated rind of ¹/₂ lemon
grated rind of ¹/₂ orange
fine sea salt and ground pepper to taste

several baking sheets lined with parchment
  paper

Preheat the oven to 300°F.

Finely dice the pork, discarding any bones, but leaving on the skin. Put into a heavy casserole with the oil, water, and strip of orange peel. Bring to a boil on top of the stove, then cover tightly. Cook in the oven for 2–3 hours, stirring occasionally and adding more water as necessary to prevent the mixture from sticking. The pork should be a nice crisp, golden brown, with plenty of rendered fat.

Leave to cool until warm, then remove the strip of orange peel. Stir in the grated lemon and orange rind, and season to taste. Turn into a small bowl, and press down the meat so the fat comes to the surface. When completely cold, cover tightly and store in the fridge. Bring back to room temperature before using.

Make the dough as given, adding the yeast dispersed in 1 tablespoon of water when you add the last of the measured water. Knead for 10 minutes, then return the dough to the bowl. Work in the pork mixture. The mixture is very heavy, sticky, and greasy, but keep on until the pork is thoroughly distributed in the dough. Cover the bowl with a clean, dry cloth and leave in a warm place until the dough is doubled in size – about 2 hours.

Toward the end of the rising time, preheat the oven to 400°F.

Using wet hands, pinch off pieces of dough the size of tennis balls, without punching down or deflating the dough. Gently place on the parchment-lined sheets – don't worry if the dough looks rough and oozing with fat. Leave for 15 minutes.

Bake for 20–25 minutes until browned and the rolls sound hollow when tapped underneath. Cool on a wire rack.

The rolls are best eaten warm within 2 days. They do not freeze very well.

* Active dry yeast is not recommended.

Bibliography

Bailey, Adrian. *The Blessings of Bread*, Paddington Press, London, 1975.

Barron, Rosemary. *The Flavors of Greece*, William Morrow, New York, 1991; Penguin, London, 1994.

Carr, Sister Frances A. *Shaker Your Plate: of Shaker Cooks and Cooking*, Sabbathday Lake, Maine, United Society of Shakers, 1985.

David, Elizabeth. *English Bread and Yeast Cookery*, Penguin, 1979.

Field, Carol. *The Italian Baker*, Harper and Row, New York, 1985.

Floris, Maria. *Bakery – Cakes and Simple Confectionery*, The Cookery Book Club of the Wine and Food Society, London, 1968.

Jaine, Tom. *Making Bread at Home*, George Weidenfeld and Nicolson, London, 1995.

Jaine, Tom. *Building a Wood-Fired Oven for Bread and Pizza*, Prospect Books, Totnes, 1997.

Kirkland, John. *The Modern Baker, Confectioner and Caterer*, The Gresham Publishing Company, London, 1907.

Leader, Daniel and Judith Blahnik. *Bread Alone*, William Morrow, New York, 1993.

Lindsay, Eldress Bertha. *Seasoned with Grace, My Generation of Shaker Cooking*, The Countryman Press, Woodstock, Vermont, 1987.

MacMillan, Norma. *In a Shaker Kitchen*, Simon & Schuster, New York, 1995.

Maisner, Heather and Michael Bateman. *The Sunday Times Book of Real Bread*, Rodale Press Ltd, Bucks, 1982.

Ortiz, Joe. *The Village Baker*, Ten Speed Press, Berkeley, California, 1993.

Ojakangas, Beatrice. *The Great Scandinavian Baking Book*, Little, Brown, Boston, 1988.

Paige, Jeffrey S. *The Shaker Kitchen*, Clarkson N Potter, New York, 1994.

Rambali, Paul. *Boulangerie – the Craft and Culture of Baking in France*, Macmillan, New York, 1994.

Robertson, Laurel. *The Laurel's Kitchen Bread Book – a Guide to Wholegrain Baking*, Random House, New York, 1984.

Roden, Claudia. *The Book of Jewish Food*, Alfred Knopf, New York, 1997; Viking, London, 1997.

Sarkhel, Udit. *The Bombay Brasserie Cookbook*, Pavilion, London, 1997.

Silverton, Nancy. *Breads from the La Brea Bakery*, Villard, New York, 1996.

Skees, Suzanne. *God Among the Shakers*, Hyperion, New York, 1998.

Sreedharan, Das. *Fresh Flavours of India*, Conran Octopus, London, 1999.

Thorne, John. *Outlaw Cook*, North Point Press, Farrar Strauss Giroux, New York, 1992; Prospect Books, Totnes, 1999.

Thorne, John. *Simple Cooking*, as above, 1987.

Wood, Ed. *World Sourdoughs from Antiquity*, Ten Speed Press, Berkeley, California, 1996; London, 1997.

Directory

MILLS

Branscombe Manor Mill and Old Bakery
The mill, owned by the National Trust, is open Sundays 2 to 5p.m. April to October. The Old Bakery tea shop is open daily 11a.m. to 5p.m. Easter to October. Branscombe, Seaton, Devon EX12 3DB, England. Tel (mill) 01392 881 691; (tea shop) 01297 680 333.

Brumwell Milling
Stoneground organic bread flour, rye and spelt flours, cormeal; price list available. 328 East Second Street, Sumner, LA 50674. Tel 319-578-8106.

Butte Creek Mill
Stoneground bread flour, buckwheat flour, cornmeal; price list available. P.O. Box 561, Eagle Point, OR 97524. Tel 503-826-3531.

Cann Mills
Good range of organic and stoneground flours, rye, whole-wheat and Maltstar, all popular with local bakers. Shaftesbury, Dorset ST7 0BL, England. Tel 01747 852 475.

Doves Farm
Wide range of locally grown and organic flours, including stoneground, spelt, an excellent rye flour, and specialist range of flours, including gluten-free, pizza, brown rice, and buckwheat. Telephone for complete stocklist and stockists; mail order also available. Salisbury Road, Hungerford, Berks RG17 0RF, England. Tel 01488 684 880.

Gray's Grist Mill
Organic stoneground flours and meal available by mail order. Write or telephone for up-to-date details and before visiting, as the mill is undergoing changes. P.O. Box 422, Adamsville, RI 02801. (From the Boston/Providence area take Rte 195 to Rte 24 South to Rte 81 South. Follow this to its end, then left into Adamsville Rd.) Tel/Fax 508-636-6075. http://burning-electrons.com./GRAYS.

The Great Valley Mills
Stoneground bread flour, rye and semolina flours, steel-cut oats; catalog available. R.D.3, Country Line Road, Box 1111, Barto, PA 19504. Tel 800-688-6455.

Isinglass Mill
Stoneground organic and non-organic whole-wheat flour, wheaten flour, organic white and brown flours, and organic brown, white, and rye flours are available by mail order. The Deeps, Crossabeg, Wexford, Eire. Tel 053 28226.

Letheringset Mill
Miller Mike Thurlow produces wonderful stoneground 100% whole-wheat flour at his lovingly restored watermill. Good shop with wide range of flours and organic produce, plus mill tours and advice. Telephone for opening times and mail order details. Letheringset, Holt, Norfolk NR25 7YD, England. Tel 01263 713 153.

Little Salkeld Watermill
All organic flours, bio-dynamic also available, including stoneground whole-wheat, 85% wheatmeal, barley, and rye. Telephone for opening times and mail order details. Little Salkeld, Penrith, Cumbria CA10 1NW, England. Tel 01768 881 523.

Maud Foster Windmill
The mill shop sells organic flours and porridge oats. The tea room serves morning coffee, lunches, and afternoon teas, with baked goods made from their own flour. Telephone for opening times and mail order details. The mill is just off the A16/A52 Grimsby–Skegness road in Boston, Lincs, England. Tel 01205 352 188.

New Hope Mills
Stoneground bread flour, buckwheat, rye, and spelt flours, cornmeal; catalog available. R.R.2, P.O. Box 269A, Moravia, NY 13118. Tel 315-497-0783.

Otterton Mill
The miller takes guided tours for groups, which have to be booked, but there is a mill museum and full explanations of the working of the mill. Also a craft shop, and barn bakery and duckery restaurant which specialize in breads and cakes made with their organic flour as well as organic produce. The mill is open every day, 10:30a.m. to 5:30p.m. Easter to end October; 11a.m. to 4p.m. November to Easter. Otterton, Budleigh Salterton, Devon, England. Tel 01395 568 521/567 041.

Shipton Mill
The full range of flours is available by mail order, although there is a minimum order of 5 kilos in total made up from any of the different flours. Call Sue Perrett at Shipton Mill, Long Newton, Tetbury, Glos GL8 8RP, England. Tel 01666 505 050; Fax 01666 504 666.

Stafford County Flour Mills Co.
Unbleached white and whole-wheat flours. P.O. Box 7, Hudson, KS 67545. Tel 316-458-4121.

War Eagle Mill
Stoneground organic bread flour, buckwheat and rye flours, cornmeal; catalog available. Route 5, Box 411, Rogers, AR 72756. Tel 501-789-5343.

BAKERIES

Familie Arnold-Arnold
Backerei-Konditorei
3901 Simplon-Dorf, Switzerland

Bakoven
175 Ashburnham Road
Ham, Richmond, Surrey TW10 7MR, England
Tel (020) 8948 6040

Bock
40 rue de Gasperich
Luxembourg

The Flour Bag
Burford Street
Lechlade, Nr. Burford, Glos GL7 3AP, England
Tel 01367 252 322

Franciscan Friars of Hungary Bakery
21 Central Street
Bangor, ME 04401
Tel 207-947-3770
fbse@Juno.com

The Hi-Rise Bread Co.
208 Concord
Cambridge, MA 02138
Tel 617-876-8766

Maison Jocteur
Le Boulanger de l'Ile Barbe
Lyon, France 69009 Saint-Rambert
Tel 04 78 83 98 35

Tzia Matilda snc.
Via Lanusei 21
08030 Gergei (Nu), Sardinia
Tel 0782 808098

Panetteria F.lli Matta
Via Marconi 123
Gergei (Nu), Sardinia
Tel 0782 808202/808871

Oberweis
1 ZA Cloche d'Or
Rue Guillame, Kroll, Luxembourg
Tel 40 31 40-1
and 19–21 Grande Rue, Luxembourg
Tel 47 07 03

Patrick LePort
La Boulangerie Savoyarde
73630 Ecole en Bauges, France
Tel 04 79 54 82 74; Fax 04 79 54 86 51
Note: The bakery is in the middle of the tiny village
south of Annecy. The shop is halfway down the
entrance at the side – look out for the small roadside
sign. Bread available 1 to 6:30p.m. Monday to Friday.

Vete-Katten
Kungsgaten 55
111 22 Stockholm, Sweden
Tel 08/208405

The Village Bakery
Melmerby
Penrith, Cumbria CA10 1HE, England
Tel 01768 881 515

OVENS

Beehive ovens
For information on beehive terracotta ovens contact:
Cesol Tiles, 11 Bushell Business Centre, Hithercroft
Road, Wallingford, Oxon OX10 9DD, England.
Tel 01491 825249; Fax 01491 825147.

Paul Merry
Write or telephone for details of Paul's brick ovens
and consultancy, and his breadmaking courses. Rose
Cottage, Long Marton, Appleby, Cumbria CA16 6BJ,
England. Tel/Fax 01768 361 102.

Reinhart von Zschock
Designer of cast ovens (with Paul Merry) and
European stove designer and builder. The Ceramic
Stove Company, Ruskin Mill, Nailsworth, Stroud, Glos
GL6 0LA, England. Tel 01453 833 931.

Tandoor ovens
For information on fixed and portable *tandoors*, in
various sizes, for UK or export, contact: The Clay Oven
Company, 164A Dukes Road, London W3 OSL,
England. Tel (020) 8896 2696.

EQUIPMENT AND INGREDIENTS

The Baker's Catalogue
American mail-order catalog for the dedicated home
baker, offering the proper tools and equipment, an
extensive range of flours, grains, and seeds, and hard-
to-find ingredients. Produced by The King Arthur
Flour Company. Contact them at P.O. Box 876,
Norwich, VT 05055-0876.Tel 800-827-6836. The
Baker's Store, on Rte 5 South in Norwich, is open
7 days a week. Tel 802-649-3361 for details.

Bridge Kitchenware
Professional bakeware, cookware, and tools; catalog
available. 214 E. 52nd Street, New York, NY 10022.
Tel 800-274-3435.

Dean & Deluca
Specialty bakeware, cookware and tools, as well as
dried and candied fruit and peel. Catalog available
from their mail order department, 560 Broadway,
New York, NY 10012. Tel 800-221-7714.

Maid of Scandinavia
Specialty bakeware and tools; catalog available.
3244 Raleigh Avenue, Minneapolis, MN 55416.
Tel 800-328-6722.

Pete's Spice and Everything Nice
Bread flours, buckwheat, rye, semolina and spelt
flours, cornmeal, dried and candied fruit and peel;
catalog available. 174 First Avenue, New York, NY
10009. Tel 212-254-8773.

Sourdoughs International
Ed Wood's dried sourdough cultures from around the
world are available by mail order. He offers nine different cultures, including: one that originated with
the California Gold Rush of 1849; one from an old
Yukon gold prospector; another from Hurghada, a
village on the Red Sea and one from Giza, both in
Egypt; a 200-year-old culture from Austria; one 150
years old from a Paris bakery; and one from a small
town south of Moscow. Contact him at Sourdoughs
International, PO Box 670, Cascade, ID 83611. For a
brochure, Tel 800-888-9567 or Fax 208-382-3129.
www.sourdo.com/.

Williams-Sonoma
Bakeware, cookware,and tools; catalog available.
P.O. Box 7456, San Francisco, CA 94120-7456.
Tel 800-541-2233.

OTHER ADDRESSES

Canterbury Shaker Village
Open daily May through October, weekends April,
November, and December. The Village is situated
about 15 miles north of Concord (on I-93 take exit 18
and follow the many signs). Canterbury, NH 03224.
Tel 603-783-9511. www.shakers.org.

The Shakers of Sabbathday Lake
For more information, write to The Shaker Society,
707 Shaker Road, New Gloucester, ME 04260. For
details of tours, shop opening times, and workshops:
www.maine.com/shakerlibrary.

Rasa Samudra Restaurant
5 Charlotte Street, London W1P 1HD, England.
Tel (020) 7637 0222.

Sarkhels Restaurant
199 Replingham Road, Southfields, London SW18
5LY, England. Tel (020) 8870 1483.

La Tante Claire
The Berkeley, Wilton Place, London SW1 7RL,
England. Tel (020) 7823 2003.

Index

Acknowledgments

This book would not have been written without help from a considerable number of people:

in the UK
Norma MacMillan and Paul Welti, Barbara Levy, John Wallace, Jenni Muir, Stuart Cooper, Peter Howard, Jeni Wright. Alan and Daniel Hertz, Jann Neilson, Yvonne Jenkins and Sharon Turner, Gareth Spencer Jones and Tricia Sleigh, Hilary Leathes, Otto Stromfelt, Claire Parker.
John Lister and Clive Mellum, Pierre Koffmann, Andrew Whitley, Paul Merry, Tom Jaine, Maurice Bichard, Rosemary Barron, Rosemary Rowson, Christine Sherriff, Desna Greenhow, Gert Kusche and Marcus Hampton, Das Sreedharan, Udit Sarkhel, Maurice and Nanette Chaplais, The Roskilly family, Gill Dandy and Kurt Bettin, Michelle Kershaw, Elaine Hallgarten. Barbro Hunter-McAusland, Boel Benson and Ann-Charlotte Carlsson of the Swedish Trade and Travel Council. Jill Brand, Julia Spence, Kyle Hayes. Our thanks to Gerrit Buntrock for manipulating photographs.

in France
Patrick LePort, Paul Bocuse.

in Luxembourg
Jeff and Pit Oberweis, Fernand Bock.

in Sardinia
A big thank you to our guides, Kailani Soares and Mariano Angius, of Angius Organics, Signora Ghiani, Mariella Giovanni Daniele and Simone Contu, the Matta family, Signora Speranza Carai and Guiseppe Scintu, the Mayor of Gergei.

in Sweden
Beatrice Grill and Per Saletti, Magnus Johansson, Ulf Edlund. Lee Persson and Ingrid Eriksson of Svenska Dagbladet, Marita Witander and Helena Martinsson at Skansen.

in Switzerland
Bernhard, Ann-Rose and Peter Augsberger, Rolf Eggel, Urs and Mathilda Arnold-Theiler.

in the USA
Annette and Will Hertz, the Morgenstern family, Jeff Paige and the staff at Canterbury Village, the Shaker Society at Sabbathday Lake, Rene Becker, Tim McTague, Brother Donald and Brother Kenneth, Ya-yoi Tsuchitani, Caroll and Ben Boltin. Barbara Walker. Chad Mooney.